# TERRORISM

## Titles of Related Interest

Charters & Tugwell   *Armies in Low-Intensity Conflict*

Hartmann & Wendzel   *Defending America's Security*

Joes   *From the Barrel of a Gun*

Laffin   *The World in Conflict*

Leventhal & Alexander   *Nuclear Terrorism*

Selth   *Against Every Human Law: The Terrorist Threat to Diplomacy*

Taylor   *The Terrorist*

## Related Periodicals*

*Armed Forces Journal International*

*Defense Analysis*

*Middle East Strategic Studies Quarterly*

*Survival*

*Sample copies available upon request

# TERRORISM
## The Newest Face of Warfare

■

## DONALD J. HANLE

*First Volume of the Series*
Yonah Alexander, *General Editor*

Pergamon-Brassey's
*TERRORISM*
Library

PERGAMON-BRASSEY'S
International Defense Publishers, Inc.

Washington · New York · London · Oxford
Beijing · Frankfurt · São Paulo · Sydney · Tokyo · Toronto

| U.S.A. (Editorial) | Pergamon-Brassey's International Defense Publishers, Inc. 8000 Westpark Drive, Fourth Floor, McLean, Virginia 22102, U.S.A. |
| --- | --- |
| (Orders) | Pergamon Press Inc., Maxwell House, Fairview Park, Elmsford, New York 10523, U.S.A. |
| U.K. (Editorial) | Brassey's Defence Publishers Ltd., 24 Gray's Inn Road, London WC1X 8HR, England |
| (Orders) | Brassey's Defence Publishers, Headington Hill Hall, Oxford OX3 0BW, England |
| PEOPLE'S REPUBLIC OF CHINA | Pergamon Press, Room 4037, Qianmen Hotel, Beijing, People's Republic of China |
| FEDERAL REPUBLIC OF GERMANY | Pergamon Press GmbH, Hammerweg 6, D-6242 Kronberg, Federal Republic of Germany |
| BRAZIL | Pergamon Editora Ltda, Rua Eça de Queiros, 346, CEP 04011, Paraiso, São Paulo, Brazil |
| AUSTRALIA | Pergamon-Brassey's Defence Publishers Ltd., P.O. Box 544, Potts Point, N.S.W. 2011, Australia |
| JAPAN | Pergamon Press, 5th Floor, Matsuoka Central Building, 1-7-1 Nishishinjuku, Shinjuku-ku, Tokyo 160, Japan |
| CANADA | Pergamon Press Canada, Suite No. 271, 253 College Street, Toronto, Ontario, Canada M5T 1R5 |

Pergamon-Brassey's books are available at special discounts for bulk purchases for sales promotions, premiums, fund-raising, or education use through the

Special Sales Director,
Macmillan Publishing Company
866 Third Avenue
New York, NY 10022.

**British Library Cataloguing in Publication Data**

Hanle, Donald J.
Terrorism.-(Pergamon-Brassey's terrorism library)
1. Terrorism
I. Title
322.4′2

ISBN 0-08-036742-9

**Library of Congress Cataloging-in-Publication Data**

Hanle, Donald J.
Terrorism : the newest face of warfare / Donald J. Hanle.
p.    cm.—(Pergamon-Brassey's terrorism library : 1st v.)
Bibliography: p.
ISBN 0-08-036742-9 :
1. Terrorism.  I. Title.  II. Series.
HV6431.H35  1989
303.6′25—dc20

89-32291
CIP

Printed in the United States of America
10  9  8  7  6  5  4  3  2  1

*To my wife, Donna Dare, who believed.*

# Contents

■

# Foreword:
# Pergamon-Brassey's
# Terrorism Library

■

Terrorism, as a process of deliberate employment of psychological intimidation and physical violence by sovereign states and sub-national groups to attain strategic and political objectives in violation of law, is not new in history. In modern times, along with the nuclear age, we are in the midst of the new "age of terrorism" with all its frightening consequences for the continuity of civilized order.

Indeed, terrorism has been a permanent fixture of contemporary life. It poses a variety of threats, including those related to the safety and welfare of ordinary people, the stability of the state system, the health and pace of economic development, and the expansion and even the survival of democracy. Today's terrorists are better organized, more professional, and better equipped than their historical counterparts. Technological developments offer new targets and new capabilities. Tomorrow's terrorists might resort to chemical, biological, or nuclear violence to achieve mass disruption or political turmoil.

In light of this likelihood, Pergamon-Brassey's has developed its

Terrorism Library. The purpose of this series is to offer books, written or edited by recognized experts, on a variety of subjects including the causation and control of terrorism; national, regional, and global perspectives on terrorism; and specific case studies. Although each volume will stand on its own merit, the Terrorism Library will provide a comprehensive intellectual and professional framework for better understanding the nature, scope, intensity, and consequences of the threat of modern terrorism and what society can do to cope with this phenomenon in the 1990s.

Professor Yonah Alexander
Institute for Studies in
International Terrorism, State
University of New York, and the
Elliott School of International
Affairs, the George Washington
University
*General Editor*

# Introduction

∎

*T*errorism: The Newest Face of Warfare seeks to answer the question, is terrorism a form of war? As will be seen, there is no simple answer to this simple question. Certainly terrorism appears in many ways to be a form of war, at least to the casual observer. Indeed, many politicians, political scientists, journalists, and even military officers often refer to terrorism as warfare—a mode of war. But is terrorism really war? And if so, what ramifications does this have concerning strategies for neutralizing this threat? Before answering these questions, it is, of course, first necessary to come to an understanding of just what is meant by the terms *war* and *terrorism*. It is here that the complexity of the question at hand comes to light. With a quick glimpse at the table of contents the reader will note that it requires four of ten chapters simply to isolate, define, and come to an understanding of this phenomenon called war. It takes an additional chapter to define terrorism. Thus, at least 50 percent of this book is required to define the terms.

This situation is caused by several factors, not the least of which is the complexity of war itself. There is, at least in the West, little consensus on what war truly is. Indeed, each discipline—sociology, ideology, psychology, political science, etc.—has a totally separate approach to studying this phenomenon, each focusing on different aspects, identifying different causes, and having different parameters for what *is* war and what *is not*. It became quickly apparent, therefore, that to select only one of these disciplines and to accept its parameters as a definition of war would be too arbitrary. That is, the risk of creating a tautology would be too great, wherein definition *w* equals definition *t* and therefore the two are equivalent.

This book therefore rejects a unilateral approach to examining war. Rather, it lumps all the approaches together, seeking to find common denominators and then, using information that all would agree to be true, proceeds to define war. By approaching the study of war in this manner, it quickly becomes apparent that war is a dynamic process based on fundamental principles that remain constant over space and time—that is, each principle is immutable.* This is corroborated in this book by examining the works of classical military thinkers ranging from Sun Tzu to Liddell Hart as well as those who historically fall in between, most particularly Karl von Clausewitz. By sifting through these classical works we can see that all war—regardless of place or era—has the same basic purpose and relies on the same basic element—lethal force—that is manifested on both the physical and psychological planes simultaneously and is governed by the aforementioned immutable principles. In this way, war is isolated as a unique human activity, and with such criteria established, it becomes possible to ascertain whether any other human intercourse—such as terrorism—meets the parameters of war.

Before this book begins such an examination, however, one thing further needs to be explained—namely the variables in war. Although war is based on immutable principles, its outward manifestation on both the psychological and physical planes changes over time. For example, advances in technology as well as social and political structures clearly affect how wars are fought. Moreover, although all wars have

---

*The term *immutable* is used here to suggest that each principle is a constant. Thus, the principle of surprise when applied to classical or modern warfare remains the same, although the conditions and methods through which it is manifested may be drastically different.

the same basic purpose, the specific objectives they seek as well as the means used to achieve them change according to variables, such as who is the stronger, the aggressor, or the most desperate. In examining such variables this book contends that war has evolved over time, driven by a dialectical process in which new methods of war-fighting are introduced based upon new organizational, social, or technological innovations that, in turn, require combatants to have and master new skills to emerge victorious. Gaining an understanding of this evolutionary process makes it possible to explain how terrorism—which has existed for centuries—suddenly has become one of the most important methods of warfare in the modern, nuclear era.

Having achieved a thorough understanding of war, this book then turns its attention to terrorism. By borrowing much of the information presented in the four chapters on war, it becomes possible to come to an understanding of terrorism in one, relatively short chapter. What is seen is that terrorism is simply a unique method of force employment. Using this definition it is possible to identify a wide array of types of terrorism that this book groups into seven major categories: psychotic, criminal, mystical, revolutionary, repression, military, and state-sponsored. Each of these is tested against the criteria of war to ascertain which, if any, are a form of war. Surprisingly, only three types qualify—revolutionary, military, and state-sponsored.

But what does all this mean? Of what importance is the fact that repression terrorism is not war, while revolutionary terrorism is? The answer, quite simply, is in how one would go about neutralizing these two threats. This is the subject of the book's final chapter. Here we see that if, indeed, a type of terrorism is war, then it follows that it, too, rests on the same immutable principles of war as do the more classical manifestations of the phenomenon. This being the case, a type of terrorism that qualifies as a form of war should—indeed *must*—be treated as a form of war, and the methods used to neutralize it should be in consonance with those necessary to neutralize any military threat. Failure to do so would not only lead to disaster, but defeat, or at the very least, maintenance of the status quo with no hope for victory. Although many Western democratic states have begun to take steps in the right direction, more needs to be done. For although it does not currently appear that the political entities employing terrorism as warfare are on the verge of victory, neither are they on the verge of defeat. It is only by applying lethal, military force according to the principles of war that victory in this struggle becomes possible.

The importance of this book, then, is based on several factors. First, it provides substantive evidence to confirm the widely held belief that terrorism—or at least some types of it—is indeed a form of war. Secondly, armed with this understanding, appropriate responses to the types of terrorism that are forms of war become not only more apparent but, once clearly identified, can be carried out more effectively. Finally, at present there exists very little exhaustive research into terrorism as a military as opposed to a general political phenomenon. While it would be wrong to suggest this book is an exhaustive study of the military aspects of terrorism, it is the sincere hope of the author that it is at least a step toward closing this academic gap. Indeed, if this book serves to stimulate further research or discussion of terrorism as a form of war, its purpose will have been fulfilled.

# Acknowledgments

■

This book began as a debate in a graduate seminar at the University of South Carolina, and it was under the careful guidance of Professor Peter Sederberg that this concept was turned into a basic thesis. The thesis was further developed at the Naval Postgraduate School where the learned feedback and guidance of my fellow students and professors fleshed out the basic outline. Particularly important were Professor Frank Teti's guidance on the evolution of war and Professor Paul Buchanan's assistance in preparing the basic manuscript, especially in terms of organization. Additionally, I owe a great debt to Colonel Harry Summers, whose book *On Strategy* reminded me that it is not enough for a soldier to be professionally competent only in terms of technical expertise, management, and leadership, but that he or she also has a scholastic duty as well. Finally, I acknowledge the support, advice, and encouragement provided by my wife, Donna Dare, to whom this work is dedicated.

# CHAPTER 1

# WAR: FORCE, POWER, AND POLITICS

∎

## Introduction

War is a highly specialized activity having characteristics common with other forms of human intercourse but combined in a unique manner. The first characteristic is, of course, its reliance upon lethal force as its primary means. This, in itself, is certainly not unique. Many other forms of human activity also deal with lethal force, including criminal activity, capital punishment, suicide, abortion, and euthanasia. Clearly, these lie outside the pale of war. What makes war *war*, then, is not its reliance upon lethal force, but *how* it uses this force and to what *end*. This book seeks to identify the unique manner in which war combines these factors and thereby provide a means by which to measure whether certain types of terrorism are a form of war. That is to say, if it can be established that war represents a unique combination of factors or characteristics regarding *how* and *why* lethal force is employed, and if it can be established that these same factors or characteristics are present in a certain type of terrorism, then it is safe to assume the two—war and terrorism—are equivalent.

This chapter seeks to identify the first of these characteristics germane to all forms of war: to identify to what *end* lethal force is employed in war. This will provide the first element of the paradigm by which this book will measure war. To do this it is necessary to have an understanding of the four basic approaches to the study of war; this makes us aware of the different theories on the courses and purpose of war. Particularly important to the first section is determining the similarities between the four approaches, especially regarding the utility of force in the struggle for power. The second section will then focus upon the approach that, for the most part, will govern this book's analysis of war. This is the *technological* approach, which is based primarily upon the works of classical military thinkers whose expertise includes not only the function of war per se, but how force functions in war in particular. The third section will then isolate the purpose of force in war—providing the first means by which to test whether certain types of terrorism are also a form of war.

## The Approaches to the Study of War

According to Quincy Wright in his work *A Study of War*, there are four basic approaches to the study of this phenomenon: ideological, psychological, sociological, and technological.[1] Each approach suggests that war is caused by a different motive. What this section will show is that these motives are not mutually exclusive, and more important, at the highest level of abstraction, all perceive war to be caused by the same motive—the quest for power. This is clearly recognized by the technological approach, which essentially accepts the other three approaches as being valid but unable to stand alone. For this, and reasons that will be discussed later, the technological approach will provide the primary perspective of war throughout this book.

The ideological approach is the oldest approach to the study of war and is normative in its conception of it. Early writers of this school believed wars were caused by injustices, or they believed war to simply be a facet of the human condition, like language or sex, and not the creation of man. Later writers and thinkers of this approach emphasize the role of war as an instrument of justice or authority and are primarily concerned with whether it is waged with, by, and for legitimate means and ends. In the Calvinist ethic for example, "The state was ordained by God [to use war] not only to protect the good and punish the bad, but also support the true religion."[2] This essentially was a spinoff of the Catholic tradition initiated by St. Augustine in the fourth century, which asserted that "war was permissible to promote peace, that is order and justice, provided the war was initiated by a proper authority and . . . that authority had found peaceful procedures inadequate."[3]

Although man now recognizes he has "more rational" reasons for going to war, the ideological approach still plays a major role in mobilizing a populace for war. Virtually every nation goes to war convinced that it is right, that the war is just, and God is on its side. During World War II America went to war to "make the world safe for democracy." Even today, the Soviet Union has gone to great lengths in its political and military doctrine to differentiate between just and unjust wars. To the USSR, just wars are limited to those that aid the forces of socialism or are waged in defense of the Soviet Union. All other wars are, by Soviet definition, unjust.[4]

The basic weakness in this approach derives from the fact that being normative, it generally ends up describing what "should be," rather than "what is." Secondly, all normative approaches suffer from being subject to interpretation. Hence, one man's holy war is another's war of repression and aggression.

The psychological approach essentially perceives war from a behavioral perspective in which experts "take as their point of departure the behavior of individuals, and from this they draw inferences [to] the behavior of the species."[5] In other words, it sees cultures as being simply "abstractions of psychological elements in aggregates of human beings."[6] Consequently, this approach perceives war to be caused by the personal motives of individuals who band together to satiate specific personal desires by the use of force against an "out group." War begins in the minds of men for the purpose of serving the goals of individual actors, which are then translated to a broader scale.

The basic weakness of this approach is that war is an organized, group activity that includes organizations having dynamics of their own that do not lend themselves to explanations based upon individual human behavior patterns. While it provides useful insights regarding the human element as a catalyst for war, it cannot, for instance, explain why, as happened during World War I, Britain went to war with Germany because Austria invaded Serbia.

This question is easily answered by the sociological approach, which is basically a systems-theory approach to the study of war. This approach perceives war to be but one of many interactions between and within political systems. War, like any interaction, may be useful in maintaining or regulating a political system, such as that manifested in the "balance of power" that governed the nineteenth-century European state system. It can also be useful in transforming a political system, which is the purpose of those who foment a revolutionary or civil war. Using this systems-theory approach it is easy to understand how Britain became engaged in a war with Germany because of Austrian aggression. Britain wanted to maintain status quo in the interstate system, while Germany and Austria wanted to modify it. The ultimate result was the First World War.

This is not to denigrate—much less totally eliminate—the role of human beings in causing and fighting wars. The sociological approach emphasizes, however, that "any valid explanation of revolution [or war] depends upon the analyst's rising above the viewpoints of the participants to find important regularities across given historical instances. . . ."[7] According to Gordon Wood, "it is not that men's motives are unimportant; they indeed make events . . . but the purposes of men . . . are so numerous, so varied, and so contradictory that their complex interaction produces results no one intended or could even foresee."[8]

Although this approach provides a very good understanding of how war can maintain, regulate, or change social and political systems, it, like the ideological and psychological approaches, has great difficulty in explaining *how* wars are fought. That is, these approaches cannot explain why one side chooses a certain tactic or why certain types of armed forces are created over other types. For answers to questions such as these, it is necessary to use the technological approach.

As Quincy Wright notes, "The technological approach is usually exemplified by the attitude of professional military men and diplomats, in writing on strategy and diplomacy . . . [and] conceives [of] war as the use of regulated violence for political ends."[9] It is an approach comfortably shared by such "realist" thinkers as Thomas Hobbes, Francis Bacon, Niccolò Machiavelli, Karl von Clausewitz, and Hans Morgenthau. It is also the primary—although not the only—approach this book will use to investigate war and terrorism.

There are three basic reasons why the technological approach will predominate throughout this book. First, we propose to establish that terrorism is a form of war based upon its manipulation of force to meet political objectives, which is the basis of the technological approach. Second, the technological approach incorporates elements from each of the other three approaches, which can be applied when necessary and appropriate. Finally, the technological approach is the only one that adequately describes how and why wars are fought the way they are. All of these factors make the technological approach more versatile and accurate in its depiction of war.

Although the three previously mentioned approaches appear to focus on a different cause of war, at the most abstract level, they are actually identifying the same basic cause as the technological approach—the struggle for power. Whether one wishes to correct an injustice, satiate the goals of individual actors, or change the status quo within a given political or social system, power is an essential element when opposition is met. Furthermore, the side enjoying the greater power will determine the outcome. As will be shown later, having greater power does not necessarily mean having the most physical force—otherwise it would be impossible for terrorism to exist at all—but force is the dynamic element of power, and how force is applied determines which side has the greater power. The key point here is that whether the objectives have ideological, psychological, or sociological roots, force can secure and/or defend those objectives.

The utility of force is readily seen in the writings of both Machiavelli and von Clausewitz. In *The Prince*, Machiavelli admonishes "the ruler to keep in mind the preservation of his power depend[s] upon military strength."[10] Von Clausewitz is even more specific: "The decision by [force] is . . . in war what cash payment is in commerce."[11] Force, then, is the ultimate arbiter in the struggle for power; this struggle is the primary cause of war. The adherents to the technological approach perceive a Hobbesian international system that is "characterized by an absence of effective institutionalized constraints on the use of force by its members. . . ."[12] As Thomas Hobbes puts it in his work *Leviathan*,

> In all times kings and persons of sovereign authority, because of their independency, are in continual jealousies, and in the state and posture of gladiators: having their weapons pointed, and their eyes fixed on one another—that is, their forts, garrisons, and guns on the frontiers of their

kingdoms—and continual spies upon their neighbors; which is a posture of war. . . . [W]here there is no common power, there is no law, no injustice. Force and fraud are in war cardinal virtues.[13]

International relations are consequently punctuated by wars resulting from the continuous struggle between the constituent parts. It is a social system wherein force and power are useful both in achieving political goals and in defending against the demands and incursions of others. But while this clearly identifies the cause of war, it does not adequately identify what makes war a phenomenon unique from all other forms of human endeavor. For this, the specific characteristics of war must be identified, and war must be precisely defined.

## The Technological Approach

The technological approach rests upon scientific methodology. It begins "with the concrete and objective evidence of the senses and attempts to create from [this], logical structures capable of predicting events in the future and practical techniques [or fundamentals] capable of controlling them."[14] This scientific realism permits war to be logically analyzed to discern not only what causes war but how it functions. Furthermore, it makes it possible to identify the special characteristics germane to all types of warfare. These characteristics will be described in this section.

The scientific methodology of the technological approach finds early roots in the classic Greek and Roman histories of Thucydides, Polybius, and Livy. Thucydides began writing his histories of the Peloponnesian War in the fifth century B.C. It is in these essays that he proposes "that in the order of human nature, future events would resemble those which had occurred."[15] In other words, there is a pattern to history. Furthermore, Thucydides also believed that human nature is constant and that the pattern of "history will reveal the springs of human behavior."[16] Finally, Thucydides believed that human conflict was due to the motives of fear, greed, and ambition.[17]

Thucydides is suggesting that since there is a pattern to history, it is possible to analyze its course by careful observation and reasoning.

Upon closer examination he found that wars were essentially caused by human motives, which further suggests that war must serve some purpose in satisfying human desires, including those to be free from fear and to satiate greed and ambition. Although his ideas were lost during the Dark Ages, his careful recording of historical events enabled thinkers and writers of the Renaissance to "discover" and once again ponder the basic factors of history and human nature.

While Thucydides was writing his histories, a Chinese philosopher named Sun Tzu began writing his treatise *The Art of War*. In it, he reveals "an understanding of the political and philosophical fundamentals so sound and enlightening as to warrant serious study by scholars and soldiers today"[18] in the estimation of the *Encyclopedia of Military History*. Sun Tzu's basic premise can be found in the opening verse of his work: "The art of war is of vital importance to the state."[19] As Samuel B. Griffith points out in his excellent translation of Sun Tzu, "Here is recognition—and for the first time—that armed strife is not a transitory aberration, but a recurrent, conscious act and therefore susceptible to rational analysis."[20] Griffith continues,

> By relating war to the immediate political context, that is to alliances or lack of them, and to unity and stability on the home front and high morale in the army contrasted with disunity in the enemy country and low morale in his army, Sun Tzu attempted to establish a realistic basis for relative power.[21]

This was Renaissance thinking five centuries before Christ. Furthermore, Sun Tzu understood war to be an intrinsic element of politics. First, he deems national unity to be essential to military victory. Second, he proposes that war was not an end in itself, but rather a means to an end. When discussing how a war should be waged, Sun Tzu states that a wise general "creates conditions certain to produce a quick decision; for him victory is the object of war, not lengthy operations however brilliantly conducted."[22] This is essentially an appeal to the military commander to subordinate his military objectives and operations to the political objective for which the war is being waged.

Despite having been published in the West as early as 1772, the works of Sun Tzu remained relatively obscure until the early twentieth century. It was not until Sir Basil Liddell Hart was introduced to Sun

Tzu in 1927 that the Chinese philosopher was incorporated into any major Western military writings. Liddell Hart was extremely impressed with Sun Tzu, according to Griffith, crediting Sun Tzu with having "in . . . one short book . . . embodied almost as much about the fundamentals of strategy and tactics as [Hart] had covered in more than twenty books."[23]

Niccolò Machiavelli is generally considered the first modern military thinker to see war in a way similar to Sun Tzu. Like Sun Tzu, Machiavelli saw war as an organized, recurring, premeditated act that could be subjected to rational analysis.[24] As a Renaissance thinker, Machiavelli based his views on war upon the belief that behind all social activities lay basic principles and laws that are timeless and that, through logical deduction, could be discovered and applied to daily life. Machiavelli sought to support his theories by carefully studying the events of the past. He was particularly inspired by the classical histories of Thucydides, Livy, and Polybius and the military handbooks of Caesar, Frontinus, and Vegetius.

Although the principles of war will be discussed in detail later in this book, it is important to note some of the more salient observations made by Machiavelli. First, he notes the importance of morale and cohesion in achieving victory. Additionally, he emphasizes the central importance of the battle to warfare and contends that in war a state should apply all possible force available to it. Perhaps Machiavelli's most profound observation derived from the classical histories is that political power is based upon military power rather than the size of its treasury, pointing out that gold only became political power if it could be transformed into military strength. This idea was quite revolutionary at the time when Italian wars were fought with condottieri (mercenaries) who often engaged in day-long battles in which only one or two men were killed. Because waging war was a service each captain of a condottieri company provided, and because the individual soldier was the "working capital" of said companies, losses were kept to an absolute minimum, with battlefield maneuvers often deciding the victor.[25]

Machiavelli was to have a major impact upon the nineteenth- and twentieth-century military thinkers. Quincy Wright goes so far as to credit Machiavelli with influencing "a huge literature . . . of books on strategy and power politics such as those by von Clausewitz, Jomini, Mahan, and von der Goltz."[26] Each of these writers has in turn affected others, such as Liddell Hart, J.F.C. Fuller, John Keegan, and Generals

Patton, von Moltke, Guderian, Rommel, and von Schlieffen, to name a few.

As a member of the technological school, it should come as no surprise that von Clausewitz perceived war from a Machiavellian perspective. Like Machiavelli, von Clausewitz sought to ascertain and precisely define the recurring, immutable laws governing warfare.

## Clausewitz on the Purpose of War

For von Clausewitz, the purpose of war is isolated in the phrase, "War is an act of force to compel our enemy to do our will."[27] This definition, standing alone, could apply to the full spectrum of violent human interaction, from individual persons—say in a barroom brawl—to alliances of nations. But von Clausewitz quickly narrows this definition with his famous maxim, "War is the continuation of policy by other means."[28] Here we see he is referring to political entities, not merely individuals. Hence, war is the employment of force by a political entity sufficient to compel another political entity to meet a political goal or objective.

The beauty of this definition stems from the fact that it is free of any normative concepts. War exists when a political entity attempts to compel an enemy by force—irrespective of whether this force complies with regulatory laws created by man or meets a specific juridical definition. Man's law is an artificial construct. It is not an immutable law, such as the law of physics, and hence man's law may be (and often is) ignored or broken. The principles of warfare, on the other hand, apply whether man recognizes them or not. They apply whenever war exists and, therefore, are not considered normative.

This is not to infer that man's law has no impact on war. From a policy, strategic, or tactical perspective, wars are often limited by the normative values of man, but these values are effective only if all the belligerents adhere to them, and most especially, if they do not confront the principles and laws governing the use of violent force in war. As von Clausewitz notes,

> Kind-hearted people might of course think there was some ingenious way to disarm or defeat an enemy without so much bloodshed . . . pleasant as this sounds, it is a fallacy . . . war is such a dangerous business

that the mistakes [coming] from kindness are the very worst. The maximum use of force is in no way incompatible with the simultaneous use
of the intellect. If one side uses force without compunction, undeterred
by bloodshed ... while the other side refrains, the first will gain the
upper hand. That side will force the other to follow suit; each will drive
its opponent toward extremes, and the only limiting factors are the
counterpoises inherent in [the laws and principles of] war.[29]

We might conclude from von Clausewitz's line of logic that the limitations on force imposed by the normative laws of man will give way
if the situation is desperate for the political entities engaged and neither side is quickly victorious. Put in less tautological form: war becomes less subject to normative restrictions as desperation grows for
one or all the political entities involved and if the war does not end
quickly.

Another very important factor in understanding the purpose of war
from the Clausewitzian perspective is his definition of force. Using
only von Clausewitz's definition of war as stated above, it is possible
to conceive of economic or diplomatic "warfare" as is often suggested
by sociologists, psychologists, and even some political scientists. Von
Clausewitz concedes that commerce and diplomacy are much like war.
But as he quickly points out, the simple struggle of interests is not war:
"War is a clash between major interests, which is resolved by bloodshed—that is the only way in which it differs from other conflicts."[30]
He goes on to state that

physical force, therefore, is the specific means of war, and it would be
absurd to introduce into the philosophy of war ... a "principle of moderation." Our opponent will comply with our will if "either he is ...
disarmed or placed in such a position that he is threatened with being
disarmed."[31]

In effect, force is the means of war and imposing our will on the
enemy, its object. It is important to note here von Clausewitz's notion
that political objectives may be obtained in two ways: disarming the
enemy or threatening to do so. By presenting these alternatives von
Clausewitz is differentiating between physical and moral force. These
will be dealt with in greater detail in chapter 2, since they are critical
to our understanding terrorism as war. Whereas it is intuitively obvious that a disarmed enemy must submit to the victor's will, it is less
apparent why an enemy would submit if he retains the means to resist.

Yet, as will be established below, virtually no war has been fought until one side is totally defenseless.

We may conclude, then, that war at its most basic level is simply a clash of wills between two political entities. Although the physical force will determine the type and scale of the war, it is the will to fight that determines when the war begins and ends. It is this human element that takes war out of the realm of the pure physical science and permits the very weak to engage the very strong in war. Otherwise, terrorism could not exist.

## Summation

In summary, war is the result of the struggle for power between contending parties. Power is sought because it has the ability to compel one's opponent to do one's will. And force is used because it has utility in compelling and because there is no higher authority than a decision made by force. War is also a conscious, recurring, organized phenomenon, capable of being observed and rationally analyzed (Thucydides, Sun Tzu). It is purposeful, goal-oriented activity inextricably linked to politics (Sun Tzu, Machiavelli). Moreover, it differs from all other forms of human conflict in that it involves death or the threat of death (von Clausewitz). Above all, it is a clash of wills between contending parties (von Clausewitz). Consequently, the definition of war for the remainder of this book is this:

> *War is an act of lethal force between organized political entities for the purpose of achieving political goals by compelling an enemy to modify or surrender his own political objectives through weakening or destroying his will to resist.*

This represents the first element of the paradigm this book will use to test whether a certain type of terrorism qualifies as a form of war.

## Notes

1. Quincy Wright, *A Study of War,* 2 vols. (Chicago: The University of Chicago Press, 1941), p. 423.

2. Roland H. Bainton, *Christian Attitudes Toward War and Peace: A Historical Survey and Critical Re-evaluation* (New York: Abingdon Press, 1960), p. 145.

3. Wright, op. cit., p. 886.

4. Richard F. Staar, *USSR Foreign Policies After Detente* (Stanford, Calif.: Hoover Institution Press, 1985), p. 112.

5. Robert L. Pfaltzgraff and James Doherty, *Contending Theories of International Relations: A Comprehensive Survey* (New York: Harper & Row, 1981), p. 140.

6. Wright, op. cit., p. 1233.

7. Theda Skocpol, *States and Social Revolutions: A Comparative Analysis of France, Russia and China* (New York: Cambridge University Press, 1983), p. 18.

8. Gordon Wood, "The American Revolution," *Revolutions: A Comparative Study*, edited by Lawrence Kaplan (New York: Vintage Books, 1973), p. 129. As quoted in Skocpol, ibid., p. 18.

9. Wright, op. cit., p. 423.

10. Felix Gilbert, "Machiavelli: The Renaissance of the Art of War," *Makers of Modern Strategy: Military Thought From Machiavelli to Hitler*, edited by Edward M. Earle (Princeton: Princeton University Press, 1943; Princeton paperback printing, 1972), p. 3.

11. Karl von Clausewitz, *On War*, edited and translated by Michael Howard and Peter Paret (Princeton: Princeton University Press, 1976), p. 97.

12. K. J. Holsti, *International Politics: A Framework for Analysis* (Englewood Cliffs, N.J.: Prentice-Hall Inc., 1983), p. 270.

13. Thomas Hobbes, *Leviathan*, XXII, p. 65. As quoted in Will and Ariel Durant, *The Story of Civilization*, vol. 8, *The Age of Louis XIV* (New York: Simon & Schuster Inc., 1963), p. 555.

14. Wright, op. cit., p. 426.

15. Thucydides, *The Peloponnesian Wars*, translated by Benjamin Jowett, revised and abridged by P. A. Brunt (New York: Washington Square Press, 1963), p. xxix.

16. Ibid.

17. Ibid., p. xxx.

18. R. Ernest Dupuy and Trevor N. Dupuy, *The Encyclopedia of Military His-

*tory: From 3600 B.C. to the Present* (New York: Harper & Row, Publishers Inc., 1970), p. 19.

19. Sun Tzu, *The Art of War*, edited and translated by Samuel B. Griffith (London: Oxford University Press, 1963; Oxford University Press Paperback, 1971), p. 63.

20. Ibid., p. 39.

21. Ibid., pp. 39–40.

22. Ibid., p. 41.

23. Ibid., p. vii.

24. Wright, op. cit., p. 426.

25. Gilbert, op. cit., p. 14.

26. Wright, op. cit., p. 427.

27. von Clausewitz, op. cit., p. 75.

28. Ibid., p. 87.

29. Ibid., p. 76.

30. Ibid., p. 149.

31. H. Rothfels, "Clausewitz," *Makers of Modern Strategy: Military Thought from Machiavelli to Hitler*, op. cit., p. 102.

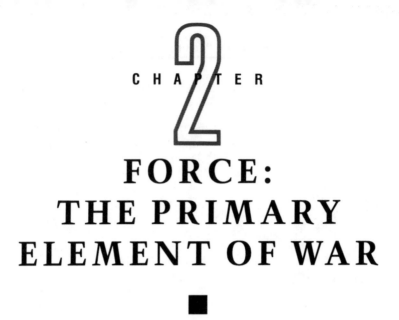

CHAPTER 2

# FORCE:
# THE PRIMARY
# ELEMENT OF WAR

■

## Introduction

All war, regardless of when it is waged or the form it takes, rests upon a single, indispensable element—*force*. As noted earlier, it is force that separates economic or diplomatic conflicts from war. But how, exactly, does force function in war? In answering this question, this chapter will explore how force becomes power and how force operates simultaneously on the physical as well as the psychological plane. Furthermore, this chapter will examine the instruments of force in war, which include its weapon systems and military organization. Particular emphasis will be placed upon the will to fight or "moral force" as a prerequisite for the creation and maintenance of cohesive military units. This, in turn, will provide a better understanding of precisely how terrorism functions as a weapon of war by establishing how it can break down the political and social cohesion of a targeted political entity. Finally, this chapter will add criteria to the paradigm this book will use to determine which types of terrorism are a form of war.

## Force and Power

Force and power are not equivalent concepts. Clearly, force is a necessary element of power, but the amount of force available to a political entity does not necessarily indicate the amount of power it has. Japan and Saudi Arabia, for example, enjoy considerable power in the international system despite the fact that both are military pygmies. Moreover, the Vatican or scores of international corporations such as Du Pont and Exxon enjoy a great amount of power despite having no military—force-generating—capability at all. We must conclude, therefore, that power involves more than mere physical force.

Arleigh Burke, the former chief of naval operations, argues that power is made up of three essential components: *force* and *persuasion*, which are actually two extremes along the same continuum of human interaction, and *influence*, which lies somewhere in between. To Burke, force compels a nation (or other political entity) by removing any alternatives. The target must comply or cease to exist. Persuasion, on the other hand, becomes power by presenting "ideas so attractively that they not only seem valid intellectually but also induce a desired type of response."[1] He continues,

> The term "influence" connotes the forms of power between pure force and pure persuasion. Behavior is neither "forced" nor is it determined by dispassionate persuasion. Rather, the power that exercises influence obtains the desired behavior by controlling the choices available to the "influenced," [that is] . . . the possessor of power can add further advantage to the type of behavior desired [or] he can . . . impose additional sanctions upon the types of undesirable behavior.[2]

The most important thing to note here is that with the use of *influence* or *persuasion* the target can choose whether to comply and to what degree. By employing *force* the choice is removed unless the target can counter in kind.

Edward Luttwak would agree with this analysis to a point in that he also perceives force to be a component of power, although only from a static perspective. In dynamic terms, however, "force and power are not analogous at all, but they are, in a sense, opposites. One is an input and the other output, and efficiency requires the minimization of the former [force] and the maximization of the latter [power]."[3] He points out that force works by direct application on the field of battle or in active (non-combat) deployment. [But] . . . force also works indirectly (i.e., politically) since its mere presence—if recognized—may deter or compel. But the direct suasion [sic] of force, though undoubtedly a political rather than a physical phenomenon, occurs only in the narrowest "tactical" dimension.[4]

Luttwak further contends that force-in-operation is basically analogous to a physical phenomenon, equivalent to the concept of mechanical force in Newtonian physics. "Both are consumed in application; both wane over distance to a degree that is dependent on the means of conveyance or the medium of transmission. . . ."[5] Consequently, military force, like mechanical force, can only be used in one place at any given time, becomes weaker as it disperses, and weakens with distance and use. This we may call *kinetic force*.

On the other hand, power, according to Luttwak, is not subject to Newtonian physical laws. This is because power is not so much the ability to employ force as it is a perception process on the part of the target group. Power exists when the target group perceives the power-wielder can punish or reward and then acts upon those perceptions. In this manner, then, power is a subjective perception and may be described as *potential force*. Luttwak describes it this way:

> Perceived power does not diminish with distance, for it is not a physical phenomenon. For the same reason, perceived power is not consumed by use. One client king or ten can perceive the same undivided power in the empire and can be influenced by it. Nor is the quantum of this power diminished when the obedience of a further dozen kings is secured . . . by contrast, force applied to one sector to impose tranquility on one restless tribe is unavailable for use against another, any increase in the number of targets diminishes the amount of force that can be used against each.[6]

So power is not merely the amount of physical force available to the power-wielder, but rather the target group's perception that the power-wielder can grant rewards or issue punishments. Ultimately, however, power rests upon force. If one of the target groups no longer perceives the power-wielder to be able or willing to use force, that target group will probably become less and less influenced by that power-wielder. If this happens, the power-wielder may attempt to use rewards or economic sanctions to bring the rebellious group back in line with the power-wielder's policy goals—but this leaves the decision to comply up to the target group. The target group may simply reject all methods of influence attempted by the power-wielder. At this point, the power-wielding entity must decide whether to "let this one go"—with the probable result that the other, weaker target groups controlled by the power-wielder will no longer perceive it as having sufficient power to warrant continued deference—or the power-wielder can resort to punitive means involving force. The element of force, if applied successfully, will remove any alternatives the target group may have considered and will result in that group's compliance once again with the power-wielder's will. In short, force becomes power when it affects the target group's will and perceptions. We see, then, that the ultimate utility of force lies in its fundamental role in the exercise of power.

It should be apparent at this point that an entity may exert power far and away more influential than the amount of force that entity controls. Understanding this relationship between force and power is absolutely essential if one is to grasp how terrorism functions.

## Physical Force, Moral Force, and Combat Power

In the first section of this chapter it was argued that physical force became power when the target group perceived it has no alternative but to comply with the power-wielder's will. Implicit in this argument is that the target group regains or maintains its freedom of action if it can negate the power-wielder's force. This, of course, means the target group must have its own means to resist; that is, its own physical force sufficient to neutralize the influence of the power-wielder's physical force. And, when both sides employ physical force for the purpose of securing or retaining political objectives, a state of war exists.

Since wars are violent physical struggles, it stands to reason that the side enjoying greater physical force will always emerge victorious. If we measure physical force in terms of the size of the armed forces and the quality of its equipment, then determining which side will win an armed conflict can be reduced to a simple mathematical formula. Yet history is replete with examples of physically weaker military powers defeating stronger ones. What can account for this apparent contradiction?

As was suggested by Luttwak in the last section, force and power are not equivalent. It is the perception of the recipient of that force that converts it from physical force to power. It is the same in combat. Physical force becomes combat power when the recipient's actions are influenced by that force. This can occur in two ways. First, it can occur on the physical plane where the physical force physically disables the enemy, making it impossible for him to continue to fight—whether he wants to or not. Second, it can occur on the psychological plane where physical force demoralizes the enemy, making him *unwilling* to fight, even though he still has the means to do so. As will be shown, victory generally goes to the side that is able to demoralize the enemy first— regardless of the overall numerical ratio of physical forces. If the enemy's will to fight has been destroyed, no amount of physical force can change the equation. Physical force is inert unless it is animated by the will to use it.

For the purpose of this book, the will to fight will be called *moral force*. Moral force represents the ability to resist demoralization and to initiate and sustain combat in the face of great personal danger. The elements of moral force are nebulous and much more difficult to quantify than the elements of physical force. In his book *Fighting Power*, Martin van Creveld identifies the elements of moral force, which he calls "fighting power," as being "discipline and cohesion, morale and initiative, courage and toughness, the willingness to fight and the readiness, if necessary, to die."[7] The greater these elements the less vulnerable an armed force will be to demoralization. Moral force, then, is critical in determining the combat power of any belligerent.

Wars are seldom lost by the total exhaustion of the elements of physical force on one side. They are lost from the collapse and loss of moral force. The very fact that virtually all battles result in the capture of healthy combatants along with perfectly functional equipment serves as a testament to the proposition that physical force is a factor in war only as long as it remains animated by moral force. Indeed, most military commanders, strategists, and students of warfare credit moral force with being far more important to victory than physical force. Military studies are replete with arguments supporting this contention.

The great eighteenth-century military commander Maurice de Saxe believes that "the human heart is the starting point in all matters pertaining to war."[8] This was echoed almost a century later by Napoleon Bonaparte's famous maxim, "In war the moral is to the physical as three is to one."[9] And von Clausewitz puts it this way, "One might say that the physical seems little more than the wooden hilt, while moral factors are the precious metal, the real weapon. . . ."[10] Reflecting the earlier contention that war is, above all, a clash of wills, the French military thinker Ardant du Picq suggests that "in battle, two moral forces, even more than two material forces, are in conflict. The victor has often lost . . . more [physical forces] than the vanquished. . . . Moral effect inspires fear. Fear must be transformed into terror in order to conquer. . . ."[11] Even Sir Basil Liddell Hart, who admonishes his reader to remember that "the strongest will is of little use . . . inside a dead body,"[12] concedes that of the two, moral factors enjoy predominance in all military decisions.[13] And these are but a handful of the discussions by military thinkers and strategists on the superiority of moral over physical force.

The reason moral force enjoys such predominance over physical force can easily be seen by examining how physical force actually functions on the battlefield. As mentioned earlier, physical force is manifested in combat by disabling the enemy, that is, by destroying or damaging his means to fight and by killing, wounding, or capturing the enemy's combatants. But again, this is physical force being applied in strictly a physical sense. Physical force confronts physical force until one or the other is totally expended. In combat, however, the total annihilation of one of the contending forces is a relatively rare phenomenon, since the combatants on the losing side usually perceive what is happening long before the final blow and attempt to disengage. In this situation, physical force begins to exert extreme psychological pressure upon the side that perceives it is losing, and that side becomes demoralized. Demoralization, of course, immediately affects the physical force available to the demoralized army since the combatants lose courage and willingness to fight. In short, there is nothing with which to animate the physical force necessary to defeat the enemy.

This is borne out by von Clausewitz, who contends in his work that the morale of the enemy is a lucrative target. He notes that "a great destructive act inevitably exerts on all other actions, and it is exactly at such times that the moral factor is, so to speak, the most fluid element of all, and therefore spreads most easily to affect everything else."[14] He touches on this again when he says, "the loss of moral equilibrium . . . can attain such massive proportions that it overpowers everything by its irresistible force."[15]

It is not necessary, therefore, to totally disable the enemy to defeat him. Thousands of armed combatants can be influenced to stop fighting by physically compelling (killing, wounding, or capturing) a few hundred at the right place and time. Consequently, physical force is much more useful in negating the enemy's physical force on the *moral* rather than the *physical* plane. This is borne out by Liddell Hart:

> A strategist should think in terms of paralyzing, not of killing. Even on the lower plane of warfare, a man killed is merely one less, whereas a man unnerved is a highly infectious carrier of fear, capable of spreading an epidemic of panic. On a higher plane of warfare, the impression made on the mind of the opposing Commander can nullify the whole fighting power that his troops possess. And still on a higher plane, psychological pressure on the government of a country may suffice to cancel all the resources at its command—so that the sword falls from a paralyzed hand.[16]

What is important to understand here is the dynamic relationship between physical and moral force. It is this relationship that rationalizes the fact that military powers having smaller armed forces equipped with qualitatively inferior weapons can, and do, defeat those having objectively superior forces. It also explains why it is so difficult to determine the combat power of an armed force without having tested it in combat. Indeed, it is the very nebulous nature of combat power that is one of the major causes of war in the first place. As John Stoessinger notes in his book *Why Nations Go To War,*

> A leader's misperception of his adversary's power is perhaps the quintessential cause of war. It is vital to remember, however, that it is not the actual distribution of power that precipitates a war; it is the way in which a leader thinks that power is distributed. A war will start when nations disagree over their perceived strength. . . . And the war will end when the fighting nations perceive each other's strength more realistically.[17]

War, then, is a test of the physical and moral strength of the political entities waging it. Since even in a modern nation-state mobilized to fight a total war only a small percentage of the population actually bears arms, the question becomes one of how to maximize combat power with a minimum of physical force. As will be shown, there are two means of doing so: (1) adapt current technology to improve the lethality and effectiveness of the weapon systems and military formations employed and (2) maximize moral force through the creation of cohesive military organizations. Because moral force is a prerequisite for physical force, it is necessary to address moral force first.

## Military Organization and Moral Force

In the search to maximize physical force, man learned the importance of moral force. And, in the search for the best means to generate and sustain moral force in combat, man arrived at the military organization. On the physical plane, military organization permits physical force to be concentrated into combat formations that are responsive to the will of a single commander. On the moral plane, military organizations socialize the individual combatant in a manner that subordinates his will to the group and sustains his morale and courage in combat. This chapter deals with how military organizations maximize moral force.

From the moment the first military formation appeared on some forgotten, ancient battlefield what ultimately determined victory was the ability to maintain unit cohesion longer than the enemy. The instant a combat unit began to break up, its combat power rapidly dwindled to nothing, and victory was virtually assured for the side remaining intact. As technology improved the means of war, military organizations became increasingly large until, by the late eighteenth or early nineteenth century, the military organization encompassed the entire nation-state. Consequently, victory was determined not only by the cohesion of the armed forces, but of the nation-state as well. As will be shown in a later chapter, destroying a nation's cohesion is one of the major objectives of military, revolutionary, and state-sponsored terrorism. For the moment, however, it is important to understand the dynamic process of developing and sustaining moral force and cohesion in military units. This will provide a foundation for understanding the principles behind the use of force in a terroristic manner.

In their book *Crisis in Command*, Richard Gabriel and Paul Savage define unit cohesion as "the expectation that a military unit will attempt to perform its assigned orders and mission irrespective of the [combat] situation and its inevitable attendant risks."[18] But what makes men stay and fight despite those "attendant risks"? As the Spartan general Brasidas reportedly observed, "When every man is his own master in battle, he will readily find a decent excuse for saving himself."[19] And Hilaire Belloc, when writing of the battle of Poitiers, suggested, "Every member wishes to separate himself from the band when it is in danger. Indeed, the wish to decamp is always strongest . . . where the group is in greatest danger."[20] Throughout history armies have weathered these same circumstances, with some consistently doing better than others. Why do some armies maintain their cohesion longer than others?

The ancients discovered that discipline and training were elementary factors in creating and sustaining the will to fight. This, in turn, led to cohesion in battle. Consequently, endless drill and iron discipline became the lot of the ancient soldier. By the first century B.C. the Roman military system was the best in the world not because of some technical advantage but simply due to "insistence on constant training and enforcement of severe discipline."[21] Training gave the soldier and his commander confidence in his ability to his job, while discipline ensured every soldier did his job correctly in the face of extreme personal danger.

What no military organization could tolerate was a man who put his personal safety above the job he was required to do. If that man broke and ran, he could easily affect the cohesion of the whole unit. Consequently, the usual method for dealing with those who turned to flee was to inflict the ultimate measure of discipline on them—that is, kill them before they could affect the others. There were, of course, lesser punishments for lesser breaches of soldierly conduct, but clearly "organizational compulsion" and coercion became major instruments in ensuring unit cohesion in combat.

Organizational compulsion has carried forward through the centuries and is operative even in today's military organizations. In his book *The Face of Battle,* John Keegan describes the use of organizational compulsion and coercion in the battles of Agincourt (1415), Waterloo (1815), and the Somme (1916). For instance, he describes how "friendly" cavalry was used to coerce friendly infantry at Waterloo. This was accomplished by placing the cavalry behind unwilling infantry to keep the latter from breaking and running.[22] Keegan also mentions British noncommissioned officers (NCOs) shooting deserters during World War I in order to stabilize a unit in the thick of battle and dissuade any other men from deserting.[23]

Clearly without consistent and effective organizational compulsion, military discipline wanes. As George Patton observed, "There is only one sort of discipline—*perfect discipline.* If you do not enforce and maintain discipline, you are potential murderers."[24] Certainly without military discipline, unit cohesion is impossible. A classic example of this is the U.S. Army in the Vietnam War. During that war, organizational compulsion was drastically curtailed. Two examples of this are sufficient to support this contention: (1) the limited prosecution of actual and suspected assaults upon superiors by subordinates and (2) the failure to adequately deal with "combat refusals."

During the last three years of American involvement in Vietnam, there were, according to Gabriel and Savage, 363 cases of assault with explosives against superiors and another 118 cases that were deemed probable assaults. Of these 481 cases, less than 10 percent resulted in the offender being apprehended and brought to trial. Equally important was the treatment of mutiny during the war. Despite the progressive increase of "combat refusals" from 68 in 1968 to approximately 245 in 1970, there was virtually no administrative change in how to deal with the problem. Certainly there were no executions of the type described by Keegan. The ultimate result, of course, is that by the time the American Army left Vietnam, its military cohesion was in a state of advanced disintegration.[25] The lack of consistent and effective organizational compulsion was clearly a contributing factor.

Aside from organizational compulsion, there are three other major factors in the generation of moral force and unit cohesion. These are *group (peer) pressure, the survival instinct,* and *leadership.* It was the French military thinker Ardant du Picq who first began to examine the concept of group pressure as a factor in group cohesion. During the mid-nineteenth century he proposed that "success in war depends upon individual valor . . . and this in turn depends upon mutual moral pressure and mutual supervision of men 'who know each other well.'"[26] This line of reasoning was again taken up during World War II by the military historian General S.L.A. Marshall. Examining du Picq's hypothesis as it functioned on the modern battlefield, Marshall found that group pressure was one of the primary cohesive elements in American military units. In *Men Against Fire,* he writes:

> Whenever one surveys the forces of the battlefield, it is to see that fear is general among men, but to observe further that men are commonly loathe that their fear will be expressed in specific acts which their comrades will recognize as cowardice . . . . When a soldier is known to men around him, he . . . has reason to fear losing the one thing he is likely to value more highly than life—his reputation as a man among men.[27]

The key factor in both du Picq's and Marshall's observations is that group pressure—the desire not to let one's comrades down or show cowardice—is only operative if the actor is well known and also an accepted member of the group. Consequently, both Marshall and du

Picq conclude that armies must organize in a manner to allow such a relationship to build among the men. This idea has been reinforced by Morris Janowitz who examined cohesion and disintegration in the German Wehrmacht during World War II. In this study Janowitz notes,

> It appears that a soldier's ability to resist is a function of the capacity of his immediate primary group [his squad or section] to avoid social disintegration. When that individual's immediate group, and its supporting formations, met his basic organic needs, offered him affection and esteem . . . supplied him with a sense of power and adequately regulated his relations with authority, *the element of self concern* in battle . . . was minimized.[28]

Janowitz concludes his study by observing that the remarkable cohesion of the German Army was due in large part to its careful nurturing of the primary group.[29] Perhaps the major factor in making sure these groups were formed was the unique German replacement system. Unlike the American system whereby combat units remained on the front lines for protracted periods and were kept up to strength by a steady stream of individual replacements, the German system rotated whole divisions out of the front lines, which allowed the reconstitution of the primary group before the unit returned to combat. The efficacy of the German system can be readily seen by the relative combat effectiveness of the Wehrmacht and the U.S. Army during World War II. In fifty combat engagements between 1942 and 1945 the average combat effectiveness of similarly equipped combat units of roughly equal size was 1:1.55.[30] That is to say, on the average, German combat units were 20 percent more effective than American units of similar size and like equipment. Certainly, the American replacement system, which hindered the formation of primary groups, contributed to this disparity.

The third major element in creating and maintaining group cohesion is far more primordial than the first two. It is, paradoxically enough, the survival instinct. Whereas organizational compulsion and peer group pressure are particularly effective in getting men to the battlefield and function in certain ways to keep men fighting, once on the battlefield a man's survival instinct becomes an additional factor. If a man is placed in a situation where he cannot physically disengage the enemy due to the mere fact that safety is too far away, the survival instinct can make a man a ferocious fighter—particularly if it is a fight-

or-die situation. Since he perceives that he cannot run away with any hope of success, the soldier determines his only hope of survival is to stay with his unit and subdue the enemy. It is what du Picq refers to as "escape by attack."[31] Unit cohesion is thereby enhanced by the soldier's perception that his unit offers him security.

The fourth and final instrument of group cohesion is military leadership. As Gabriel and Savage succinctly put it, "One factor virtually guaranteeing poor military performance is bad leadership and its destructive effort upon group cohesion."[32] A good leader, of course, has the opposite effect. His primary function in combat, besides carrying out the orders of his superiors, is to maintain the cohesion of his unit. He does this by sustaining his men's courage and morale through a combination of coercion and leadership by example. To be effective, the leader requires two elements: respect and loyalty of his men. This is secured in many ways, but three of the more important are (1) that the men are aware the leader is concerned about their welfare, (2) that the leader shows he is willing to share the same risks and sacrifices as his men, and (3) that the men perceive the leader to be a competent combat commander who is unlikely to risk his men's lives needlessly.[33] When units are led by such men, they can endure incredible hardships and face hopeless odds without losing their cohesion. Despite the fact that their entire nation was crumbling around them, soldiers of the German Wehrmacht fought tenaciously to the very last. As Janowitz notes, the German soldier was "likely to go on fighting, providing he had the necessary weapons, as long as the group possessed leadership with which he could identify himself, and as long as he gave affection to and received affection from [his primary group]."[34]

Organizational compulsion, group pressure, the survival instinct, and leadership are, then, the primary components of moral force and unit cohesion at the combat unit level. But these organizational dynamics also play important roles in higher echelons, even into the governmental structure itself. Obviously the belligerent best able to mobilize its war-fighting resources in the most efficient and effective manner will enjoy a greater advantage over an enemy that does not or cannot. As with combat power on the battlefield, moral force is the primary factor in mobilizing a city-state, kingdom, or nation-state for war. Just as the combat unit must be a cohesive body, so must the political entity that sends it into combat. It is interesting to note that the French Revolutionary Convention relied on all four of the component factors of unit cohesion when, on August 23, 1794, it called for a levy en masse. The leadership component, of course, was provided by the convention. The other three can be clearly seen in the order itself.

> From now until such time as its enemies have been driven out of the territory of the Republic [*survival instinct*] all Frenchmen are permanently requisitioned for the service of the armies [*organizational compulsion*]. The young shall go and fight, the married men shall forge weapons and transport food, the women shall make tents and clothes and serve in the hospitals, the old men shall [go] . . . into public places to rouse the courage of warriors and preach hatred of kings and the unity of the nation [*group pressure*].[35]

Even the most powerful nation on earth cannot ignore the need for organizational cohesion, particularly among the government, the armed forces, and the people of which they are made. Harry Summers in his book *On Strategy* points out how the failure to mobilize the will of the people eventually resulted in the U.S. defeat in Vietnam despite the latter's extreme military weakness.[36] When America's moral force gave way, national cohesion failed, and the military might of the United States rapidly dwindled until it was no longer a match for a tiny, third world nation.

To summarize this section, then, we have seen the central role played by moral force in the generation and maintenance of combat power. Moreover, moral force is enhanced by organizational compulsion, group pressure, survival instinct, and leadership; all of which help maximize unit cohesion. Cohesion is a critical factor in all echelons of war, for without it, the organization melts away into disjointed individual parts, each seeking its own interests over the good of the whole. Finally, and most important, this section establishes that the most effective use of physical force is not in the negation of the enemy's physical force directly, but by the destruction of his moral force. If the will to use it is no longer there, physical force is meaningless. It is upon this concept that terrorism functions. It makes possible the generation of immense political power with minuscule military force.

## Weapon Systems: The Instruments of Force

Weapon systems are the means of war. They facilitate the conversion of moral force—the will to fight—into physical force. In the last section it was argued that military organizations permit the generation of the greatest possible physical force by concentrating it into cohesive military formations that are responsive to the will of a single commander. Certainly it is true that the side able to maintain its cohesion the longest will emerge victorious. But although cohesion is maintained by moral force, it is destroyed by the use or the threat of the use of physical force. It stands to reason, therefore, that the more lethal the physical force the greater its influence upon cohesion. Once both sides had developed cohesive military units ancient commanders realized that what could give them an edge on the enemy was to make their individual soldiers more deadly than their counterparts. The most obvious way to do this, of course, was by the simple expedient of equipping the soldier with better weaponry.

The *Dictionary of Weapons and Military Terms* defines a weapon as "an instrument of combat, either offensive or defensive, used to destroy, injure, defeat or threaten an enemy."[37] These may be categorized according to two widely recognized functional groupings: shock and fire. This section will address the different purposes and capabilities of each of these types of weapons, which, in turn, will aid in understanding why terrorists employ physical force in the manner they do.

Fire weapons "are devices for getting at a distant enemy while . . . actually or wishfully remaining safe from his striking power."[38] Fire weapons generally rely upon the use of projectiles or missiles and can be anything from a rock to an intercontinental ballistic missile. As technology improved, explosive devices were added, making mine warfare a new element in the fire-weapon inventory. Although they are quite useful in war, all fire weapons have a definite weakness. As the sociologist Turney-High observes,

> Fire weapons may be able to drive an enemy from a position . . . they may also be used defensively to minimize the strength of an enemy assault before the moment of contact. Prohibitive fire may also prevent an enemy from occupying a locality, but it is costly and of limited effectiveness. In spite of all these virtues, fire troops can [occupy] but can hold a position in the open only with difficulty. Fire fighters may hold with effectiveness only behind . . . cover. Fire, and fire [alone,] is hopeless if the enemy ever makes contact.[39]

Although Turney-High is primarily speaking of war in the age before gunpowder, his observations still apply today. Fire troops in modern armies consist primary of artillery and air forces, neither of which can hold their positions alone when confronted with shock forces. Consequently, fire troops are considered combat *support* forces, to denote their specialized and somewhat limited function in combat.

According to Turney-High, "It is shock or the threat of shock which works one's will on the enemy. The victor in a fire fight is a long way from his objective; the victor in a shock fight is right there."[40] It is shock weapons—clubs, swords, bayonets, mounted knights, tanks, and so on—that enable the combatant to take and hold territory. As will be shown in the chapter on the principles of war, occupying the enemy's territory is one of the primary means of disarming him since it denies that territory's resources to him and permits you to exploit them for your own war effort.

Seizing territory also provides you with a bargaining chip at the peace table, and if the enemy prizes that territory highly enough, you will have great leverage compelling him to make political concessions. As will be seen, terrorist shock operations invariably seek to seize a piece of enemy "territory" to force the target entity to make political concessions—even if that "territory" is only a single airliner or even a single hostage for whom the targeted entity is responsible. Consequently, of the two, pure shock weapons have greater utility than pure fire. This goes far in explaining why combatants expose themselves to fire to seize an objective. Fire by itself can render a piece of real estate (bridge, fortification, city, etc.) useless for a time, but shock forces may seize them for their own use. Nuclear fire weapons, of course, enjoy unprecedented destructive capacity, but still, they can only deny—not seize—territory.

Another advantage shock weapons have over fire is that shock weapons are able to capture prisoners. Fire weapons are able to compel the enemy by wounding or killing, but the enemy has the option of leaving the target area or digging in to mitigate the effectiveness of fire weapons. Shock weapons remove these options. Either the enemy defeats the shock attack or he leaves his position. If he does not, or cannot leave, the enemy is made a prisoner. As World War II clearly illustrates, capturing prisoners is the most effective and efficient means to physically destroy the enemy's combat power. By concentrating armored shock forces to break through and surround the enemy's armed forces, they often surrender without fighting due to their inability to be resupplied or reinforced. For instance, in the spring of 1940 the Germans captured over a million French, British, Dutch, and Belgian prisoners in three short weeks, while losing only 60,000 casualties in return.[41] Nor was this an isolated case. It was repeated by the Germans in the summer of 1941 when they invaded Russia, by the Soviets at Stalingrad in 1942, and by the Anglo-Allied forces in France in 1944. By the end of World War II, nearly every major power was using armored shock forces to neutralize large elements of the enemy's forces by surrounding and capturing them.

Not only do shock forces enjoy a greater capacity for neutralizing the enemy's physical forces, but they also have a larger impact on enemy morale than fire weapons. Although artillery and aerial bombardment can undermine enemy morale, as mentioned above, their effects can be mitigated by either leaving the target area or finding suitable cover. Additionally, studies of people who lived in cities suffering aerial bombardment during World War II reveal that sustained or regular bombardments did not break the enemy's morale, but merely numbed and inured them to further violence.[42] As Alexander McKee notes in his book *Dresden 1945*, civilian populations incurred incredible destruction without having their morale "crack."[43] Moreover, John Keegan describes the seven-day-long artillery bombardment prior to the infantry attack in the battle of the Somme as a failure, despite firing over 1.5 million artillery shells into a 50-square-mile area.[44] When the British attacked, not only were the vast majority of the Germans still alive, but few, if any, were demoralized.

Shock weapons, on the other hand, have a much greater effect on morale. This is no doubt due, in part, to the ability of shock attack to press the issue to the ultimate decision. At the moment a shock attack begins, both the attacker and defender know that only one or the other will emerge victorious. And, as argued in the last section, it is the side that manages to keep from becoming demoralized the longest that will emerge the victor.

These, then, are the two basic weapon types and how they function in war. Of the two, shock weapons are superior because they can seize territory, can capture prisoners, and have a larger impact on the enemy's morale. Fire forces, on the other hand, permit a belligerent to hit the enemy from a distance while remaining under cover and thereby reduce the risk to the side that employs them. Except for nuclear weapons, fire weapons tend to be the primary weapon of weaker forces fighting defensively, while shock remains the primary weapon for attack. Used defensively, fire weapons generally only add to the cost of an enemy's desired objective. Fire weapons, by themselves, seldom compel the enemy to surrender his political goals, particularly if they are defensive.

## Summation

Force is the primary element of war. Only by force is one side able to compel an enemy to modify or surrender his political goals. It is in the act of compelling that force is converted to power. But force may exist in one of two states—kinetic or potential. Kinetic force physically compels by removing all alternatives and options the target body may be considering, compelling it to act in accordance with the force-wielder's will. Potential force, on the other hand, operates on the psychological plane, inducing the target to act in accordance with the force-wielder's will on the understanding that if he does not, potential force will be converted to kinetic force. Force, therefore, can be of two types—moral or physical. It is the dynamic interaction of these two that determines a belligerent's combat power, and of the two, moral force is by far the most important.

Moral force represents the ability to animate physical force, converting it from potential to kinetic energy, and, equally important, the ability to resist demoralization in the face of the enemy's physical force. In short, without moral force, physical force is impossible. But of the two types of force, moral force is by far the more vulnerable and the more costly if it fails. Thousands or, as in the example of the German blitzkrieg into France in May 1940, even millions of combatants can be rendered useless by destroying their will to resist. This brings to mind once against Liddell Hart's comment that "the strategist should think in terms of paralyzing, not of killing." In other words, the enemy's moral force should be specifically targeted. By the same token friendly moral force should be nurtured and protected at all costs.

The best means of creating and sustaining moral force in combat is through building cohesive military organizations. These organizations inculcate moral force in the individual combatant by four methods: organizational compulsion, group pressure, survival instinct, and leadership. Organizational compulsion involves the judicious use of discipline and coercion to make the soldier do what he normally would not do were he left to his own instincts. Group pressure is in many ways the most important method. It socializes the soldier into a small body of trusted comrades the soldier needs and relies upon and who need and rely upon him. These bonds of mutual support appear to go further than any other factor in assuring a unit's cohesion holds in the face of great personal danger. Survival instinct builds in the soldier the feeling that safety lies in his unit. Leadership, of course, is required to make certain the other three elements exist and in the correct mixture to maximize moral force—both to resist being influenced by the enemy's physical force and to generate the maximum friendly physical force as well.

The instruments of physical force are shock and fire weapons. Fire weapons permit the user to attack the enemy from cover and from a distance thereby reducing the risk to the user. But fire weapons are unable to seize territory held by the enemy and by themselves cannot hold friendly territory being attacked by enemy shock forces. Shock forces are the decisive weapon. When shock forces are employed, a decision is reached. Either the attack fails or the enemy is killed, captured, or forced to retreat. But shock forces must expose themselves to enemy fire and are therefore more costly to employ than fire troops. As will be shown later, shock is an instrument that must be very carefully applied by extremely weak terrorist forces but, as in conventional warfare, is also the weapon that pays the highest dividends if properly employed.

## Notes

1. Arleigh Burke, "Power and Peace," *Peace and War in the Modern Age: Premises, Myths and Realities,* edited by Frank R. Barnett, William C. Mott, and John C. Neff. (Garden City, N.Y.: Doubleday & Co., Inc., 1965; Anchor Books edition, 1965), p. 19.

2. Ibid., p. 20.

3. Edward N. Luttwak, *The Grand Strategy of the Roman Empire: From the First Century A.D. to the Third* (Baltimore: The Johns Hopkins University Press, 1976; Johns Hopkins paperback edition, 1981), p. 196.

4. Ibid.

5. Ibid., pp. 196–97.

6. Ibid., p. 198.

7. Martin van Creveld, *Fighting Power: German and U.S. Army Performance, 1939–1945* (Westport, Conn.: Greenwood Press, 1982), p. 3.

8. Maurice de Saxe, *Mes Reveries* (1732) As quoted in Robert D. Heinl, Jr., *Dictionary of Military and Naval Quotations* (Annapolis, Md.: The United States Naval Institute, 1985), p. 196.

9. Sir Basil Liddell Hart, *Strategy* (New York: Praeger Publishers, Inc., 1968), p. 24. Quoting Napoleon Bonaparte.

10. Karl von Clausewitz, *On War*, edited and translated by Michael Howard and Peter Paret (Princeton: Princeton University Press, 1976), p. 185.

11. Ardant du Picq, *Etudes sur le Combat* (Paris, 1914), pp. 121–23. As quoted in J. F. C. Fuller, *The Conduct of War, 1789–1961* (New York: Funk & Wagnalls Inc., 1961; Minerva Press, 1968), pp. 121–22.

12. Liddell Hart, op. cit., p. 24.

13. Ibid.

14. von Clausewitz, op. cit., p. 47.

15. Ibid., p. 232.

16. Ibid., p. 228.

17. John G. Stoessinger, *Why Nations Go To War*. 4th ed. (New York: St. Martin's Press, Inc., 1985), p. 210.

18. Richard Gabriel and Paul Savage, *Crisis in Command: Mismanagement in the Army* (New York: Hill and Wang, 1978; reprint edition, 1979), pp. 31–32.

19. Robert D. Heinl, Jr., *Dictionary of Military and Naval Quotations* (Annapolis, Md.: The United States Naval Institute Press, 1985), p. 90. Quoting Brasidas of Sparta to the Lacadaemonian Army, 423 B.C.

20. Hilaire Belloc, *Poitiers* (London: 1913), p. 112. As quoted in Harry H. Turney-High, *Primitive War: Its Practice and Concepts* (Columbia, S.C.: The University of South Carolina Press, 1949; second edition, 1971), p. 29.

21. R. Ernest Dupuy and Trevor N. Dupuy, *The Encyclopedia of Military History: From 3500 B.C. to the Present* (New York: Harper & Row, Publishers Inc., 1970), p. 72.

22. John Keegan, *The Face of Battle: A Study of Agincourt, Waterloo and the Somme* (New York: The Viking Press, 1976; Penguin Books, 1985), pp. 330–31.

23. Ibid., p. 282.

24. George S. Patton, Jr., "Instructions to Third Army Corps and Division Commanders" (1944). As quoted in Heinl, op. cit., p. 94.

25. See Gabriel and Savage, op. cit., pp. 43–45, 50.

26. Stefan T. Possony and Etienne Mantoux, "DuPicq and Foch: The Military School," *Makers of Modern Strategy: Military Thought from Machiavelli to*

*Hitler,* edited by Edward M. Earle (Princeton: Princeton University Press, 1943; Princeton paperback printing, 1973), p. 210.

27. Keegan, op. cit., pp. 71–72. Quoting S.L.A. Marshall from his book, *Men Against Fire.*

28. Morris Janowitz, *Military Conflict: Essays in the Institutional Analysis of War and Peace* (London: Sage Publications, Ltd., 1975), p. 178. (Emphasis added.)

29. Ibid., p. 183.

30. van Creveld, op. cit., pp. 5–9.

31. Possony and Mantoux, op. cit., pp. 211–12.

32. Gabriel and Savage, op. cit., p. 51.

33. Ibid., p. 55.

34. Janowitz, op. cit., p. 181.

35. Will and Ariel Durant, *The Story of Civilization,* vol. 11, *The Age of Napoleon* (Simon & Schuster, Inc., 1975), p. 63.

36. Harry G. Summers, Jr., *On Strategy: A Critical Analysis of the Vietnam War* (Novato, Calif.: Presidio Press, 1982; 4th reprinting, 1984), pp. 12–13.

37. John Quick, *Dictionary of Weapons and Military Terms* (New York: McGraw-Hill Book Co., 1973), p. 498.

38. Harry H. Turney-High. *Primitive War: Its Practice and Concepts* (Columbia, S.C.: The University of South Carolina Press, 1949; second edition, 1971), p. 10.

39. Ibid., p. 12.

40. Ibid., pp. 12–13.

41. Brian Bond, "Battle of France," *Decisive Battles of the 20th Century: Land, Sea and Air,* edited by Noble Frankland and Christopher Dowling (New York: David McKay Co., Inc., 1976), p. 110.

42. P. E. Vernon, "Psychological Effect of Air Raids," *Journal of Abnormal and Social Psychology, 1941,* p. 36 and pp. 457–76. As quoted in Grant Wardlaw, *Political Terrorism: Theory, Tactics and Countermeasures* (Cambridge: Cambridge University Press, 1984), pp. 35–36.

43. Alexander McKee, *Dresden 1945: The Devil's Tinderbox* (London: Souvenir Press, Ltd., 1982), pp. 58–59.

44. Keegan, op. cit., p. 235.

# 3

# THE PRINCIPLES OF WAR: FACTORS GOVERNING THE USE OF FORCE IN WAR

■

## Introduction

Although von Clausewitz is most widely known for his proposition that war is linked and subordinate to politics, from the technological/ realist perspective his most important contribution to understanding war are his principles of war. These principles govern the use and manipulation of force by the political entity in the quest for power and are the fundamental rules that provide guidance on how to employ military force to maximize the chances of success in war.

These principles will be divided into two basic types: (1) those that govern the use of force in terms of achieving a political victory and (2) those that govern the maximization of friendly force against enemy force on the field of battle. The first we shall call the *principles of war* and the second the *principles of combat*. What is important to understand from the outset is that both types of principles apply and are operational regardless of whether the war is total or limited, long or short, conventional or unconventional, or even nuclear.

This chapter will introduce five major principles of war found in von Clausewitz's book *On War*. These five are not necessarily exhaustive, since von Clausewitz posited many others. But these five establish how force should be applied to achieve the political end for which the war is being waged. Once these have been introduced and discussed in detail, we will then examine what we have labeled the seven principles of combat. Each will be defined and discussed from the perspective of von Clausewitz, as well as many other military writers. These seven principles essentially govern how physical force is to be applied to counter and overcome the enemy's physical force on the battlefield.

## Five Major Principles of War

According to von Clausewitz, there is only one means of war, and that is through the *principle of engagement* or armed combat. Von Clausewitz considers this to be the preeminent principle of war that drives all else. This is reflected in his statement that

> however many forms combat takes, however far it may be removed from the brute discharge of hatred and enmity of a physical encounter, however many forces may intrude which themselves are not part of the fighting, it is inherent in the very concept of war that everything that occurs must originally derive from combat.[1]

By coupling von Clausewitz's preeminent principle of war with his definition of war presented in chapter 1 we quickly see that war is a physical struggle between political entities that is resolved by only one means—*armed combat*. That is to say that war exists only when there is a clash of arms between opposing political entities, each wishing to compel the other. Consequently, if armed force is applied on only one side—such as the Nazi genocide campaign against the Jews during World War II—then it is not a form of war. This distinction will become extremely helpful in distinguishing between the types of terrorism that are or are not a form of war.

To von Clausewitz, however, war was not merely random clashes upon random battlefields, but rather combat for a desired end. To achieve the desired results from combat it is necessary not merely to win a victory but to win a victory from which further victories are assured or at least probable. This brings us to four additional principles of war: *the objective, the center of gravity, the defense,* and *the offense.* These are what inform us of when, where, and how to engage an opponent not only to win a battle, but to achieve the purpose for which the war is being fought. These five principles combine to provide the driving factors behind all warfare.

Although the engagement is the preeminent principle of the *means* of war, the military or operational objective is the most important principle of the *purpose* of war. It is the objective that subordinates war to policy. It ensures that policy is correctly translated into force—that the engagement will result in the realization of policy goals. According to von Clausewitz,

> No one starts a war—or rather no one in his right senses ought to do so—without first being clear in his mind what he intends to achieve by that war and how he intends to conduct it, the former is its political purpose; the latter its operational objective. This is the governing principle which will set its course, prescribe the scale of means and effort which is required, and make its influence felt . . . down to the smallest operational detail.[2]

Liddell Hart concurs with von Clausewitz, stating, "In discussing the subject of 'the objective' in war it is essential to be clear about . . . the distinction between the political and military objective. The two are different, but not separate. For nations do not wage war for war's sake, but in pursuance of policy. The military objective is only the means to a political end."[3] He goes on to admonish us, however, that "history shows that gaining a military victory is not in itself equivalent to gaining the object of policy."[4] According to U.S. Army Field Manual 100-5,

> There is no simple formula for winning wars. Defeating enemy forces in battle will not always insure victory. Other national instruments of power and persuasion will influence or even determine the results of wars. Wars cannot be won, however, without a national will and military forces equal to the task. Although successful military operations do not guarantee victory, they are an indispensable part of winning.[5]

Thus, the problem becomes one of determining which military objective will achieve the political purpose for which the war is being fought.

Von Clausewitz was aware of this problem and to meet it conceived his second great principle of war: the *center of gravity*. Basically, the center of gravity is "that point in the enemy's organism—military, political, social, etc.—at which, should he be defeated, or should he lose it, the whole structure of national power will collapse."[6] It should be stressed that the center of gravity will vary from enemy to enemy depending upon military, political, and social circumstances. Von Clausewitz offers these examples:

> For Alexander, Gustavus Adolphus, Charles XII, and Frederick the Great the center of gravity was their army. If the army had been destroyed, they would have all gone down in history as failures. In countries subject to domestic strife, the center of gravity is generally the capital. In small countries that rely on larger ones, it is usually the army of their protector. Among alliances, it lies in the community of interest, and in popular uprising it is the personalities of the leaders and public opinion. It is against these our energies should be directed.[7]

To arrive at the military objective, a political entity at war with another must reduce the substance of the enemy's power to the fewest possible sources—preferably to only one. This will expose the enemy's center of gravity, which should then become the primary military objective. Failure to do so will invariably result in military defeat and the inability to achieve the political purpose of the war. According to Harry Summers, this is precisely why the United States lost the war in Vietnam:

> We had adopted a strategy that focused on none of the *possible* North Vietnamese centers of gravity—their army, their capital, the army of their protector, the community of interest with their allies, or public opinion. The center of gravity could not be the North Vietnamese Army because we had made a conscious decision not to invade North Vietnam to seek and destroy its armed forces. For the same reason it could not be Hanoi, the North Vietnamese capital. Our desire to limit the conflict and our fear of direct Soviet and Chinese involvement prevented us from destroying the "army of their protector" . . . the same fears prevented us from striking at the community of interest among North Vietnam, the Soviet Union and China. "The personalities of the leaders" and "public opinion" were never targets the United States could exploit. Instead, by seeing the Viet Cong as a separate entity rather than an instrument of North Vietnam, we chose a center of gravity which in fact did not exist [as] . . . was demonstrated during TET-68, when, even though they were virtually destroyed, the war continued unabated.[8]

Other than selecting and concentrating on the wrong center of gravity, von Clausewitz identifies three more barriers to achieving victory. First, he admits there may be instances where it is impossible to reduce several centers of gravity to one. When this is so, there

> is admittedly no alternative but to act as if there were two wars or even more, each with its own object. This assumes the existence of several independent opponents, and consequently great superiority on their part. When this is the case to defeat the enemy is [probably] out of the question.[9]

But as von Clausewitz points out, such cases are usually rare. The second barrier is the strength of your forces. These must be strong enough to score a decisive victory over the enemy's forces and to be able to make the effort necessary to pursue victory to the point where "the balance is beyond redress."[10] The final barrier is the political environment. To assure victory you must make certain your political position is so secure that success will not bring further enemies against you who could force you to abandon your efforts against your original opponent.

Selecting and concentrating on the correct center of gravity is obviously simply a function of good military intelligence, planning, and political resolve. The remaining three barriers—strength of your forces, multiple centers of gravity, and the political environment—are more problematic. They are particularly important to this book in that they almost perfectly describe the situation in which the modern political terrorist is likely to find himself. Although this point will be elaborated upon later, it is important to note that relative to the terrorist, the enemy usually enjoys massive superiority in political and military power. Although the enemy appears to have many centers of gravity, as will be seen, these can be reduced to one: namely, the target entity's forces of coercion. The military forces available to the terrorist are extremely weak and completely incapable of overcoming its enemy's armed forces except in the most limited tactical sense. In addition, terrorists are virtually always in a weak political position vis-à-vis their enemy. How, then, is it possible for the weaker side to emerge victorious? Von Clausewitz provides us with two answers: the factor of *time* and the *principle of defense.*

Of all the resources used on the field of battle, time is the only one that is not renewable or reconquerable. To Napoleon, time is the most critical factor in war. He states, "In the art of war, as in mechanics, time is the grand element between weight and force."[11] "The loss of time is irreparable in war . . . operations only fail through delays."[12] Thus, "strategy is the art of making use of time and space . . . space we can recover, lost time never."[13] This establishes the importance of time in war, but it does not explain why time benefits the weaker over the stronger belligerent.

As von Clausewitz points out, at first glance it would appear that time is mutually beneficial to both belligerents. Upon closer scrutiny, it becomes obvious that the stronger belligerent has little to gain from prolonging the war. By not achieving a quick victory the stronger political entity affords the weaker belligerent an opportunity to wear down the stronger foe—both physically and morally. Given enough time, the weaker power may be able to strengthen its own combat power, erode that of its enemy and/or create a more favorable political environment. Gaining time is, therefore, critical to the weaker belligerent, and buying time is one of the primary purposes of the *principle of defense*. Indeed, for von Clausewitz, the purpose of defense is simple preservation:

> It is easier to hold ground than to take it. It follows that defense is easier than attack, assuming both sides have equal means. [But] just what is it that makes preservation and protection so much easier? It is the fact that time which is allowed to pass unused accumulates to the credit of the defender. He reaps where he did not sow. Any omission of attack— whether from bad judgment, fear, or indolence—accrues to the defender's benefit.[14]

Having established that defense is easier than offense, von Clausewitz concludes that the defense is the stronger form of war. Sun Tzu also came to the same conclusion. He declares, "Invincibility lies in the defense; the possibility of victory in the attack. One defends when his strength is inadequate; he attacks when it is abundant."[15]

In effect, though weaker than your opponent, you may, by electing to fight defensively, offset his superiority. Even victorious attackers experience great wastage of their armed forces as they are spread over the conquered territory for garrison and police purposes. Perhaps one of the best descriptions of this phenomenon is given by General Horace Porter in his discussion of the Union Army of the Potomac's last offensive against the Confederate Army of Northern Virginia during the American Civil War. He notes that although the Union Army consisted of nearly twice the number of troops of its Confederate counterpart commanded by Robert E. Lee—116,000 to 70,000—the advantages were with the latter because he was on the defensive. Porter writes,

> Those familiar with military operations . . . will concede that, notwithstanding Lee's inferiority in numbers, the advantages were, nevertheless, in his favor . . . . Having interior lines, he was able to move by shorter marches, and to act constantly on the defensive . . . forc[ing] the invading army continually to assault fortified positions . . . . Lee and his officers were familiar with every foot of ground, and every inhabitant was eager to give them information. His army was in a friendly country, from which provisions could be drawn from all directions, and few troops had to be detached to guard lines of supply. The Union army, on the contrary, was unfamiliar with the country, was without accurate maps, could seldom secure trustworthy guides, and had to detach large bodies of troops to guard its long lines of communication, protect its supply trains, and conduct wounded to points of safety.[16]

As can be easily seen from the above, the attacker is continuously spread thinner and grows relatively weaker, while the defender grows increasingly strong compared to the attacker. During this phase, the defender should not remain passive but do everything possible to increase the attacker's expenditure of effort in all aspects of his warmaking resources. As von Clausewitz puts it, the defense is not merely "a simple shield, but a shield made up of well-directed blows."[17] U.S. Army Field Manual 100-5 echoes von Clausewitz when it states,

> Some military theorists think defense is the stronger form of war because denying success is easier than achieving it. Indeed, the defender does have significant advantages over the attacker. In most cases he not only knows the ground better, but having occupied it first, he has strengthened his position and massed his forces. He is under the cover of his own artillery and air defense. Once the battle begins, the defender fights from cover against an exposed enemy . . . [and] the effects of obstacles, airpower, and conventional weapons on exposed troops . . . favor the defender.[18]

According to von Clausewitz, the ultimate purpose of the defense is negative. That is, it is oriented primarily toward negating the offense and preserving the defense.[19] This is not done by mere passive defense, but by counterattacking when and where possible. This makes the offensive forces increase their expenditure of effort and slowly wears them down. As von Clausewitz notes, since

> the defense is the stronger form of war, yet has a negative object, it follows that it should be used only so long as weakness compels, and be abandoned as soon as we are strong enough to pursue a positive object. When one has used defensive measures successfully, a more favorable balance is usually created; thus, the natural course in war is to begin defensively and end by attacking.[20]

In other words, only by eventually taking the offensive can one hope to achieve victory. This is true even if your political goals are totally defensive and your only purpose for waging war is self-preservation.

A perfect example of the need for the offensive in a "purely defensive" war is the 1948 Arab-Israeli conflict. Within hours of becoming a sovereign nation-state, Israel was invaded by the armies of Egypt, Jordan, and Syria. As Israeli General Y. Yadin describes it, these forces ". . . were halted, and those of Egypt and Syria were hurled back beyond the original frontiers of Palestine. The formidable British-trained Arab legion of Jordan fought the Jews on more or less even terms, [but] . . . by the end of the year, Israel had [re]established her frontiers by force of arms over virtually all of the terrain which had been allotted her [by the UN] before the war. . . ." Only by counterattacking—going over to the offensive—could Israel have maintained its territory and sovereignty.[21]

It is the *principle of the offense*, then, that enables you to achieve victory. Whereas defense has a negative purpose—preservation—the offense has a positive one—conquest. And, it is the offense that enables the belligerent to increase his capacity to wage war. It does this by destroying the enemy's fighting forces, securing decisive terrain, depriving the enemy of resources (and alternately, gaining those resources for the attacker), gaining information, and deceiving or diverting the enemy's strength. The noted military historian Hew Strachan appears to contradict von Clausewitz by calling the offense the stronger form of war "as it affirms morale and only it can lead to victory. The defense is weaker because it . . . yields the initiative to the enemy, and is therefore acceptable only as a prelude to a counter-attack."[22] Upon closer scrutiny it is apparent that Strachan means it is the more *decisive* form of war, since the offense is the only means to achieve victory. But what, exactly, is it that makes this form of warfare so decisive?

This is a particularly difficult question in view of the fact that we have already claimed that the defense is stronger because of the various advantages that accrue to it. Actually, Strachan gives us a hint when he states that the "defense . . . yields the initiative to the enemy." U.S. Field Manual 100-5 emphasizes that the initiative is the only significant advantage the attacker possesses. "If the attacker loses the initiative, even temporarily, he will jeopardize the success of the entire operation."[23] It is imperative, therefore, that we fully understand this phenomenon before delving more deeply into the principle of the offense.

Von Clausewitz is strangely silent on the concept of the initiative. This is not to say he was unaware of it, but that he used the term very sparingly, preferring instead to discuss its component parts: speed, surprise, and concentration of effort. Consequently, we will rely on the U.S. Army's definition, which states, "Initiative implies an offensive spirit in the conduct of all operations. The underlying purpose of [which] . . . is to seize or retain independence of action."[24] In other words, make the enemy react to your plans; keep him off balance, confused, and disorganized and thereby vulnerable to attacks at unexpected places and times or from unexpected directions. This makes it possible to overcome the advantage enjoyed by the defender. As Sun Tzu observes, "A confused army leads to another's victory."[25]

It is the ability to seize the initiative and ensure independence of action that leads directly to victory and therefore makes the offense the decisive form of warfare. This, however, leads us to two basic questions: why would one of the belligerents adopt the defensive form of warfare in the first place, and secondly, once having launched an offensive, why abandon it and allow the defender the opportunity to counterattack? The answer to both questions, as suggested earlier, is a matter of relative physical strength at a given time. The defender does not voluntarily select the defense as a means of fighting but is compelled to do so by his relative physical weakness. Nor does the attacker voluntarily give up the offensive but is compelled to do so at certain places and times by the loss of local superiority. If this occurs often enough, the attack may be considered "spent" or, as von Clausewitz puts it, has reached the *culminating point of victory,* and a certain equilibrium settles over the war until one side builds enough strength to launch or renew the attack.[26] Both of these factors are important in understanding why terrorists use certain methods of fighting. We will digress a moment to gain a better understanding of each.

We have pointed out on several occasions that the defender gains certain advantages over the attacker and that it is the defender's weakness that compels him to seek this posture. A quick example will be sufficient to establish why this is so. J.F.C. Fuller, in analyzing Marshal Foch's book *The Principles of War*, attacks Foch's contention that improved firepower is to the attacker's advantage. Fuller points out the basic fallacy in Foch's assumption that a rifle in the hands of an attacking soldier is equivalent to a similar rifle in the hands of a defending soldier if the latter is using cover. He states, "To mention one fact out of several, because [the] defender lying prone will [physically] offer one-eighth [the] target of [the] advancing assailant, the assailant's hits must be reduced by seven-eighths."[27] Therefore, based on cover alone, the defender enjoys seven times the superiority over the attacker, and if the outcome were to rely only upon firepower alone—which, of course, it does not—the attacker would sustain seven casualties for every casualty sustained by the defender assuming both sides are equally proficient in marksmanship. Even given the mitigating factors of surprise and speed, it is apparent the attacker must be substantially stronger than the defender if the offensive is to be successful. Thus, the weaker belligerent is compelled to seek the "force-multiplying" qualities of the defense or be quickly overwhelmed.

To the physically stronger, then, goes the privilege of taking the offense. But as we noted earlier, even the defender may—indeed must—launch counterattacks or lose the war. This implies the defender is able to gain superiority over the attackers so that their roles, at least temporarily, are reversed. This is what von Clausewitz refers to as the "culminating point of the attack."[28] This situation is possible due to the fact that the attacker generally faces a greater expenditure of effort than does the defender. Von Clausewitz observes that, while

it is possible in the course of the attack for superiority to increase . . . usually it will be reduced. The attacker is purchasing advantages that may become valuable at the peace table, but he must pay for them on the spot with his fighting forces. If the superior strength of the attack—which diminishes day by day—leads to peace, the object will have been attained . . . most of them [however] only lead up to the point where their remaining strength is just enough to maintain a defense and wait for peace. Beyond that point, the scale turns and the reaction follows with a force that is usually much stronger than the original attacks.[29]

A perfect example of this scenario is the war in the Pacific during World War II when the Japanese attacked as long as they were able and then reverted to the defensive while the ever-increasing power of the United States and its allies came to bear. We can conclude, therefore, that it is incumbent upon the attacker to use his rapidly waning superiority in strength to achieve a decisive victory over the defender before the culmination point is reached. What von Clausewitz is suggesting is that war is basically a negative-sum game where both sides usually lose strength in every operation. While the defender loses forces, installations, resources, cohesion, and morale when facing a continuously successful offensive, the attacker's strength is eroded by garrisoning occupied territory, lengthening supply lines that cause delays in replenishing losses, and so on. The secret to victory, of course, is to cause your enemy to lose at a faster rate than you do.[30]

As we discussed earlier, both sides are attempting to gain and/or maintain superiority in their war-making assets by maximizing the other's expenditure of effort. The side enjoying the greater military strength will elect to employ the principle of the offense, since it is the most decisive means of eroding an opponent's remaining military strength and the only means of achieving victory in war. We may conclude, then, that the most important factor in war is to gain and maintain superior military strength, or as von Clausewitz writes, "The best strategy is always to be very strong; first in general, and then at the decisive point."[31] If we analyze this last statement closely, it becomes evident that it is possible to be strong in general and weak at the decisive point or even vice versa. Put in more military terminology, it is possible to be strong strategically and be weak tactically and vice versa. This would explain how the defender, who is by definition the weaker belligerent, can launch a counterattack. The defender may be weak strategically but may be able to gain tactical (i.e., local) superiority at the decisive point. We will discuss how to achieve local superiority in more detail when we examine the *principles of combat*. For the moment, it will be helpful to gain a better understanding of the difference between strategic and tactical warfare.

Von Clausewitz differentiated the concepts of strategic and tactical in terms of their ability to achieve the war's political objective. "In other words," writes von Clausewitz, "the offensive is strategic when it leads directly to the political objective—the purpose for which the war is being waged. When it does not lead directly to the objective it is subsidiary and its value tactical rather than strategic."[32] Quincy Wright offers this definition:

> The management of military operations in direct contact with the enemy in order to win battle is called "tactics." The management of operations so as to effect such contact under the maximum advantage . . . is called "strategy."[33]

There are probably scores of other definitions as well, and they often contradict one another. In general, however, strategy involves employing forces to secure military and political objectives that will have a direct bearing on the enemy's collapse, and tactics involve forces in direct contact with the enemy and whose purpose is to secure objectives from which further military operations are not only possible but are enhanced.

As we look at these concepts more closely, it becomes apparent that one can wage war differently on a tactical and a strategic level—i.e., tactical offense and strategic defense. Very weak belligerents such as guerrillas and terrorists are too weak to secure strategic objectives and win the war outright. Therefore, they must operate on the strategic defensive—that is, with the strategic objective of negating their own total destruction by the enemy. But, they are also capable of launching tactical offensives, seeking tactical military victories with the aim of increasing the enemy's expenditure of effort, wearing him down physically and morally, and hoping to eventually achieve sufficient strength to launch a strategic offensive.

Von der Goltz, a noted nineteenth-century military strategist and student of von Clausewitz, summed up the four combinations of strategy, tactics, offense, and defense, including the maximum results that could be expected from each in a simple matrix. This is shown in table 1.

From this table it becomes apparent that if the enemy is allowed to continuously fight offensively at both the strategic and tactical levels, the defender is doomed to defeat. Therefore, the defender must conduct tactical offensives as often as possible or be forced to surrender political goals and cease fighting. The question becomes one of how to establish local superiority in order to launch a tactical offensive. This is where the remaining principles of war come into play.

TABLE 1    Von der Goltz Matrix

| Strategic Defense Tactical Defense | Strategic Defense Tactical Offense |
|---|---|
| Complete absence of decision. [*The best the defender can hope for is continued existence.*] | Victory on the battlefield without general results for the campaign or war. [*At best a portion of the enemy forces are defeated.*] |

| Strategic Offense Tactical Defense | Strategic Offense Tactical Offense |
|---|---|
| General situation favorable for victory with limited results since the righting power of the enemy is unimpaired. [*Enemy forces still exist.*] | Destruction of the enemy, conquest of his territory. [*A total military victory from which the political goal(s) for which the war is being waged can be achieved.*] |

SOURCE: Baron von der Goltz, *The Conduct of War: A Brief Study of Its Most Important Principles and Forms*, translated by Joseph T. Dickman (Kansas City, Missouri: The Franklin Hudson Publishing Co., 1896), p. 32. As quoted in Summers, op. cit., p. 110. (Author's additions in italics.)

## The Seven Principles of Combat

Thus far we have identified five major principles of war. They are *the engagement, the objective, the center of gravity, the defense,* and *the offense.* The remaining seven principles of war govern the actual employment of combat forces for the purpose of securing, maintaining, or exploiting superiority in combat power at the strategic or tactical level. These seven principles are *mass, economy of force, maneuver, unity of command, security, surprise,* and *simplicity.*

As already intimated, there is a subtle difference between these seven and the first five principles of war. These seven are primarily concerned with how to maximize combat power for the purpose of winning an engagement. This is sometimes referred to as *force multiplication* and essentially concerns the enhancement of combat efficiency and effectiveness in achieving specific military objectives.

Some purists may argue that the military objective is also a force multiplier in that it prevents combat power from being wasted on non-essential missions. Although this is true, we will shortly see that this concept is subsumed within the principles of mass, economy of force, and unity of command, which among them ensure that combat power is focused on the right place and ensures the effort is coordinated with minimum combat power wasted on peripheral areas. Given this, we can conclude that the objective is the desired *end* while the seven principles just introduced are the *means*. For the purpose of this book, these seven principles will be called henceforth the *principles of combat* and the original five will be called the *principles of war.*

The short definitions shown in table 2 below are taken from U.S. Army Field Manual 100-1 *The Army.* This manual admonishes, "It must be understood . . . these principles are interdependent and interrelated. No single principle can be blindly adhered to, or observed, to the exclusion of the others; none can assure victory in battle without reinforcement from one or more of the others."[34]

These principles are able to work because it is impossible for the enemy to be equally strong everywhere you may wish to attack. Consequently, even if your enemy has overall superiority, you may, by correctly employing these principles, concentrate superior combat power at a given point, surprise, and overwhelm the enemy forces located there. Such an action may be a simple ambush of an enemy supply

**TABLE 2**    Principles of Combat

---

**Mass**—concentrate combat power at the decisive place and time.

**Economy of Force**—allocate minimum essential combat power to secondary efforts.

**Maneuver**—place the enemy in a position of disadvantage through the flexible application of combat power.

**Unity of Command**—for every objective there should be unity of effort under one responsible commander.

**Security**—never permit the enemy to acquire an unexpected advantage.

**Surprise**—strike the enemy at a time and/or place and in a manner for which he is unprepared.

**Simplicity**—prepare clear, uncomplicated plans and clear, concise orders to ensure a thorough understanding of all participants.

---

SOURCE: Field Manual 100–1, chapter 3. As quoted in Summers, op. cit., pp. 199–204.

column, or it may be a major offensive on an unexpected avenue of advance. Sun Tzu succinctly describes these principles as follows:

> If I am able to determine the enemy's dispositions while at the same time I conceal my own, I can concentrate while he divides [to search for me]. I can use my entire strength to attack a fraction of his. There I will be superior. Then, if I am able to use many to strike few at a selected point, those I deal with will be in dire straits.[35]

What Sun Tzu has described is a simple plan, using *mass* to strike at a selected point where he knows he will have superior combat power. The plan uses *maneuver* to concentrate his forces and *security* and *surprise* to avoid the main enemy forces and strike where the enemy least expects him. Since Sun Tzu is speaking in the first person, we may assume he is employing *unity of command.* The only principle not specifically touched on here is *economy of force,* although we may also assume Sun Tzu has dispatched a minimal force to keep the enemy's main forces busy while Sun Tzu's main force lands its blow on his selected target. In this way, then, it is possible for generally weaker forces to attack stronger ones. Now let us look at each principle in more detail.

Mass has long been recognized as a major principle of combat. According to von Clausewitz, "An impartial student of modern war must admit that superior numbers are becoming more decisive with each passing day. The principle of bringing maximum possible strength to the decisive engagement must therefore rank higher than it did in the past."[36] The military thinker Antoine Jomini believed the center and the heart of all military operations "consists of putting into action the greatest possible number of forces at the decisive point in the theater of operations . . . [by using] the correct line of operations."[37]

During World War II this concept was borne out by the Germans, who mastered the principle of mass in their blitzkrieg strategy. They called the decisive point where the main effort was concentrated the *schwerpunkt.*[38] This point was either lightly defended or able to be quickly overwhelmed by combined armor, artillery, and air attacks. In this way the Germans repeatedly gained superiority in combat power at a decisive point and time.

Economy of force is generally considered reciprocal to the principle of mass.[39] It refers to the notion of not wasting forces on secondary, tactical objectives. To concentrate forces to meet the principle of mass, it becomes necessary to weaken forces elsewhere. As Sun Tzu observes, "For if he prepares to the front his rear will be weak, and if to the rear his front will be fragile . . . and when he prepares everywhere, he will be weak everywhere."[40]

Von Clausewitz noted the importance of economically employing your forces to ensure none is wasted or idle, particularly during an engagement. He states, "When the time for action comes, the first requirement should be that all parts must act: even the least appropriate [action] will occupy some of the enemy's forces and reduce his overall strength, while completely inactive troops are [unilaterally] neutralized. . . ."[41] In other words, since victory usually goes to the side that is consistently able to bring superior combat power to bear, wasting forces on mundane, secondary tasks or "trying everywhere to be strong" will erode the combat power available to you at the critical point and time.

Maneuvering your forces so as to place the enemy in a disadvantaged position while maintaining flexibility allows you to "sustain the initiative, to exploit success, to preserve freedom of action and reduce your own vulnerability."[42] Sun Tzu called speed the "essence of war"[43] and admonished the commander of numerically weak forces to be able to avoid stronger forces.[44] Few would argue the need for offensive forces to have mobility. Certainly the most heralded use of maneuver on the field of battle this century is, once again, the German blitzkriegs of World War II where "vastly improved mobile ordnance, fast tanks . . . and other cross-country vehicles combined to produce a doctrine of mobile warfare at speeds here-to-fore impossible."[45] The defense, too, can use mobility to maintain flexibility and to preserve freedom of action. This is shown in the concept of the *elastic defense,* which

> entails the complete abandonment of the perimeter with its fortifications and associated infrastructure. Instead, defense is to rely exclusively on mobile forces, which should be at least as mobile as those of the offense. The two fight on equal footing: the defense can be as concentrated as the offense, since it need not assign any troops to . . . protect territory; on the other hand, the defense thereby sacrifices all tactical advantages normally inherent in its role (except knowledge of terrain), since neither side can choose its ground, let alone fortify it in advance.[46]

As we will see later, maneuver is the paramount principle of combat used by guerrillas and terrorists as they fight their wars of evasion and surprise.

Unity of command is as old as war itself, but as war has become more complex, this principle has often been forgotten. Von Moltke warns us, "No war council could direct an army, the Chief of Staff should be the only adviser to the commander ... even a faulty plan, provided it was executed firmly, was preferable to a synthetic product."[47] Harry Summers sees the lack of unity of command to be one of the primary causes of the U.S. defeat in Vietnam. Quoting former Under Secretary of the Air Force Townsend Hoopes, Summers writes, "In his criticism of the Vietnam War, Hoopes notes that the United States was actually fighting 'three separate or only loosely related struggles.' There was the large scale, conventional war, ... there was the confused 'pacification' effort, ... and there was the curiously remote air war against North Vietnam."[48] Summers continues,

> In comparison with the Korean War (especially in the early period) where all of the strategic direction came from General MacArthur's GHQ Far East Command, there was no equivalent headquarters for the Vietnam War. General Westmoreland was only the tactical commander—the equivalent of the Eighth Army Commander in the Korean War. Part of the strategic direction (especially air and naval matters) came from Honolulu, part came from Washington and there was no coordinated unity of effort.[49]

As Ambassador Robert W. Komer concluded, "The bureaucratic fact is that below the Presidential level everybody was responsible [for the Vietnam War]."[50]

Security is the principle that denies the enemy the advantage of surprise. In the quote above by Sun Tzu the enemy had to divide his forces to search for Sun Tzu's army, while Sun Tzu, knowing the location of the enemy, was able to select one portion of the dispersed enemy army and overwhelm it. Security means, then, denying the enemy information about your own forces—which some call deception. Sun Tzu contends that "all warfare is based on deception. Therefore, when capable, feign incapacity; when active, inactivity. When near, make it appear you are far away; when far away, that you are near. Offer the enemy a bait to lure him; feign disorder and strike him."[51]

Surprise is possibly the ultimate force-multiplier. Von Clausewitz credits surprise with being "the means to gain superiority."[52] It allows the commander to mass forces at an unexpected point and can result in victories far exceeding that which could be expected from the same amount of force had the enemy been alerted. History is replete with examples of this; two of the most famous being the Trojan Horse and Pearl Harbor. But as von Clausewitz stresses, the true advantage to surprise is its psychological impact on the enemy. "Whenever it is achieved on a grand scale," he writes, "it confuses the enemy and lowers his morale; many examples, great and small, show how this in turn multiplies the results."[53]

The principle of simplicity essentially ties all the other principles together, including the five principles of war (the engagement, the objective, the center of gravity, the defense, and the offense). It is as Harry Summers calls it, a "litmus test,"[54] the purpose of which is to make sure that all echelons have a clear understanding of what they are to do and how they are to do it. As von Clausewitz notes, in war "everything looks simple; the knowledge required does not look remarkable, the strategic options are so obvious that by comparison the simplest problem of higher mathematics has an impressive scientific dignity."[55] He concludes, however, that although the military is a very simple and relatively easily managed machine, "we should bear in mind that none of its components is of one piece: each part is composed of individuals, every one of whom retains his potential for friction and misunderstanding."[56]

These, then, are the seven principles of combat. When properly employed they make it possible for even very weak forces to attack—at least at the tactical level—an enemy that enjoys an overall overwhelming strategic superiority in combat power. As we will see later, these principles—particularly mass, security, and surprise—allow terrorists to achieve victories of far greater importance than their extremely limited numbers would suggest possible.

## Summation: The Three Test Criteria of Warfare

The summary of this chapter will also summarize the first part of this book pertaining to the basic, immutable elements of war that will be used in the coming chapters to test whether a specific form of terrorism is a form of war. These three criteria were derived by analyzing war from its most basic level of abstraction and through the eyes of a wide spectrum of classical military thinkers. In this way, no single individual opinion colored the outcome; it helped to ensure these characteristics are, in fact, a valid test of whether any given activity constitutes warfare.

The first, and probably most widely accepted, criterion is summed up in von Clausewitz's famous dictum, "War is the continuation of policy by other means." In other words, war involves the employment of lethal force for a political end. As will be seen in chapter 6, however, there can be some question as to what constitutes a political end. Consequently, two further criteria will be employed to test whether an activity is a form of war; both entail an examination not to what end, but rather by what means this force is employed.

The second criterion used in this test is to determine whether the activity employs force on the moral plane. This is done by ascertaining if an entity's cohesion is being targeted. Cohesion is used as a determining factor since it, more than any other element in war, signifies the moral and psychological bonds that bind human beings to higher sociological organisms. Although traditional examinations of this phenomenon tend to focus only upon the combat unit, given the nature of modern war as well as the unique features of terrorism, we will expand the level of analysis to include any political entity—subnational, national, empire, alliance system, etc.—that employs force for a common political end recognized and embraced by all of the constituent parts.

The third and final immutable factor of war we will use in this test is the employment of force against force on the physical plane. This element is essentially von Clausewitz's principle of engagement, and it is operationalized by determining whether the force employed is subject to the principles of combat that govern the manipulation of physical force against physical force in war. If it can be established that the presence or absence of these principles has no bearing on whether a given type of terrorism can achieve its specific political end, then this activity does not employ physical force against physical force and therefore is *not* a form of war.

Each of these three criteria is insufficient in and of itself to determine whether a given activity is a form of war. A specific form of terrorism can be considered a form of war only if it can satisfy all three criteria.

## Notes

1. Karl von Clausewitz, *On War*, edited and translated by Michael Howard and Peter Paret (Princeton: Princeton University Press, 1976), p. 95.

2. Ibid., p. 579.

3. Sir Basil Liddell Hart, *Strategy* (New York: Praeger Publishers, 1968), p. 351.

4. Ibid.

5. Field Manual 100-5, *Field Service Regulations—Operations* (Washington, D.C.: Government Printing Office, 1982), p. 1-1.

6. von Clausewitz, op. cit., p. 597.

7. Ibid.

8. Harry G. Summers, Jr., *On Strategy: A Critical Analysis of the Vietnam War* (Novato, Calif.: Presidio Press, 1982; 4th reprinting, 1984), p. 129.

9. von Clausewitz, op. cit., p. 592.

10. Ibid.

11. Napoleon Bonaparte, "Correspondance Inedite de Napoleon Ier, Conserve Aux Archives de la Guerre," XVIII, no. 14707, edited by Ernest Picard and Louis Tuety (1912). As quoted in J.F.C. Fuller, *The Conduct of War, 1789–1961* (New York: Funk and Wagnalls Inc., 1961; Minerva Press, 1968), p. 50.

12. Napoleon Bonaparte, "Correspondance", XII, no. 9997. As quoted in J.F.C. Fuller, op. cit., p. 50.

13. Napoleon Bonaparte, in a letter written to General Stein, written on January 7, 1814—as quoted in J.F.C. Fuller, op. cit., p. 50.

14. von Clausewitz, op. cit., p. 357.

15. Sun Tzu, *The Art of War*, edited and translated by Samuel B. Griffith (London: Oxford University Press, 1963; Oxford University Press paperback, 1971), p. 85.

16. Horace Porter, *Campaigning With Grant* (New York: 1897; Da Capo Press, Inc., 1986), pp. 39–40.

17. von Clausewitz, op. cit., p. 357.

18. Field Manual 100-5, op. cit., p. 10-3.

19. von Clausewitz, op. cit., p. 358.

20. Ibid.

21. Y. Yadin, "A Strategic Analysis of Last Year's Battles," *The Israeli Force's Journal*, September, 1949. As presented in appendix II to Liddell Hart, op. cit., pp. 396–401.

22. Hew Strachan, *European Armies and the Conduct of War*, 2d edition (London: Allen Unwin, Inc., 1983), pp. 1–2.

23. Field Manual 100-5 op. cit., p. 8-5.

24. Ibid., p. 2-2.

25. Sun Tzu, op. cit., p. 82.

26. von Clausewitz, op. cit., p. 528.

27. J. F. C. Fuller, op. cit., p. 123.

28. von Clausewitz, op. cit., p. 528.

29. Ibid.

30. Ibid., pp. 566–67.

31. Ibid., p. 204.

32. Ibid., p. 143.

33. Quincy Wright, *A Study of War*, 2 vols. (Chicago: The University of Chicago Press, 1941), pp. 291–92.

34. "Principles of War and the Operational Dimension," Field Manual 100-1, *The Army* (Washington, D.C.: Government Printing Office, 1981) chapter 3. As quoted in Summers, op. cit., p. 204.

35. Sun Tzu, op. cit., p. 98.

36. von Clausewitz, op. cit., p. 282.

37. Antoine H. Jomini, *Precis d l'art de la Guerre* (Paris, 1938) p. 254. As quoted in Craine Brinton, Gordon Cragi, and Felix Gilvert, "Jomini," *Makers of Modern Strategy: Military Thought from Machiavelli to Hitler*, edited by Edward M. Earle (Princeton: Princeton University Press, 1943; Princeton paperback printing, 1973), p. 86.

38. Len Deighton, *Blitzkrieg: From the Rise of Hitler to the Fall of Dunkirk* (New York: Alfred A. Knopf, Inc., 1980), p. 157.

39. Field Manual 100-5, op. cit., p. B-2.

40. Sun Tzu, op. cit., p. 57.

41. von Clausewitz, op. cit., p. 213.

42. Field Manual 100-5, op. cit., p. B-3.

43. Sun Tzu, op. cit., p. 134.

44. Ibid., p. 80.

45. R. Ernest Dupuy and Trevor N. Dupuy, *The Encyclopedia of Military History: From 3500 B.C. to the Present* (New York: Harper & Row Publishers, Inc., 1970), p. 1017.

46. Edward N. Luttwak, *The Grand Strategy of the Roman Empire: From the First Century A.D. to the Third* (Baltimore: The Johns Hopkins University Press, 1976; Johns Hopkins paperback edition, 1981), pp. 130–31.

47. Hajo Holborn, "Moltke and Schlieffen: The Prussian-German School," *Makers of Modern Strategy: Military Thought from Machiavelli to Hitler*, edited by Edward M. Earle (Princeton: Princeton University Press, 1943; Princeton paperback printing, 1973), p. 180.

48. Summers, op. cit., p. 148. Quoting Townsend Hoopes, *The Limits of Intervention* (New York: David McKay Co. Inc., 1969), p. 3.

49. Summers, op. cit., p. 148.

50. R. W. Komer, *Bureaucracy Does Its Thing: Institutional Constraints on US-GVN Performance in Vietnam* (Santa Monica: Rand Corporation, August 1972), pp. ix, 75–84. (As quoted in Summers, op. cit., p. 147.)

51. Sun Tzu, op. cit., p. 67.

52. von Clausewitz, op. cit., p. 198.

53. Ibid.

54. Summers, op. cit., p. 163.

55. von Clausewitz, op. cit., p. 119.

56. Ibid.

# 4

# VARIABLE ELEMENTS AND FACTORS IN WAR

■

## Introduction

To this point we have discussed only those elements and factors in war that remain constant regardless of time or space. In this chapter we will examine some of the nonconstant elements of warfare that play a major role in determining how lethal force is most effectively employed. First, we will examine the six characteristics that influence the type of war a belligerent may wage. This is important since, for instance, the factors governing a conventional, total war of annihilation are quite different from those that govern a limited war of attrition and evasion—the type of war in which terrorism plays a major role. Consequently, understanding the different types of war and the variable characteristics upon which they rest will be quite helpful in isolating when terrorism is most effective. Following this, we will take a brief look at the process by which modern warfare has evolved. As will be seen through this analysis, each era or phase in this evolutionary process has resulted from the introduction of a new war-fighting skill that is critical to maximizing combat force in war. What is important here is that the conditions germane to the use of the type of war-fighting skills in which terrorism may play a major role does not occur until the latest phase of modern warfare's evolution. This latest phase, which is governed by what we have labeled *social warfare,* will be the subject of the third section of this chapter. Here we will analyze the goals and means of social warfare as well as isolate terrorism's role within this form of war. All three sections will provide not only a better understanding of war per se, but also the role of terroristic force within war as well. Equally important, this chapter will also provide a better foundation for understanding why terrorism exists and how it functions.

## Types of War

Wars can be classified in two ways: (1) by the objectives sought in the war and (2) by the methods used. In the former, the objectives can be either total or limited, which in turn determines the amount of force necessary to achieve victory. The second method involves determining how that force is employed. Political entities enjoying relatively large amounts of armed force may employ that force in positional warfare to seize and hold territory. Weaker political entities, however, must employ their forces in wars of evasion. In such wars the belligerent's armed forces do not attempt to seize and hold terrain but rather employ security and maneuver to evade the enemy's stronger armed forces, hitting only when and where local superiority can be assured. War can also be waged by annihilating the enemy's armed forces in battle or eroding his political, economic, social, and military resources in a war of attrition. It should be pointed out here that these six possible types of war are not mutually exclusive. For instance, while a war may only be *total* or *limited* at any given time, it is entirely possible that in a large war a belligerent may be fighting a *positional* war of *annihilation* in one theater of operations and a *positional* or even an *evasive* war of *attrition* in another theater. This section will address these six characteristics of war to provide a better understanding of what terrorism is trying to accomplish and why it operates the way it does.

In its most abstract form the purpose of war is to render your opponent powerless to resist your will by destroying his war-fighting capabilities or, as von Clausewitz puts it, to *"disarm* him." Disarming the enemy consists of three main objectives "which between them cover everything: the armed forces, the country and the enemy's will."[1] He continues,

> The fighting forces must be destroyed: that is they must be put in such a condition that they can no longer carry on the fight. The country must be occupied; otherwise the enemy could raise fresh forces. Yet both of these may be done and the war . . . cannot be considered [won] so long as the enemy's will has not been broken.[2]

These, then, are the military or operational objectives of total war. The political objective of such a war is to eliminate one of the belligerents as a political entity. There are, however, wars for lesser purposes, and these are known as limited wars. Limited wars are far and away the most common type of war found in history. General David Palmer has observed,

> Most wars, it can be argued, have been limited. One can dig way back in history to say [that] the final Punic War—when Rome defeated Carthage, slaughtered the population, razed the city, plowed under the ruins and sowed the furrows with salt—was not in any way limited . . . but it is hard to find other examples; in some manner or other a limiting factor was always present.[3]

This, however, is taking the concept of total war a bit far and restricts it to an overly narrow definition. Most military scholars would probably agree that what von Clausewitz meant by total war is one in which the political entity governing a nation is destroyed and replaced by one more amenable to the victor, such as the American Revolutionary War or the coalition wars against Napoleon. Yet even with this less narrow definition, General Palmer's contention remains correct; there have indeed been far more limited than total wars throughout history. As von Clausewitz himself said, "The object of war in the abstract . . . the disarming of the enemy, is rarely attained in practice and is not a condition necessary to peace."[4] But in a limited war, what is the "condition necessary to peace"? Von Clausewitz answers this question by saying,

Not every war need be fought until one side collapses. When the motives and tensions of war are slight . . . the very faintest prospect of defeat might be enough to cause one side to yield. If from the very start [one] side feels this is probable, it will obviously concentrate on bringing [this] about . . . rather than take the long way around and totally defeat the enemy. War is not an act of senseless passion but is controlled by a political objective, the value of this objective must determine the sacrifices made for it in magnitude and duration. Once the expenditure of effort exceeds the value of the political object, the object must be renounced and peace must follow.[5]

In a limited war, then, each belligerent seeks not to render the other totally powerless, but rather to continuously raise the cost of continuing the war until the side less willing to sustain such cost(s) concedes victory to the other. Although total war achieves its purpose by rendering the enemy powerless, a limited war accomplishes its objective by making the cost of victory greater than the opponent is willing to bear. It is interesting to note that von Clausewitz saw the basic means for achieving victory to be essentially the same whether one is waging a total or limited form of war. He believed the best way to assure victory in war is to maximize your enemy's expenditure of effort while minimizing your own.[6] Consequently, in a total war you erode your enemy's power base so that he becomes *unable* to fight, and in a limited war you maximize his cost(s) until he becomes *unwilling* to continue to fight. According to von Clausewitz there are three primary methods of influencing the enemy's expenditure of effort:

> The first of these is the seizure of enemy territory not with the object of retaining it but in order to exact financial contributions or lay it waste. The second method is to give priority to operations that will increase the enemy's suffering . . . . The third, and by far the most important method . . . is to wear down the enemy . . . [by] using the duration of the war to bring about a gradual exhaustion of his physical and moral resistance.[7]

The key to this line of logic is, of course, to create a situation wherein the enemy perceives the cost of continuing the war to be greater than any gains he might expect should he continue to fight. As Liddell Hart notes, "Perseverance in war is only justifiable if there is a good chance of a good end—the prospect of a peace that will balance the sum of human misery incurred in the struggle."[8] This factor is operational whether you are on the offensive or the defensive. If you are attacking it is in your best interest that the enemy surrender long before his physical forces are exhausted. And if you are on the defensive, your primary objective is to make the continuance of the war too expensive for the enemy to pursue it further and therefore surrender or modify his original objective. In either case, the common denominator is the enemy's will to fight. Von Clausewitz bears this out when he writes, "If . . . we consider the total concept of victory, we find that it consists of three elements: 1) the enemy's greater loss of material strength, 2) his loss of morale [and] 3) his open admission of the above by giving up his intention."[9]

We may therefore conclude that wars are won by using physical forces to affect an enemy's will to resist. And, as von Clausewitz suggests, this can be done either by total means through the destruction of the enemy's armed forces or by limited means, in which victory is achieved by increasing the enemy's expenditure of effort. Consequently, victory in a limited war is not only dependent upon the will of the soldiers in the field to continue fighting, but also on the will of all those necessary to keep those soldiers in the field—particularly civilian workers. But as the military historian and student of von Clausewitz Hans Delbruck has pointed out, not only could victory in a limited war be achieved through affecting enemy civilian morale, but the same could occur in a total war.[10] Thus, it is possible—as in World War I—to achieve total victory without decisively defeating the enemy's army in the field. Delbruck has labeled the strategy designed to engage and destroy the enemy's armed forces "the strategy of annihilation." The second strategy Delbruck calls "the strategy of exhaustion or attrition."[11]

The strategy of annihilation is the prerogative of the stronger belligerent. This strategy represents the use of physical force on the physical plane to destroy the enemy's armed forces, making him *unable* to continue to fight. The strategy of attrition, however, is employed by belligerents who do not enjoy sufficient power to engage and decisively defeat the enemy's armed forces in open conflict. In this form of war "the battle is no longer the sole aim of strategy; it is merely one of several equally effective means of attaining political ends of the war and is essentially no more important than the occupation of territory, the destruction of crops or commerce, and the blockade."[12] The importance of this fact is that the means von Clausewitz describes in waging a limited war may be applied to a total war as well.

Delbruck and von Clausewitz, however, were describing conventional wars of position in relation to these types of war. That is, a form of war wherein both sides have sufficient strength to take and/or hold territory. But for the *very* weak, wars of position are exceedingly dangerous. Very weak political entities, therefore, should wage wars of evasion rather than position. As Barrie Paskins and Michael Dockrill have noted, "One . . . [wages] evasive land warfare . . . because one lacks the military strength to wage the kind of land war that employs concentrations of military force [able to fight] . . . decisive battles."[13]

A belligerent waging a war of evasion does its best to avoid being attacked and, by the same token, only engaging the enemy when and where it has achieved local superiority. This is perhaps best stated in Mao Tse-Tung's sixteen-character slogan, "When the enemy advances, we retreat. When the enemy halts, we harass. When the enemy seeks to avoid battle, we attack. When the enemy retreats, we pursue."[14] The key, of course, is to exhaust the enemy physically and morally, while preserving your own very weak and vulnerable forces.

Wars, therefore, can be categorized by several, often overlapping categories. A war can have a total political objective calling for the complete destruction of a targeted political entity, or a war can have a limited political objective in which a political entity is simply forced to modify or surrender a given political goal. Additionally, wars can be waged with two basic strategies: annihilation or attrition. Although both ultimately depend upon destroying the enemy's will to resist to secure victory, a war of annihilation seeks to achieve this demoralization primarily through destroying the enemy's armed forces, whereas a war of attrition involves the erosion not only of the enemy's military, but economic, political, and social resources as well. Finally, wars can be of a positional nature (with both sides taking and/or holding territory) or evasive, where one side's weakness compels it to elude the enemy's armed forces. These categorizations are presented in table 3.

Depending upon the objectives of each belligerent, it is possible for each to be fighting the same war for totally different purposes and thresholds of victory. For instance, in the American Revolutionary War, the United States was fighting a limited, positional war of attrition in the north and a limited, evasive war of attrition in the south. Washington's ultimate objective was to force Great Britain to modify its political objectives vis-à-vis the American Colonies. Washington's strategy in the north was to hold only those strategic positions he could and to wear down the British physically and morally by hitting

**TABLE 3**    Categories of Warfare

### Political Objective

| | |
|---|---|
| • *Total*—Destroy the enemy as a political entity. | • *Limited*—Cause the enemy to abandon or modify political objectives. |

### Military Objective

| | |
|---|---|
| • *Annihilation*—Destroy the enemy's armed forces in decisive battles. | • *Attrition*—If too weak to fight a war of annihilation then use the length of the war to erode the enemy's will to fight. |

### Military Method

| | |
|---|---|
| • *Positional*—Use maneuver to seize and hold strategic terrain. | • *Evasion*—If too weak to fight a positional war then use maneuver to avoid the enemy's strength. |

the British Army when and where it was weakest—as at Trenton or Monmouth.[15] The British, on the other hand, were waging a total, positional war of annihilation in which they sought to occupy rebel territory, destroy the rebels' armed forces, and disband the American Continental Congress, restoring the Colonies to British rule. Victory for both sides was therefore based upon entirely different criteria and achieved by different means. Using these same criteria it therefore becomes apparent that terrorism—especially revolutionary terrorism—is a total, evasive war of attrition.

Determining which form of warfare to select and how to secure victory is therefore dependent upon the relative strength of your armed forces and the political objective you seek. The dynamics of victory, however, are the same no matter which type of war you are waging. It *always* entails employing your armed forces in a manner and for the purpose of ultimately destroying the enemy's will to resist. But the collapse of his will is not a given. Only by correctly employing the armed force available to you can you ensure the collapse of the enemy's will. In the last chapter we saw that employing armed force in the most effective and efficient manner was dependent upon the principles of war and combat. As the remainder of this chapter will show, armed force is also subject to variable factors in war.

## The Evolution of Modern Warfare

There are three great epochs in the evolution of warfare: (1) the primitive, (2) the classical, and (3) the modern. The primitive epoch is represented by unorganized warfare wherein human conflict was employed one-on-one in single combats between individual warriors or often in highly ceremonial circumstances.[16] The classical epoch involved all of the war-fighting skills necessary to modern warfare, ranging from physical skills to technical skills (siege warfare) to social skills (maintenance of the Roman Empire). The primary difference between classical and modern warfare is simply the level of technology. Consequently, rather than cover the evolution of warfare from prehistoric times to the present, which would entail a great deal of repetition, this section will focus only upon the current, or modern, epoch. But before we delve into the evolution of warfare per se, it is necessary to have a basic understanding of the process by which warfare evolves.

## The Dialectical Process in the Evolution of Warfare

The evolution of warfare is governed by a dialectical process wherein the existing conditions (*thesis*) meet new conditions (*antithesis*), and the two combine to form something totally new (*synthesis*). As in all dialectical processes, the seeds of the antithesis are usually present long before they become significant enough to modify the existing situation. For example, the tank provided the entente powers the technical means to neutralize the benefits accruing to trench warfare during the First World War, but these new weapons were employed in accordance with existing tactical and strategic doctrine. Hence, the effect of tanks upon the outcome of the First World War was negligible. It was not until twenty years later that the tank was to come into its own, and a new mode of warfare—the blitzkrieg—was created to fully exploit the potential of this new weapon system.

As will be seen, the catalysts for change in the modern epoch are power-enhancing mechanisms that rest upon either new organizational methods or new technology. But as the example of the tank suggests, change does not occur simply with the advent of new technology. Change happens when the structural systems supporting and employing the new technology are modified to fully exploit it. Moreover, it should be stressed again that all change in a dialectical process is a *synthesis*. That is to say, the old elements and characteristics of the previous structure remain but are subsumed by the new structure that is created. Consequently, factors that were present in the earliest forms of warfare, such as the need for physical skills, are still functioning in war today, albeit at a much less important level.

There are two major factors that determine existing structural conditions: (1) the *political organization* and (2) the *social structure* of an existing society. If the political organization is highly centralized and has extensive authority throughout the entire political structure and if that new political organization determines the new technology to be dangerous to status quo, then it can effectively halt the evolutionary process by banning this new means of war. Likewise, if the social structure is unable to absorb the new technology and convert it into military hardware with its attendant supporting elements—logistics, maintenance, production, training, etc.—then again, no change in the means of war will occur. A quick example is sufficient to support this contention.

Perhaps the classical example is the role of gunpowder in Asia as opposed to Europe. Gunpowder was invented in China in the early 1200s and was employed as a weapon of war as early as 1232. Yet, within two centuries Europe clearly had the lead in this new technology. The answer to the question of how this happened can most easily be ascertained from a structural perspective. Although the Chinese clearly had the ability to create and employ gunpowder technology, they elected not to do so. This was possible only because the dominant social elements did not want this new technology, and the political organization was sufficiently centralized to ensure that the technology was not used. The Chinese emperor simply limited the spread of gunpowder through imperial decree, thereby ensuring both political and social status quo. No such means were available in Europe, however. Although the dominant social group—the mounted knights—did not want this new technology, the political structure was extremely decentralized and proved unable to prevent the proliferation of gunpowder weaponry. As Andrew Schmookler notes,

> The central rulers of China not only had no need to strive forward, but were actually motivated to retard change: thus the natural conservatism of culture was accentuated by central control. In Europe, because there was no one to control power, the rapid deployment of power-maximiz-

ing technologies was not only possible for the system as a whole but also mandatory for each actor in the system [if it were to be able to compete and survive].[17]

Even more astounding is the case of Japan, which employed fire-arms for three-quarters of a century and then gave them up to return to the pregunpowder era. Here again, the dominant social group—the samurai—did not want this new technology because it endangered their position at the top of the social order, and the centralized government proved strong enough to eliminate firearms production altogether.[18]

The second structural factor that can prevent the adaptation and employment of new technology into warfare is the inability of a given social structure to provide the necessary division of labor that sufficient numbers of the existing populace can leave what they are currently doing and master the new technology and man its supporting structures. For example, as will be shown, modern conventional warfare is only possible with a massive bureaucracy capable of supporting large armies in the field. Bureaucracies are only possible in societies where there is sufficient division of labor so that all of the necessary food and other resources can be produced by other workers, releasing the bureaucrat to perform his specialized functions of management and coordination on a full-time basis.

Normally, however, new technology is introduced, and over time it is absorbed into the existing methods of war-fighting that, in turn, slowly modify both the social and political structures as they change to maximize the new technology. Most new technology represents a quantitative, i.e., an easily measured, objective improvement over existing weapon systems. Examples of this are the quantitative improvement between a rifle and a machine gun, or a propeller-driven versus a jet-powered aircraft. Some new technology, however, is *qualitatively* better. That is, it represents the introduction of totally new means of war-fighting requiring entirely new types of skills. Examples here include the rifle versus the sword or the radio versus messengers on horseback. The improvements here are *much* less objective in that it is difficult to determine how many swordsmen equal a rifleman or how many messengers equal a radio. When changes of this size occur, then we have a new era or phase in the evolution of war.

## The Five War Skills of Modern Warfare

The most obvious advantage a belligerent can have in war is strength in numbers. Two warriors are better than one, twenty tanks are better than ten, and so on. But combatants can be made more lethal by giving them certain equipment and the skills germane to its operation, maintenance, and employment. In cases where there is great disparity in skills and weaponry, numbers become less important for the side having the advantage of superior skills. For example, two combatants armed with machine guns are probably hundreds of times more powerful than two stone-age warriors armed with clubs. By the same token, when both sides have the same relative level of skill and equipment, then numbers again become important.

The primary factors determining which skills are not only available but paramount are the political organization and social structure of a belligerent at any given time. These create the underlying structure governing the evolution of warfare. Over time this evolution has created five distinct war skills. Moreover, it should be understood that these war skills represent not only the specific skill described but also the ability to create, wield, and maintain the necessary hardware, if any, germane to that skill. These war skills are: (1) physical skills, (2) organizational skills, (3) technical skills, (4) administrative skills, and (5) social skills. These are defined as follows:

1. *Physical Skills* represent a combatant's courage, eye-hand coordination, stamina, reflexes, and sense of timing. While this is normally associated with hand weapons in shock [nonfiring, hand-to-hand] combat, it is also germane, for instance, to modern fighter-pilots.

2. *Organizational Skills* represent the ability to create and sustain cohesive military organization responsive to the will of a single commander. The critical factor here, as was discussed in chapter 2, is the ability to socialize the combatant so that he willingly subordinates himself to the group. Equally important, these skills also permit increased tactical flexibility on the battlefield, affording the commander the ability to maneuver his forces to take advantage of the tactical situation.

3. *Technical Skills* represent the ability to adapt new technology to warfare, maximizing its effectiveness through adaptations of orga-

TABLE 4     The Evolution of Modern Warfare

|  | Physical Skill | Organizational Skill | Technical Skill | Administrative Skill | Social Skill |
|---|---|---|---|---|---|
| Medieval | [X] | − | − | − | − |
| Neo-classical | + | [X] | − | − | − |
| Early Modern | + | + | [X] | − | − |
| Late Modern | + | + | + | [X] | + |
| Nuclear | + | + | + | + | [X] |

[X] = Paramount skill of a given era.
 + = Highly important, but secondary to paramount skill.
 − = Has limited or no importance in this era of warfare.

nizational, doctrinal, and sociopolitical systems. This has become particularly crucial since the advent of gunpowder due to the requirement for combatants to master skills beyond those that can be learned on the drill field.

4. *Administrative Skills* are those enabling the belligerent to generate, sustain, and coordinate the mobilization and employment of the military resources of the modern nation-state. Aside from being able to generate massive military force, these skills also permit widely separated military forces to operate in unison against the same military objective.

5. *Social Skills* represent the ability not only to generate, harness, and employ the psychosocial resources of a friendly populace, but the ability to disrupt those of the enemy as well. Essentially, it is the ability to achieve military/political objectives by disrupting the sociopolitical cohesion of the enemy and thereby defeat him without first having to destroy his armed forces or occupy his territory.

These five skills, then, are operative to one degree or another during all eras of modern warfare. The existing structural environment, however, determines which skill is paramount in a given era. Each era and its paramount skill are depicted in table 4.

The paramount skill of a given era is the most critical factor in determining victory during that era. For example, if a force with a very solid advantage in technical skills and weaponry germane to those skills were to meet an enemy with superior organizational and physical skills, but lacking equivalent technical skills and weaponry, the former will virtually always win. Moreover the greater the superiority of the technology, the less important the organizational and physical skills. Clearly, a modern twelve-man squad armed with modern weaponry could easily defeat the Hoplite phalanxes of Alexander's Macedonian army, although these same twelve men probably enjoy neither the physical nor organizational skills of Alexander's men. Admittedly, this is an extreme example, but the concept is sound. In general, any belligerent capable of operating at a higher paramount skill level than an opponent can expect to win the conflict—providing that belligerent can sustain that advantage.

To reinforce this concept, it is important to note that someone with a higher skill potential than one germane to a given era would have little effect upon the level of warfare. For instance, a person with the administrative skills of a von Moltke or the social skills of a Mao Tse-Tung would be virtually useless in the medieval era when what won victories was the ability to field more armored knights having superior physical skills than the enemy. Von Moltke's administrative skills are irrelevant until the advent of the railroad, telegraph, and mass mobilization, whereas Mao would have been entirely superfluous in an era where field armies operated independently from the populace, requiring none of the home-front support of the nineteenth- and twentieth-century armies.

## The Evolutionary Phases of Modern Warfare

In the remainder of this section, we will briefly examine each era in the evolution of modern warfare. What should become apparent is that the paramount characteristic of the previous era remains an important element of each era in the evolutionary process. Equally important, a belligerent using a less complex or earlier form of warfare has very little hope of defeating a belligerent using a higher level. This fact will become extremely important when, in later chapters, we examine ways and means to defeat the latest form of social warfare—terrorism.

It should be noted that although this section examines the evolution of warfare in Western Europe, elsewhere there were parallel evolutionary processes going on at the same time. For example, Byzantium did not succumb to the Dark Ages with the fall of Rome, but maintained its empire with a military system every bit as complex as that of the Roman Imperial system. Indeed, it was not until 1453 that the Byzantine Empire succumbed to the social forces unleashed by the Islamic Ottoman Turks. Rather than digressing to describe every exception, then, for the sake of space and clarity, this section will focus only upon one evolutionary process located in one geographical area—Western Europe.

**The Roman Military System.** Medieval warfare represents the initial thesis in the evolution of modern warfare. It represents a virtual return to preclassical, primitive warfare wherein the single, sufficient skill combatants required to achieve victory was superior physical skills. Indeed, as the renowned military historian C. W. C. Oman observes, "The young Frankish noble deemed his military education complete when he could sit his charger firmly and handle lance and shield with skill."[19] Since it was just suggested above that a less complex form of warfare resting upon a qualitatively inferior paramount skill simply cannot succeed against a more complex form of warfare, a brief digression is necessary to explain how, after 4,000 years of evolution, warfare returned almost to its very earliest form.

Few would disagree with the contention that the Roman Imperial military system was the most complex form of warfare known in the classical era. Indeed, using the model shown in table 4 above, the Roman military system included all five of the skills depicted there, with the paramount skill being social skills. Clearly, the other skills were present and important, but as you move to the left on the table, the skills become less and less important. Physical skills are the least important. For instance, as R. Ernest Dupuy and Trevor Dupuy note,

> Individually rarely more than 5'6" in height . . . the Italian legionary had a healthy respect for his huskier barbarian foes. In fact, until the time of Caesar, the almost unreasoning Roman fear of Gauls and Germans . . . was reflected in the individual emotions of even veteran soldiers. Yet they [also] realized that regular formations and discipline made them militarily superior to the barbarians. . . .[20]

It was organizational skills that permitted the Roman legionary to defeat his physically and numerically superior counterpart. But it was technical and administrative skills that permitted the Romans to mobilize and concentrate superior combat power wherever it was needed to defend or expand the vast Roman Empire. As Luttwak points out,

Once the empire was mobilized to fight . . . it was invincible . . . . [E]ven
if the enemy could not be drawn out to fight in close combat, or out-
maneuvered in field operations, it would still be defeated by relentless
methods of Roman "engineering" warfare. . . . The ability to bring large
numbers of men on the scene of combat, to construct the required infrastructures, to provide a steady supply of food and equipment in remote and sometimes desolate places—all this reflected the high standards of Roman military organization.[21]

Still, as important as even technological and administrative skills
obviously were, it was the social skills of the Roman military system
that permitted Rome to conquer and rule an area so vast. Again as
Luttwak points out, "Above all, Romans clearly realized that the dominant dimension of power was not physical but psychological—the
product of other's perception of Roman strength rather than the use of
this strength."[22] Elsewhere Luttwak writes,

Together with money and manipulative diplomacy, forces visibly ready
to fight but held back from battle could serve to contrive disunity
among those who might jointly threaten the empire, to deter those who
would otherwise attack, and to control lands and people by intimidation—ideally to a point where sufficient security or even an effective
domination could be achieved without any use of force at all.[23]

Luttwak points out that the siege of Masada in A.D. 70–73 provides
one of the best examples of this psychological use of potential force—
what we call social force. He writes,

Faced with the resistance of a few hundred Jews on a mountain in the
Judean desert, a place of no strategic or economic importance, the Romans could have insulated the rebels by posting a few hundred men to
guard them. . . . Alternatively, the Romans could have stormed the
mountain fortress. . . . [But] the Romans did [neither] of these things. . . .
Instead, at a time when the entire Roman army had a total of only
twenty-nine legions to garrison the entire empire, one legion was developed to besiege Masada, [and] to reduce the fortress by great works
of engineering. . . . The entire three-year operation, and the very insig-
nificance of its objective, must have had an ominous impression on all
those in the East who might otherwise have been tempted to revolt. . . ."[24]

The Romans, then, assured their military supremacy ultimately by
relying upon social skills. By employing these skills effectively they

were able to destroy the sociopolitical cohesion of their enemies before their potential military might could be brought to bear against Rome. It was a system that was to work quite well for nearly three centuries.

Although the collapse of the Roman Empire is due to myriad complex and interdependent factors, one of the most important is a gradual erosion of the Roman military system. As Rome began to rely more and more exclusively upon its social skills to weaken and neutralize potential enemies, the other war-fighting skills began to wane. By A.D. 378 the Romans were no longer able to field cohesive infantry forces with sufficient discipline to withstand a cavalry charge. According to Oman, "Though seldom wanting in courage, the troops of the fourth century had lost the self-reliance and cohesion of the old Roman infantry. . . ."[25] Thus, when the social skills gave way due to internal neglect and general decay, there were no other skills above sheer physical skills of the Roman legionary to fall back upon. In short, the entire system collapsed, and 4,000 years of military evolution returned virtually to the starting point. It is upon this foundation that the modern military system was to be built, and the first stone in that foundation was the medieval military system.

**Medieval Warfare.** As was stated above, the paramount skill in the medieval military system is the physical skill of the individual combatant. Little attempt was made to create cohesive, disciplined formation subject to the will of a single commander. Oman described medieval armies this way:

> Assembled with difficulty, insubordinate, unable to maneuver, ready to melt away from its standard the moment that its short period of service was over, a feudal force represented an assemblage of unsoldierlike qualities such as have seldom been known to coexist. . . . As it was impossible to combine the movements of many small bodies when the troops were neither disciplined nor accustomed to act together, it was usual to form the cavalry into three great masses, or *"battles"* . . . and launch them at the enemy. . . . [Morever, even] the most ordinary [tactical] precautions, such as directing a reserve on a critical point . . . or selecting a good position in which to [fight] . . . were considered instances of surpassing military skill.[26]

There are some, like Terence Wise, who suggest that assessments such as these are overstated and that disciplined medieval armies, including many having cohesive infantry units, existed and fared well in the warfare of that age. Certainly the Saxon housecarls who fought dismounted behind a shield wall at the Battle of Hastings in 1066 were disciplined infantry. Indeed, these 3,000 heavy infantry accompanied by an equal number of Fyrd levies held off repeated charges by 8,000 Norman, Breton, and Flemish heavy cavalry for eight hours before they finally broke. And when they did break ranks it was to *charge* the enemy.[27] Still, such disciplined battles were the exception rather than the rule. And as Wise himself notes,

> The main problem seems not to have been the fighting quality of the troops, but the inability to maintain discipline over them once battles commenced, [since] loyalties within an army were widely divided, the nobles were jealous of each other and arrogant towards the infantry, and even kings could not control such internally divided armies. Because of this [it often happened] . . . that after the first charge a *battle degenerated into a series of individual combats* in which even leaders took part.[28]

This extremely limited system of fighting was not due to any technical limitation, but rather to the sociopolitical structure of the period. First, mounted knights came almost exclusively from the landed aristocracy who, living far from central authority and protected by castle walls, were virtually independent political entities in their own right. Indeed, as Schmookler notes, it was not until the advent of gunpowder that kings were able to establish effective centralized political control.

> It has been observed that the centralization of power by European monarchs at the expense of the once autonomous nobles was made possible by the changes in technology of warfare that enabled the attacker to violate the security of fortified castles.[29]

So long as the noble lords retained any independence from the king, it was unlikely they would perceive him to be anything other than simply a "first among equals." Under such conditions, the creation of cohesive, disciplined military units, wherein the knights willingly subordinated themselves in a setting of formalized command and control, was not possible.

The alternative—the creation of alternate military forces capable of fighting the knight on more or less equal terms—was also unlikely under the given social and economic structure of the time. First there was a labor shortage, requiring every able-bodied person (other than the aristocracy, of course) to spend virtually every waking hour in the production of food. Therefore, little time or energy was left to train these food producers in the art of soldiering. Secondly, there would be extreme resistance by the noble knights to any alternate form of warfare that might threaten their political or social stature. Warfare could only evolve, therefore, if the sociopolitical system upon which it rested also changed. As shall be seen, this is precisely what occurred. So long as feudalism remained, however, victory in war went to the side having the greatest number with a superior physical skill level.

**Neo-classical Warfare.** As with the emergence of classical warfare over primitive warfare in prehistoric times, the emergence of neo-classical warfare over medieval warfare was not due to some technical advantage, but rather to superior discipline and organization. Indeed, as Dyer writes, "The first army almost certainly carried weapons no different from those that hunters had been using on animals and on each other for thousands of years. . . . Its strength did not lie in mere numbers; what made it an army was discipline and organization . . . it was the most awesome concentration of power the human world had ever seen, and nothing except another army could hope to resist it."[30] Superior discipline and organization are what we have labeled *organizational skills*. Since the creation and maintenance of cohesive military units were adequately described in chapter 2, no discussion of this dynamic process need detain us here. It is sufficient to reiterate that the strength of this military system is that it subordinates the will of the individual combatant to that of the commander. It is the operation of all these individuals in concert that makes the army superior to less cohesive means of war. Moreover, it provides the commander with the ability to perform at least some tactical maneuvering on the battlefield, giving the neo-classical army a degree of flexibility not enjoyed by its medieval counterpart.

It is interesting to note that the antithesis of medieval warfare was based initially upon two different military systems; one relying upon shock and the other relying upon fire weaponry. The system relying upon shock weaponry is embodied in the massive phalanxes of pikemen from the Swiss Confederation, and the other system relied upon a combination of the English longbow and mounted or dismounted knights working in unison. Since the longbow-knight combination represents the initial step away from the medieval system, it is to this that we first turn our attention.

Although the origins of the longbow remain obscure, the English knights learned to respect this formidable weapon in the wars against Wales,[31] where the Welsh warriors caused many casualties among the English heavy cavalry. The English king was so impressed with the weapon that he created a corps of English bowmen, and it was these who were to destroy the flower of French chivalry at the battles of Crecy, Poitiers, and Agincourt. As Wise notes,

> The longbow had proved so devastating because . . . it had greater penetration power than any other weapon and a rapidity of fire which enabled a skilled bowman to fire a dozen unaimed arrows a minute. [Since] . . . carrying a heavily armored knight, a horse might cover a hundred yards a minute . . . every archer could have fired 36 arrows. . . . At Crecy there were 5,500 archers and during the French advances [the English] must have fired thirty volleys of 5,500 arrows [165,000 arrows total].[32]

Wise and others are quick to point out, however, that as formidable as the longbow was, bowmen could not stand up to cavalry alone. Consequently, English bowmen were always employed in concert with dismounted knights. As Wise suggests, it was probably only the incredible arrogance and lack of discipline of the French chivalry that permitted the outnumbered English to win at Crecy and Agincourt, since those French knights who successfully weathered the clouds of arrows and reached the English lines felt it was beneath their dignity to fight commoners and attacked the dismounted English knights instead of the bowmen.[33] At Poitiers the French dismounted their own heavy cavalry and attempted to close with the English on foot. The end result was simply to expose the French knights to arrow-fire for a much longer time, and when the French finally reached the English lines they were in ragged formations, exhausted, and scarcely capable of heavy hand-to-hand fighting with their better-rested foes. The inescapable conclusion to be drawn of course is that the French repeatedly lost not so much because they were employing an inferior military system, since it is unlikely that the outnumbered and more lightly armed archers could have defeated mounted knights in shock combat, but that the French simply misused the system they had. Of course, we would be remiss not to note that one main reason for fighting medieval conflicts was to capture opponents and hold them for ransom. It is doubtful, therefore, that a knight of any nationality would have wasted precious time and energy fighting and capturing a "worthless" commoner.

Although the longbow clearly represented a threat to the mounted knight, and consequently to medieval warfare, by itself this weapon did not entail a true antithesis to this form of warfare. It is evident, for instance, that the English chivalry came to terms and ultimately worked in unison with the weapon. The Swiss phalanxes, on the other hand, represented a true antithesis to the mounted knight—one that the knights were incapable of defeating, regardless of how well the knights were employed.

It should come as no surprise that the reemergence of massed infantry made up of well-trained and disciplined citizen soldiers should occur in Switzerland where the sociopolitical structure of feudalism first began to unravel. It was here in the wars of independence from the Holy Roman Empire that the relatively weak Swiss Confederation of Canons solved the problem of limited money and manpower not by relying on a handful of expensive mounted knights to fight their wars, but by using the same amount of limited funds to field much larger cohesive armies made up of Swiss citizenry. Each male citizen was to become a soldier, spending much of his off-time learning formation drill and the manual of arms for the pike. Free time was available due to improved farming methods that permitted an increase in the division of labor.[34] This, in turn, permitted the emergence of fledgling bourgeoisie who were independent of the landed aristocracy. Not only that, but the bourgeoisie rapidly began to accumulate wealth, and soon the center of power was moved from the castles of the noble lords to the towns where the money was.

The military system created by the Swiss was simple. It was, essentially, a return to the ancient Greek phalanx of massed pikemen. Its secret of success lay in the fact that, so long as the pikemen held their ground, not even the charge of heavy cavalry could break their serried ranks because horses will not willingly charge into a row of unwavering spear points.[35] Moreover, the phalanx enjoyed considerably more tactical flexibility than the *battles* in which the mounted knights operated. Whereas the commander of a *battle* had difficulty forming his formation in the first place and once formed had only one tactical option—the charge, or straight-ahead attack—the commander of a phalanx could move with relative ease forward, to the rear, and to either flank. Still, once contact was made, the phalanx commander's role became that of a common soldier since, just as when *battles* of mounted cavalry met, command and control became impossible. This is substantiated by Martin Van Creveld who writes,

Once armies had met and were, as the saying went, "pushing shield to shield," there was nothing more a commander could do; so he picked up his own shield and joined the fray. Of any attempt to coordinate various movements, much less to exercise control or change dispositions during the engagement itself, there could be no question whatsoever.[36]

That the phalanx was superior to mounted cavalry there can be no doubt. Austrian mounted knights were unable to break the phalanx in their first encounter with it at the Battle of Mongarten (A.D. 1315).[37] And, by the Battle of Sempach, some seventy-one years later, the knights came to realize that they were equally helpless against the phalanx when fighting dismounted.[38] Perhaps the ultimate testament to the superiority of neo-classical over medieval methods of warfare is the Battle of St. Jacob (A.D. 1444). It was here that a single Swiss phalanx of no more than 1,000 men *attacked* a French army of more than 15,000. Oman describes the battle this way:

> They attacked . . . broke [the French] center and were then surrounded by its overwhelming numbers. Compelled to form a [square] in order to resist the tremendous cavalry charges directed against them they remained rooted at the spot for the remainder of the day. . . . Not until evening was the fighting over, and then 2,000 [French] lay dead around the heap of Swiss corpses in the center.[39]

Although the Swiss were eventually wiped out in this battle, the horrible cost to the French caused them to abandon their invasion of Switzerland and go home. Even outnumbered 15 to 1 the organized phalanx was a formidable weapon against the much less organized feudal cavalry using a less complex form of warfare.

Although vestiges of the armored knight were to remain in use well into the early modern age, the phalanx and longbow marked the end of feudal chivalry. Both the bow and the phalanx made warfare much more egalitarian, wherein dismounted commoners now had the means to defeat the horse-mounted aristocrat. For the purpose of this book both systems—but especially the Swiss phalanx—establish the superiority of organized warfare over forms relying predominantly upon pure physical skill. They also represent something more sinister as well—the first step in the dehumanization of war. No longer was war a fight between two equals who may even know each other, but between articulated masses. Dyer puts it this way:

When the packed formations of well drilled men collided . . . what happened was quite impersonal, though every man died his own death. It was not the traditional combat between individual warriors. The soldiers were pressed forward by the ranks behind them against the anonymous strangers in that part of the enemy line facing them, and though in the end it was pairs of individuals who thrust at each other with spears for a few moments until one went down, there was nothing personal in the exchange.[40]

The phalanx was the first step away from war on a human scale. And the longbow represented a second step in that direction. It was a technological device—albeit one requiring years of practice to master—that could in one swift motion destroy a combatant having far more training and vastly superior physical skills. As will be seen, this dehumanization of war has increased drastically with each new era in the evolution of modern warfare.

The phalanx and the bow, then, reigned supreme on European battlefields until a technical innovation made them obsolete. That innovation was the advent of gunpowder and the development of field artillery.

**Early Modern Warfare.** In early modern warfare a new skill was added to war—the technological skill. The need for this new skill for victory was to have a profound effect on the nature of war. To begin with, it was the first skill needed in modern warfare that could not be gained upon the drill field. Although the majority of the combatants still went through repeated training to gain and improve skills in hand-to-hand combat, and to make absolutely certain every man in a formation was able to move in perfect unison with his comrades, there was now also a need for the technically skilled combatant, who had to be trained in the sciences, particularly chemistry, mathematics, and ballistics. Secondly, technical warfare employed military devices that consumed supplies at an alarming rate. This, in turn, required armies to think and operate in terms of maintaining lines of supply as well as traditional lines of communication with some central depot or other supply source. Consequently, in addition to the classical combatant, warfare in the technical, early modern age required practical scientists known as artillerists and communication/transportation experts known as logisticians.

That victory was no longer to be gained by physical and organizational skills alone was proved time and again in battles of the fifteenth and sixteenth centuries. Even the vaunted Swiss pike phalanxes were no match for armies having technical skills, even if the technically superior army had organizationally inferior combat units. A case in point is the Battle of Marignano (A.D. 1515) where the Swiss phalanx, made up of men armed solely with pikes and other shock weapons, were swept from the battlefield by an army consisting of only artillery and the same heavy cavalry the Swiss had repeatedly beaten in the past. Oman describes the battle this way:

> The system which [the French] . . . employed was to deliver charge after charge of cavalry on the flanks of the Swiss columns while the artillery played upon them from the front. The [attacks] by the cavalry, though they never succeeded in breaking the phalanx, forced it to halt and form the [square]. . . . Of course these attacks would by themselves be fruitless; it was the fact that they checked the advance of the Swiss, and obliged them to stand halted under artillery fire that settled the [issue].[41]

Clearly, the tightly packed phalanx armed only with shock weapons was no match for artillery. One hit could, as Oman notes, "plough through its dense ranks [disabling up to] . . . 20 men. . . ."[42]

Equally important, artillery now made the offensive once again the predominant form of war. No longer could dukes and princes defy the central authority of the king by hiding behind the impregnable walls of a fortified castle. By the middle of the sixteenth century armies could be armed with artillery capable of firing iron shot weighing over 1,000 pounds.[43] No stone wall, regardless of its thickness, could withstand such pounding. Moreover, artillery and small arms were far more expensive than the sword and pike had been, thus, only political entities enjoying great wealth, such as kings, could purchase sufficient quantities to arm an entire army. Both factors tended to cause a general centralization of power as the kings gradually enforced their will upon the reluctant feudal lords.

Another important factor is that, as with the longbow, early muskets provided even the lowest-born commoner the means to fight on equal or better terms with the aristocratic mounted knights. Unlike the bow, however, the musket required only weeks rather than years to master. Consequently, anyone having sufficient money to arm and equip an army with firearms could, in a matter of months, create combat power superior to that of armies dependent upon mounted knights or other combatants whose primary factor of lethality was based upon physical skill with a shock weapon that had taken years to master. In short, the technologically armed combatant was not only more effective in terms of lethality on the battlefield, but he was also more efficient in terms of training time over his classically armed and trained opponent.

This improved lethality was not without trade-offs, however. Perhaps the most important drawback of the technologically armed army was its increased dependence upon lines of supply. This, in turn, was to have a profound effect upon how war was to be waged. According to Theodore Ropp,

> The [classical] soldier did not use up his equipment in battle. Javelins or arrows could be manufactured or repaired on the spot by the blacksmiths and soldiers. Shot and powder on the other hand, were both expendable and irreplaceable. What was lost or shot away had to be provided by some central authority. . . . But it was these difficulties of supply and transportation which first set sixteenth century soldiers to thinking about *strategy* . . . [as opposed to simply] . . . tactics.[44]

No longer was it sufficient for a commander to understand the relatively simple mechanics of defeating an enemy on the battlefield. He must also understand strategy—the best means to bring a battle about in a manner that would protect his own lines of communications and supply while threatening those of his enemy. This, along with the increasing complexity in numbers and types of technological means employed, required commanders and their officers to be full-time professional soldiers. This in turn led to the need for military academies to teach the officers the technical skills required in the art and science of war.

As the early modern era was to show by the time it entered full stride in the Thirty Years' War, victory still went to the side able to maintain its cohesion, but disrupting the enemy's cohesion was becoming increasingly dependent upon technological means. It was the commander best able to employ these technical means that most often emerged the victor. In this way, a pattern was established that was to remain in effect until the present era in the evolution of warfare: new technology is introduced, then organizational means are found to maximize the effectiveness of the new technology.

The Swedish king Gustavus Adolphus was perhaps the first military commander to make effective organizational changes to maximize the new gunpowder technology. For instance, he placed musketeers in the pike phalanxes, giving these formations both a shock and fire capability. He standardized the caliber of all artillery, placed them entirely under military command, and made them smaller and more mobile so they could be employed more easily and more effectively on the battlefield. In short, Gustavus Adolphus's army was the first to make firepower a truly effective offensive weapon on the battlefield. According to Dyer, "the musket volleys and cannon fire of Gustavus Adolphus' army could shatter a formation of pikemen from a hundred yards away, without ever coming into physical contact with it."[45] These innovations were so effective that by the end of the Thirty Years' War in 1648 nearly every European army had adopted these same techniques.

By 1700 virtually all infantrymen were armed with muskets. In this way, although physical and organizational skills were still necessary, every soldier required a certain amount of technical skill to emerge victorious in combat. For instance, an infantryman had to perform fifty-four separate movements in precisely the correct order to load and fire his weapon.[46] The eminent military historian Henry Lumpkin describes a typical eighteenth-century battle this way;

> After a comparatively short artillery exchange, one or both [sides] would move forward at the quick march. . . . At 100 yards . . . [or closer], volleys were exchanged, three to five rounds per minute. This intense fire would continue point-blank until the commanding officer of one of the forces engaged . . . decided to order a bayonet charge. This usually occurred when the opposing side obviously had begun to wilt under the fire storm. . . . The essence of this kind of fighting . . . was fire discipline—troops so trained that they would stand unflinching and take heavy losses while delivering a greater volume of fire at a greater speed than the enemy.[47]

To fight such battles one required not only professional officers, but professional, long-service soldiers trained in the effective use of their weapon and in close-order drill. As Dyer notes, this efficiency under stress could only be achieved through literally thousands of hours of repetitive drilling.[48] This was clearly beyond the ability of part-time citizen soldiers such as those employed by the Swiss Confederation. Thus, what began as an efficient means to produce highly lethal combatants in the shortest possible time by providing them with a technical device obviating the necessity of years of training to hone physical skills ultimately resulted in the creation of the need for other, equally time-consuming training. Still, the inescapable fact was that a man armed with a musket enjoyed greater lethality than either the individual warrior knight or a soldier armed solely with a shock weapon. What made him deadlier still were the tactical innovations introduced by Gustavus Adolphus and improved upon by other great captains such as Frederick the Great and Napoleon.

These tactical innovations should not be confused with the concept of organizational skills introduced in the neo-classical era. Though they are related, they are different. These innovations were entirely dependent upon considerations of maximizing physical, not moral, force. Moreover, these changes were adopted to employ most effectively the technology of the day. For instance, decisions as to whether to have fourteen ranks or six ranks depended upon how fast soldiers in each rank could load and fire so as to have a constant rolling barrage of volley fire. In this way, these tactical innovations should be considered simply an adjunct or subelement of the technical skills an army required during this era.

Organizational as well as physical skills were, of course, still extremely important during this era. This was particularly true if both sides enjoyed equivalent technical skills and tactical innovations. In such cases, as Lumpkin's description of an eighteenth-century battle shows, the side that first began to break under fire usually felt the shock of a bayonet attack thereafter. In short the coup de grace was usually delivered in a manner germane to the neo-classical era; one with which the Swiss pikemen would be entirely comfortable and probably superior to any eighteenth-century army. Still, all things being equal, it was superior technical skills that provided the edge in determining victory in the early modern era.

**Late Modern Warfare.** By the early nineteenth century a new paramount skill began to be felt in war. This is what we have labeled *administrative skills*. These skills not only make it possible to mobilize all of the necessary resources of a nation-state to fight a war, they also permit the command, control, and coordination of widely separated military forces making it possible for them to be employed in unison against the same military objective. Two technological inventions made this possible: (1) the railroad and (2) the telegraph. These, coupled with modern bureaucratic management techniques, made modern mass warfare possible.

The railroad was the first major improvement in military transportation in nearly 4,000 years. Previously, soldiers had to rely solely upon muscle power of men and animals to move their supplies and equipment. Until the early modern era, this served as a hindrance and nuisance, but was rarely catastrophic for armies before the advent of gunpowder weaponry. Afterwards, however, armies became increasingly tied down to their lines of supply, particularly as armies tried to carry food, fodder, and munitions with them on every campaign. This posed considerable problems since there was an increase in things that had to be carried but no improvements in the means to do so. Martin Blumenson and James Stokesbury make the following observations on the speed and carrying capacity of an army in the pre-industrial era:

> The marching man in the Hittite armies moved at the same speed as his later counterparts in the armies of Frederick the Great. He could carry about the same weight of material—sixty pounds . . . [over an extended period]—and he required the same amount of [food, shelter, and other equipment]. . . . [Moreover], the train of the army was tied to the speed of oxen or bullocks, and they could go only about twelve miles a day without breaking down; even then they needed a day's rest every fourth day. The oxen could therefore go [only] thirty-six miles in four days, though the soldiers [who could go easily 15 miles a day] could march sixty miles in the same time. . . .[49]

Blumenson and Stokesbury go on to note that the British Army in Spain during the Napoleonic wars continued to operate at this leisurely pace even as late as 1813.[50] Napoleon was the first to break away from these encumbering supply columns by making his men carry their munitions—shot and powder—while having them forage for their food. In this way Napoleon's armies were marching 60 miles every four days while other European armies were barely able to make 36 miles in the same time. Moreover, Napoleon was less concerned about his lines of supply and therefore had much greater freedom of action than his counterparts.

Another major drawback in supplying a moving army was that unless large amounts of food and fodder were brought with you, the maximum size of an army that could live off the land in a given vicinity was 20,000 men.[51] Armies larger than this had to move in widely dispersed columns of no more than 20,000 men each and then come together to fight a battle. Napoleon solved this problem by creating the corps d'armee, each of which actually represented a small army having its own infantry, cavalry, and artillery units attached. The first corps to encounter the enemy was expected to be able to fight a defensive holding action for at least a day until the other corps could be notified and rushed to the point of action.[52] But as Martin van Creveld points out, before the advent of modern communications technology, only a man with the genius and energy of a Napoleon could really hope to effectively command and control such widely dispersed forces.[53] Indeed, even Napoleon occasionally lost control over these forces. For instance he reportedly was unable to maintain control of up to five of his eight corps engaged against the Prussian Army at the double battle of Jena-Auerstadt in 1806.[54] Still, Napoleon did succeed in a manner that far surpassed any of his contemporaries, and the secret of his success appears to have rested on two important innovations: (1) the creation of self-contained, mission-oriented strategic units, each with its own commander and staff and made up of all three combat arms,[55] and (2) the creation of a general headquarters that took care of the ever-growing administrative problems and details germane to coordinating, controlling, and supplying these widely separated combat units. These two elements combined were to be the foundation stones of the late modern methods of warfare.

As the American Civil War illustrates, victory in late modern warfare usually went to the side best able to mobilize and coordinate the employment of the greatest number of soldiers over the longest period of time. Few would argue with the contention that, particularly early in the war, the Confederate Army enjoyed the same technical skills and probably enjoyed superior organizational skills compared to the Union Army. But now that it was possible to have the administrative ability to mobilize an entire nation for war, the days of a war being decided by one cataclysmic battle were over. Now what mattered *most* was quantity, not quality. In other words, the decisive factor came not from the ability to field and sustain a technically and organizationally superior army, but rather the ability to field and sustain the greatest number of such armies against the enemy. As Sir Michael Howard has observed, the

> masters of operational strategy were to be found, not in the victorious armies of the North, but among the leaders of the South. . . . [Consequently] the victory of the North was due not to the operational capabilities of its generals, but its capacity to mobilize its superior industrial strength and manpower into armies which [could be employed] in such strength that the operational skills of their adversaries were rendered almost irrelevant.[56]

Even more important, an administratively superior army could also defeat an army that was technically superior in many ways. Perhaps the best example of this is the Franco-Prussian War. Although the Prussians enjoyed technical superiority in some of its field artillery, the French clearly had the technical lead in infantry weapons with the chassepot rifle, which could accurately fire nearly three times as far as the Prussian needlegun and the *mitrailleuse,* an early form of the machine gun. Despite these French technical advantages, the Prussians decisively defeated every French field army within three months of the opening campaign.

The ease and swiftness of the French defeat is clearly related to administrative failures. First, the French were only able to mobilize 224,000 men in the same time the Germans mobilized 475,000. According to Dupuy and Dupuy this disparity was largely due to the fact that "German mobilization and troop concentrations followed a definite, well-directed plan, which utilized the railway net to the full . . . [while] French mobilization was haphazard and incomplete."[57] Additionally, whereas each Prussian army had established general headquarters fully capable of supporting their subordinate corps and other units, the French only belatedly created two armies by arbitrarily combining corps together, leaving the army commanders to operate as best they could by using one of their corps headquarters staff to double as an army general staff.[58] All of this not only made a shambles of the mobilization of the French army but also drastically hindered effective command and control once the army was assembled. Michael Howard describes the French mobilization this way:

> Thus a plan already faulty in principle was further marred by faults in execution; and as the army assembled around Metz and Strasbourg it found itself lacking not only in men but the most elementary supplies. The trouble lay, not in the inadequacy of stocks, but in the arrangements for their distribution. . . . Meanwhile, the German [mobilization] had gone on as planned.[59]

Administrative skill, then, governed who would emerge victorious in the wars of the late modern era. By World War I the French had corrected the faults in their mobilization plans and methods of command and control. Since both sides were roughly equivalent in administrative skills, the war ground on until the massive influx of American manpower and resources tipped the scales against Germany. As Ropp notes, "Surprisingly . . . neither the French nor the German commands attempted to use their cavalry in 1914 to disrupt the enemy's mobilization."[60] This oversight was corrected by the Germans in World War II; by employing blitzkrieg tactics they were able to surround and cut off large portions of the enemy's army, robbing the enemy commander of his operational control of these isolated pockets and neutralizing any administrative skills the enemy might enjoy. Unfortunately for the Axis, the Germans were unable to disrupt administrative skills over intercontinental distances. Once again, as in World War I, the industrial might of the United States proved decisive. And this, of course, was primarily dependent upon bureaucratic/administrative skills capable of coordinating the millions of tasks necessary to build, train, deploy, employ, sustain, and control U.S. armed forces operating on a massive, global scale.

As in the American Civil War, victory was ultimately a factor of quantity over quality, especially in Europe. German tanks were better armed and armored than American. German jet fighters and guided missiles far surpassed anything the Allies had. Clearly, then, the side that could produce the most over the longest period of time and effectively employ it against the enemy in well-coordinated efforts would almost always emerge victorious—providing they could maintain that advantage. As will be seen in the next section, maintaining this advantage was heavily dependent upon not only developing and maintaining the correct bureaucratic/administrative mechanisms of command and control, but also upon the willingness of those within this system to continue to support it.

**War in the Nuclear Era.** The major factor governing warfare in the nuclear era is, of course, nuclear weaponry. Ironically, the paramount skill germane to this era does not devolve from the use of these awesomely destructive weapons, but rather from the *threat* of their use. Consequently, they, like the Roman legions of the high classical era, establish the environment in which force is employed. That is, like the legions, nuclear weapons are virtually omnipotent once put into action, and all who might consider standing against them are fully aware of the probable consequences of doing so. In this way, nuclear weaponry functions as potential force and therefore operates primarily in the psychological versus the physical plane. As a result, the paramount skill in the nuclear era involves not so much the mobilization and employment of military resources as social skills.

As was stated earlier in this chapter, social skills represent the ability to mobilize and sustain the sociopolitical resources of a friendly populace while undermining, disrupting, and destroying those of the enemy *without first having to destroy his armed forces.* This last part is critical due to what we have labeled the *Brodie Paradox.*

The Brodie Paradox stems from the irony that nuclear weaponry is so devastatingly effective and efficient that for two nuclear powers to go to war with one another is tantamount to virtual national suicide for both parties. Consequently, as Bernard Brodie concluded during the late 1940s, warfare involving the mutual exchange of nuclear weapons may not even be warfare at all—at least in any classical sense of the term. Indeed, when he applied to atomic warfare von Clausewitz's dictum that "war is a continuation of policy by other means," Brodie quickly surmised that there is simply no rational political objective sufficient to justify the immense destruction of nuclear warfare conducted on a massive, global scale. Furthermore, even "limited" nuclear warfare between nuclear-equipped powers has little utility since it could quite easily and uncontrollably escalate into global, thermonuclear war. Another political scientist, William Kaufman, expands upon Brodie's contention and observes that

> traditional strategy, along with its weapons and axioms, held that the idea of war was to destroy the enemy's will to fight. . . . [But] in an era when both combatants have long-range multimegaton nuclear weapons in their arsenals . . . the traditional military objectives could not be gained without committing national suicide in the process, thus nullifying any Pyrrhic victory [that] might have been achieved.[61]

In short, nuclear war cannot be fought in any traditional manner since there are simply no objectives "commensurate with the horribly destructive magnitude of all out nuclear war."[62] Consequently, this, the most effective and efficient technical means to wage war, in the end, has virtually no utility at all in actual warfare. Nuclear-equipped states are therefore compelled to wage war by limited means and for limited objectives, applying lethal force by a means and in an area where it is not perceived to be a direct, unambiguous threat to another nuclear state.

The unexpected means of warfare in the nuclear era has become sociopolitical rather than purely military. Moreover, the utility of limited wars involving internal conflicts between factions within a given state has increased dramatically. Such wars rely upon revolutions, insurgencies, and civil wars employing conventional guerrilla and terrorist means. The purpose of these conflicts is to gain or maintain control of the populace of a given political entity. We call this type of warfare *social warfare.*

Since social warfare will be discussed in detail in the next section, it is sufficient to note here that the paramount skill in this form of warfare is social skill. Certainly the other skills remain important; the combatants must meet at least minimum physical skills and be able to maintain cohesive military units. The belligerents must also be able to supply their armed forces with relatively modern technical means and afford both the combatants and those who support them with the necessary technical skills to employ and maintain this technology. Finally, the belligerents must be able to mobilize armed forces and project and sustain these forces over long distances, in year-round campaigns, and in coordinated efforts. This, of course, requires administrative/bureaucratic skills. But as the American Revolutionary and Vietnam wars show, the ability to field consistently superior force and win field engagements does not assure victory.

Perhaps the first war in modern warfare in which social skills played the predominant role is the American Revolutionary War. Despite winning nineteen of the thirty-one major engagements of the American Revolutionary War, fighting two more to a draw, and winning thirty-seven additional minor engagements, the British still lost the war.[63] This was certainly not due to any lack of military capability or inferior physical, organizational, technical, or administrative skills, but rather it was due to inferior social skills. According to Lumpkin,

> After comparatively easy captures of Savannah and Charleston, the British . . . committed one serious error after another. They overestimated the numbers of Loyalists who would flock to their aid. They antagonized thoroughly the very people upon whose eventual support they must depend if victory were to be achieved. . . . [Moreover], as it became increasingly clear that the British could not protect their adherents or control the hinterland, an ever growing number of southerners supported the partisans. . . . Both sides made blunders, but the British mistakes could not be remedied. When they failed to subjugate Georgia and South Carolina and win over . . . the majority of the people, the British lost not only the war in the South but the final and best chance to subdue the thirteen colonies.[64]

The same basic conclusion can be drawn for other wars in which social skills were the predominant factor, such as Vietnam, Algeria, China, Nicaragua, and Cuba. This is clearly seen in the following observation made by Harry Summers about Vietnam:

> One of the most frustrating aspects of the Vietnam War from the Army's point of view is that as far as logistics and tactics were concerned we succeeded in everything we set out to do. At the height of the war the Army was able to move almost a million soldiers a year in and out of Vietnam, feed them, clothe them, supply them with arms and ammunition, and generally sustain them better than any Army had ever been sustained in the field. . . . On the battlefield itself, the Army was unbeatable. In engagement after engagement the forces of the Viet Cong and North Vietnamese were thrown back with terrible losses. Yet in the end, it was North Vietnam, not the United States that emerged victorious.[65]

The conclusion to be drawn here is both evident and inescapable. The advantage the Americans enjoyed over the British and the Vietnamese over the Americans was not technical or organizational or administrative, but simply social. Just as an army whose paramount skill is organizational cannot hope to defeat an army having a technical paramount skill, so too, an army relying upon technical and administrative skills cannot hope to defeat a belligerent whose paramount skill is social. Moreover, as shall be seen in the coming chapters, relying upon administrative, technical, or organizational skills to combat the means of social warfare—which can include both guerrilla and terrorist methods—are both ineffective and inappropriate.

## Social Warfare

Social warfare is a distinct subtype requiring its own paramount skill, which in turn affects how force can best be employed. Although social warfare has existed since the early classical epoch and was greatly relied upon by the Roman Empire, it has generally been regarded as a simple adjunct to the main business of war-fighting. Only after the advent of nuclear weaponry and the Brodie Paradox did social warfare become a primary means of waging war in the modern epoch.

Although there are exceptions, such as the Arab-Israeli conflicts, most conflicts between nuclear-equipped powers or their allies fall into the category of social warfare. This section will briefly analyze social warfare, first as it evolved in the prenuclear eras and then how it has developed in light of the Brodie Paradox. From this analysis we will gain a better understanding of precisely what this form of warfare seeks to achieve and how it does so. This, in turn, provides a foundation for understanding why terrorism exists and how it can present a military challenge to the modern nation-state.

## Social Warfare Before the Nuclear Era

To have a fuller understanding of social warfare, it is helpful to examine the state from a structural perspective. The state, according to Barry Buzan, consists of three primary components: (1) physical, (2) institutional, and (3) metaphysical.[66] The physical component is the territory and people existing within and subject to the state's authority. The institutional component consists of the institutions of law and government. Finally, and most important, the metaphysical component is the concept or the idea of the state acknowledged and accepted by the populace itself. As Buzan notes,

> We can infer from [this] . . . that the state exists, or has its essence, primarily on the social rather than on the physical plane. In other words, the state is more a metaphysical entity, an idea held in common by a group of people, than it is a physical organism.[67]

Given this, we can see that should any one of these components cease to exist, the state can no longer function as a sovereign entity within the international milieu. Of course, the most important component is the common idea of the state. Indeed, as the Armenian, South Moluccan, and Palestinian irredenta have clearly shown, even without sovereign territory the *idea* of the state—embodied in revolutionary terrorism—is sufficient to make its presence felt within the international system.

It is clear, then, that the most effective attack on the state is not limited to destroying the state's physical assets of territory and people, nor to disrupting its institutional assets of command and control, but should also entail an assault upon the state on the social or moral plane. This is particularly true if the state in question is already experiencing internal difficulties pertaining to questions of legitimacy of the ruling regime, or the existing ideology or form of government. Again, according to Buzan, "The distinguishing feature of weak states is their high level of concern with domestically generated threats to the security of the government."[68] This represents a very clear weakness that should be capitalized upon by anyone seeking to wage war upon that state.

The idea that a state could employ social forces within a targeted entity as a weapon and means of war is a very old one. As Samuel Griffith points out, Sun Tzu was well aware of the importance of national unity and cohesion in any struggle between nations. Indeed, Sun Tzu stressed that no war be undertaken before the enemy is politically destabilized. Summing up Sun Tzu's remarks Griffith writes,

> Sun Tzu believed . . . war was to be preceded by measures designed to make it easy to win. The master conqueror frustrated the enemy's plans and broke up his alliances. He created cleavages between sovereign and ministers, superiors and inferiors, commanders and subordinates. His spies were everywhere, gathering information, sowing dissension, and nurturing subversion. The enemy was isolated and demoralized; his will to resist broken. Thus without battle his army was conquered, his cities taken and his state overthrown.[69]

Using social forces to destabilize and weaken political opponents is therefore an ancient ploy, and down through the centuries there have been many examples of political struggles between two sovereign political entities being resolved in such a manner. It has proven most effective in situations where the cleavages noted by Sun Tzu already exist, are extremely pronounced, and are irreconcilable.

These cleavages represent potential weaknesses in the structural cohesion of a given political entity and provide a rough idea of how polarization might occur should that cohesion be disrupted. From a structural perspective these cleavages can occur vertically, horizontally, or on both axes simultaneously. Vertical cleavages are social in nature, representing such factors as race, religion, ideology, and nationality. Horizontal cleavages are those that prevent political mobility between the ruled and the rulers. These cleavages are most pronounced, of course, when they occur on both planes simultaneously; that is, when a group is excluded from integrating into society by some vertical cleavage and from participating in the political process at the same time. As will be seen, such situations provide excellent opportunities for those willing to exploit them.

These factors are important in any war, but they are particularly crucial in wars in which neither belligerent has sufficient combat power to secure victory through a war of annihilation. In such cases, both belligerents end up waging a war of attrition wherein technical military means lose much of their importance in securing victory. In such a war, military means derive their importance primarily from a defensive perspective—i.e., they are important only to the point that they are able to *deny* victory to the enemy. It is here that weaknesses in a belligerent's social structure becomes critical in determining victory. This is particularly true if the existing social cleavages are so salient that a belligerent can harness disgruntled social forces within the enemy camp. A few historical examples are sufficient to demonstrate how this functions.

One early example of a state effectively harnessing and employing internal social forces against a political entity is Queen Elizabeth I's support of the Dutch rebels in the Spanish Netherlands during the sixteenth century. According to Will and Ariel Durant, Elizabeth "planned to support the revolt of the Netherlands sufficiently to keep them from surrendering to Spain or bequeathing themselves to France. For as long as the revolt continued Spain would [be diverted] and stay out of England."[70]

As Elizabeth quickly realized, enlisting the aid of these social forces made combatting Spanish policies an extremely efficient prospect. At the price of a relatively small amount of gold coin, Elizabeth had a fanatically dedicated army that not only did the bulk of the fighting and dying but also diverted vast amounts of Spanish political, economic, and military resources. In the end, the revolt in the Netherlands tipped the scales in England's favor. According to Theodore Ropp, "The Dutch revolt played the same role in the decline of Spain as the Spanish revolt was to play in the fall of Napoleon. It was the 'running sore' which drained off Spanish soldiers, Spanish morale, and Spanish money."[71]

As this example clearly shows, social forces can be harnessed and converted into political/military power. Moreover, they are efficient, promising very large returns for a relatively small investment. And, as shown, the employment of social forces can even be quite decisive. Equally important, ignoring these social forces can be disastrous. Perhaps the best example of this is Hitler's invasion of the Soviet Union on June 22, 1941.

The Soviet state that awaited Hitler's onslaught consisted of a patchwork of disaffected peoples very clearly delineated by horizontal and vertical cleavages. Millions had died during Stalin's collectivization of Soviet agriculture and political purges. According to J. F. C. Fuller,

> In 1941, in the Ukraine, White Russia and the Baltic States alone, some 40,000,000 people yearned for liberation; therefore in order to disintegrate the colossus, all Hitler had to do was to cross the Russian frontier as a liberator, and terminate collectivization. It would have won over to him, not only minorities, but it would also have dissolved Stalin's armies, because they so largely consisted of collectivized serfs.[72]

In the first weeks following the invasion the Germans were received as liberators. Everywhere, particularly in the Baltic States and the Ukraine, German soldiers were greeted by cheering happy people. By December nearly 2.5 million Soviet soldiers had surrendered, many wishing to join Germany's crusade against Bolshevism.[73] Then came Heinrich Himmler's special action detachments called the *Sichereitdienst* or SD, whose purpose was the subjugation of the inhabitants of the newly conquered territories. It was the incredibly brutal methods employed by the SD that saved the politically bankrupt ideology of Bolshevism. As one contemporary German observer noted, "By rousing the Russian people to a Napoleonic fervor we enabled the Bolsheviks to achieve a political consolidation beyond their wildest dreams and provided their cause with the halo of a 'patriotic war.'"[74]

The results, of course, were catastrophic for Germany. Ignoring these social factors was a supreme error on the part of Hitler and his Nazi regime, and the lesson it provides is clear. Not only can social factors be harnessed by an outside sovereign power, failure to do so can quickly lead to disaster.

There are limitations, however, in any attempt to harness and direct social forces located in the enemy camp. The three major drawbacks are (1) the social forces generally have objectives of their own that may not be compatible with those of the sponsoring state, (2) these forces are often unpredictable and are difficult to control, and (3) often these social forces take years or even decades to develop to the point they can be considered an important factor. All three of these factors are readily seen by returning to the English conflict with Spain in the sixteenth century.

The English quickly learned by their support of the Dutch rebels in the Spanish Netherlands that today's ideological ally can become tomorrow's nationalist enemy. English support of their Protestant Dutch brethren undoubtedly was a decisive factor in the latter's overthrow of the Catholic Spanish colonial yoke. The end result for England, however, was not the creation of a natural ally, but a new economic and military rival. Within one hundred years, Holland and England would go to war three times as both nations sought to gain supremacy of the seas.

The Spanish also found that social forces are often very unpredictable and difficult to control. About the same time the English began to back the Protestant Dutch rebels, the Spanish began to support the Catholic rebels in Scotland and Ireland. Although these rebels would eventually divert vast amounts of English political and military resources, at the time of the Spanish Armada in 1588 they were still not a significant factor. Indeed, as the Spanish sailors from the defeated armada quickly learned, Ireland was no safe haven. Shipwrecked crews and landing parties alike were hacked to pieces by the same Irish Catholic peasantry that Spain sought to use against England.

Time is also a factor. While they are efficient, social forces often require years, even decades, to generate enough power to be decisive. Certainly more was settled between Spain and England during the ten-day naval battle of the Spanish Armada than in the previous ten years of internecine warfare in the Netherlands. Nations all too often simply do not have time to harness and employ even existing social forces, much less expend years of careful nurturing in the hopes of creating such forces. Thus, for the most part, nations tend to rely upon their own military instrument to resolve disputes and achieve political objectives. They might be less efficient over the long run, but they have been more decisive and effective when an immediate decision was necessary and desired.

Even as continued technological advancements made warfare increasingly costly, unlimited, total warfare remained an integral element of national policy well into the present century. There were many, of course, who did question the utility of total war under modern conditions even before the turn of the century. Some students of warfare like Ivan S. Bloch were well aware of the horrible costs of total war between states armed with modern weaponry. Well before the outbreak of World War I, Bloch had written that the terrible costs of such warfare rendered it counterproductive. Citing the incredible, unprecedented slaughter, the slowly moving armies engaged in long and indecisive battles and the incredible strain on the civil populace to sustain such a war, Bloch questioned whether the social fabric of any nation could withstand the stresses of modern warfare.[75] Of course, ephemeral psychological and sociological factors continued to be employed whenever possible but were generally simply an adjunct to conventional warfare. Military men understandably tended to rely more heavily upon the more tangible and more easily calculated technical aspects of armed conflict. The results from a "whiff of grapeshot" were simply far more easy to calculate, direct, and control than the actions of the rabble of the street. The prospect of using social forces as the predominant means of warfare was, for the time being, simply out of the question.

Even nations born of revolution and built on an ideological foundation calling for the export of social revolution, such as the Soviet Union, relied almost exclusively upon its military instrument to consolidate and expand its own revolution. Although Lenin had initially created the Red Army not as an army of the state but as an army of the world proletariat, when the revolution did not spread of its own accord across the rest of Europe, revolutionary rhetoric quickly gave way to the pragmatic requirements of defending the Soviet state. Until a mere forty years ago, the primary means of expanding the socialist revolution was through the employment of the Soviet Army. As will be seen, these conditions were to change with the advent of nuclear weaponry, however.

## Social Warfare in the Nuclear Era

As was seen earlier in this chapter, nuclear weaponry brought about a profound change in the nature of warfare. Indeed, as established by the Brodie Paradox, a nuclear power cannot employ its military instrument against another nuclear power due to the fear of uncontrolled escalation to full-scale nuclear war wherein "victory" is unachievable in any classical definition of the term. In short, even limited conventional warfare between nuclear powers has to be avoided because the results are too unpredictable; the situation too unstable. Clearly, lethal force has to come in some other form if it is to have any utility in achieving policy goals.

Ironically, what had been the least stable and most unpredictable means of employing lethal force for political ends has now become the most stable. Rather than rely upon unlimited total warfare requiring the mobilization of the full spectrum of a nation's military, economic, political, and social resources, states are employing low-intensity conflicts often using surrogate military forces.

Many nuclear equipped nations have sought to capitalize on the utility of low-intensity conflicts, but it is the Soviet Union that has probably best operationalized the employment of social forces for the attainment of foreign policy objectives. Two Soviet operational concepts are particularly helpful here: (1) *the correlation of forces* and (2) *wars of national liberation.*

The correlation of forces is not equivalent to Western notions of the balance of power. This latter concept relies almost exclusively upon measurements of military power. Although military power is a major element of the correlation of forces, this concept includes much more. According to A. Sergiyev,

> The foreign policy potential of a state depends not only upon its own forces and internal resources but, to a considerable extent, on such factors as the existence of reliable socio-political allies among other states, national contingents of congenial classes, mass international movements and other political forces active in the world scene.[76]

From this it is clear that the Soviets understand that political power is not only subject to the availability of resources of the state initiating foreign policy actions, but also dependent upon the sociopolitical environment in which those resources operate. Vernon Aspaturian puts it this way:

> Soviet leaders, in short, have long recognized that social conflicts, tensions, frustrations and resentments . . . conceal tremendous reserves of pent-up social power, which can be detected by dialectical analysis and then tapped, mobilized, and transmuted into concrete political power subject to the manipulation of Soviet [foreign] policy.[77]

Correlation of forces considerations are, therefore, carefully factored into any Soviet foreign policy decision, and major commitments of Soviet resources are extremely unlikely if the sociopolitical environment does not augur well for the rapid achievement of a given policy objective. There is, however, one very important factor that would prevent

Soviet commitment to a given foreign policy objective even if the local correlation of forces were ripe for exploitation, and that is if such an objective would directly threaten the security of the Soviet state. It is here that the concept of wars of national liberation comes into play.

The importance of wars of national liberation is that they permit the USSR to support the expansion of socialism without directly involving the Soviet state. The local, indigenous population provides the bulk of the necessary power in the form of combatants and support organizations, while the USSR supplies weapons—often laundered through a third nation—and offers training and technical expertise. As Khrushchev repeatedly emphasized, these wars were not to be equated with wars between states, but rather were wars of indigenous popular uprising to throw off the "bonds of imperialist tyranny."[78]

In this way, the Soviet Union is able to "peacefully coexist" within the fraternity of nation-states, while undermining it. William Odom points out that *"peace* to the Soviet Union . . . means the destruction of all nonsocialist states . . . without [resorting to] interstate wars."[79] He continues to underscore this point by stating, "Peaceful coexistence in the Soviet definition is continuation of the international class struggle by other than direct military means whenever possible."[80] In other words, to wage the conflict and win the victory by employing indigenous revolutionary movements to serve as surrogate military/ political forces in the struggle against capitalism. And, given its utility in revolutionary warfare, terrorism is often included in these Soviet-sponsored conflicts.

The objective of the Soviet Union, then, is total: the destruction of all nonsocialist states. Its means, however, are limited. That is, the USSR is waging a total war of attrition against the Western powers in which the political, military, economic, and social resources of the targeted nations are slowly eroded by an ever-increasing expenditure of effort to contain the agitated social forces located in the areas Western governments still control. In short, it represents national revolutionary warfare expanded to global proportions with the ultimate objective being to create conditions wherein the targeted entity is weakened by internal strife and ultimately collapses of its own weight or is easily conquered by conventional military means.

The Soviet model, therefore, provides a means of understanding surrogate warfare in terms of exploiting local, indigenous social forces for political objectives. Equally important, it establishes that surrogate warfare is operative under current structural conditions governed by the threat of nuclear warfare. It is important to note, of course, that the Soviet Union is not the only nation to engage in surrogate warfare. Other nations can and do benefit from the same conditions the Soviets have so clearly operationalized. The United States supports the Nicaraguan Contras and the Mujahadeen in Afghanistan to contain the spread of Marxism. Libya, Syria, and Iran support various Islamic factions against Israel and the West. But there is a considerable range in the type of surrogate forces available to be supported. These range from conventional forces employed by allied states—such as the Soviet use of Cuban forces in Angola and Ethiopia—to guerrilla forces, to terrorism.

The conditions of the nuclear era have made it possible to employ terrorism as a viable means to effect policy goals. This is particularly true regarding conflicts between nuclear-equipped powers and their allies. As the French author R. Gaucher has observed, "The truth is, at a time when it is difficult to mobilize great masses of people without provoking a global conflict with irreparable damage, terrorism tends to become a substitute for [classical] war."[81]

There are some who even suggest that state-sponsored terrorism is a new form of world war. For instance, the Dutch political scientist Hylke Tromp believes that surrogate terrorism is a "third World War which has assumed the completely unexpected form of 'protracted' warfare by terroristic methods. . . ."[82] Terrorism, then, is clearly considered by many to be a viable means of conflict resolution under current conditions of the nuclear era.

## Summation

Although all warfare is based upon immutable laws and principles, the methods of warfare vary according to the objectives sought, the means employed, and the conditions that govern the era in which the war is being waged. As shown in table 3, war can be classified according to six characteristics: (1) total, (2) limited, (3) positional, (4) evasion, (5) annihilation, and (6) attrition. It is the various combinations of these six characteristics that determine the type of war being waged at a given time. Additionally, depending upon the evolutionary era in which the war is being waged, different types of war-fighting skills are necessary to assure or at least enhance the chances of victory. In the unorganized warfare of the medieval era, the paramount skill was the physical skill of the primary combatant—the mounted knight. This form of warfare gave way to the organized warfare of the neo-classical era. Here the paramount skill was the ability to create and maintain cohesive battlefield combat units able to fight and maneuver at the will of a single commander—i.e., organizational skills. Neo-classical warfare gave way to early modern warfare wherein the paramount skill became the ability to field, employ, and support superior technological means of waging war. The paramount skill in late modern warfare became the ability to mobilize and coordinate the full range of war-fighting resources available to the belligerent. Although other skills remained important, even armed forces having inferior physical, organizational, and technical skills could emerge victorious providing it enjoyed superior administrative skills.

Finally, the paramount skill found in the nuclear era is social skills, which represents the belligerent's ability to directly manipulate the enemy's will to fight without first having to engage and defeat its armed forces. Again, other war-fighting skills are important—but the ultimate and sufficient requirement of military force is primarily defensive, that is, it preserves the belligerent's ability to wage the war. It is not annihilative victories, superior technical or administrative means, more cohesive combat units, or physically superior combatants that secure victory in social warfare, but rather it is the ability to wear down the resolve of the populace of the targeted entity to continue the war. As will be seen in the coming chapters, terrorism is a viable means of achieving this end.

## Notes

1. Karl von Clausewitz, *On War*, edited and translated by Michael Howard and Peter Paret (Princeton: Princeton University Press, 1976), p. 90.

2. Ibid.

3. David R. Palmer, *Summons of the Trumpet: US-Vietnam in Perspective* (San Rafael, Calif.: Presidio Press, 1978), p. xix. As quoted in Harry G. Summers, Jr., *On Strategy: A Critical Analysis of the Vietnam War* (Novato, Calif.: Presidio Press, 1982; 4th printing, 1984), p. 68.

4. Sir Basil Liddell Hart, *Strategy* (New York: Praeger Publishers, Inc., 1968), p. 354. (Quoting von Clausewitz.)

5. von Clausewitz, op. cit., pp. 91–92.

6. Ibid., p. 100.

7. Ibid., pp. 92–93.

8. Liddell Hart, op. cit., pp. 370–71.

9. von Clausewitz, op. cit., pp. 233–34.

10. Gordon A. Craig, "Delbruck: The Military Historian," *Makers of Modern Strategy: Military Thought from Machiavelli to Hitler,* edited by Edward M. Earle (Princeton: Princeton University Press, 1943; Princeton paperback printing, 1973), p. 273.

11. Ibid.

12. Ibid.

13. Barrie Paskins and Michael Dockrill, *The Ethics of War* (Minneapolis: The University of Minnesota Press, 1979), p. 88.

14. Samuel B. Griffith, ed. "Sun Tzu and Mao Tse Tung," *The Art of War* (Oxford: Oxford University Press, 1963; Oxford paperback edition, 1971), p. 51.

15. For an excellent description of George Washington's strategy of attrition see: Russell F. Weigley, *The American Way of War: A History of the United States Military Strategy and Policy* (Bloomington: Indiana University Press, 1943; Indiana University paperback edition, 1973), pp. 3–17.

16. Gwynne Dyer, *War* (New York: Crown Publishers, Inc., 1985), p. 10.

17. Andrew B. Schmookler, *The Parable of the Tribes: The Problem of Power in Social Evolution* (Berkeley: University of California Press, 1984; Houghton Mifflin Co., paperback edition, 1986), p. 109.

18. Dyer, op. cit., p. 58.

19. C. W. C. Oman, *The Art of War in the Middle Ages,* revised and edited by John H. Beeler (London: Cornell University Press paperback edition, 1973), p. 33.

20. R. Ernest Dupuy and Trevor N. Dupuy, *The Encyclopedia of Military History: From 3500 B.C. to the Present* (New York: Harper & Row Publishers, Inc., 1970), p. 99.

21. Edward N. Luttwak, *The Grand Strategy of the Roman Empire: From the First Century A.D. to the Third* (Baltimore: The Johns Hopkins University Press, 1976; John Hopkins paperback edition, 1981), p. 117.

22. Ibid., p. 3.

23. Ibid., p. 2.

24. Ibid., pp. 3–4.

25. Oman, op. cit., p. 4.

26. Ibid., pp. 57–60.

27. Richard Berg, "1066: Year of Decision," *Strategy and Tactics Magazine* no. 110 (November–December, 1986), pp. 17–21.

28. Terence Wise, *Medieval Warfare* (New York: Hastings House, Publishers, 1976), p. 105. (Emphasis added.)

29. Schmookler, op. cit., p. 95.

30. Dyer, op. cit., p. 12.

31. Wise, op. cit., pp. 110–111.

32. Ibid., p. 115.

33. Ibid., p. 114.

34. James Burke, *Connections* (Boston: Little, Brown & Co., Inc., 1978), p. 66.

35. Dyer, op. cit., p. 38.

36. Martin van Creveld, *Command in War* (Cambridge, Mass.: Harvard University Press, 1985), p. 42.

37. Oman, op. cit., p. 87.

38. Ibid., p. 92.

39. Ibid., p. 96.

40. Dyer, op. cit., p. 12.

41. Oman, op. cit., p. 113.

42. Ibid., p. 112.

43. Dyer, op. cit., p. 55.

44. Theodore Ropp, *War in the Modern World*, revised edition (New York: The Macmillan Publishing Co., Inc., 1962; Collier Books, 1985), pp. 31–32.

45. Dyer, op. cit., p. 61.

46. Hew Strachan, *European Armies and the Conduct of War*, 2d edition (London: George Allen and Unwin, Inc., 1983), p. 16.

47. Henry Lumpkin, *From Savannah to Yorktown: The American Revolution in the South* (Columbia, S.C.: The University of South Carolina Press, 1981), pp. 137–38.

48. Dyer, op. cit., p. 65.

49. Martin Blumenson and James L. Stokesbury, *Masters of the Art of Command* (Boston: Houghton Mifflin Co., 1975), pp. 6–7.

50. Ibid., p. 7.

51. Ibid., p. 8.

52. van Creveld, op. cit., p. 61.

53. Ibid., p. 62.

54. Ibid., pp. 95–96.

55. Ibid., p. 97.

56. Michael Howard, *The Causes of Wars: And Other Essays*, Second Edition (Cambridge, Mass.: Harvard University Press, 1984), p. 103.

57. Dupuy and Dupuy, op. cit., p. 832.

58. Ibid.

59. Michael Howard, *The Franco-Prussian War: The German Invasion of France, 1870–1871* (New York: The Macmillan Co., Inc., 1961; Collier Books, 1969), pp. 70 and 82.

60. Ropp, op. cit., p. 201.

61. Memo, Col. L.F. Paul to Gen. White, "Princeton Report on Massive Retaliation," no date, *Thomas White Papers*, Box 1, Correspondence (1954–57), folder LoC. As quoted in Fred Kaplan, *The Wizards of Armageddon* (New York: Simon & Schuster, Inc., 1983; Touchstone Books, 1984), pp. 197–98.

62. Kaplan, *The Wizards of Armageddon*, p. 199.

63. Lumpkin, op. cit., pp. 253–79. Major engagements are defined here as those having a total of 1,000 combatants—approximately 500 on each side—involved.

64. Ibid., p. 252.

65. Harry G. Summers, Jr., *On Strategy: A Critical Analysis of the Vietnam War* (Novato, Calif.: Presidio Press, 1982; 4th reprinting, 1984), p. 1.

66. Barry Buzan, *People, States and Fear: The National Security Problem in International Relations* (Chapel Hill: University of North Carolina Press, 1983), pp. 38–39.

67. Ibid., p. 38.

68. Ibid., p. 67.

69. Sun Tzu, *The Art of War*, edited and translated by Samuel B. Griffith (London: Oxford University Press, 1963; Oxford University Press paperback, 1971), p. 39.

70. Will and Ariel Durant, *The Story of Civilizations*, vol. 7, *The Age of Reason Begins* (New York: Simon & Schuster, Inc., 1961), p. 33.

71. Ropp, op. cit., p. 39.

72. J.F.C. Fuller, *The Conduct of War, 1789–1961* (New York: Funk & Wagnalls, Inc., 1961; Minerva Press, 1968), p. 262.

73. Ibid., p. 263.

74. Ibid., p. 264.

75. See Ivan Bloch, *The Future of War in its Technical, Economic, and Political Relations*, translated by R. C. Long (Boston, n.p., 1903).

76. A. Sergiyev, "Leninism on the Correlation of Forces as a Factor of International Relations," *International Affairs*, (May 1975), p. 103. As quoted in Vernon Aspaturian, "Soviet Global Power and the Correlation of Forces," *Problems of Communism* (May–June 1980), p. 10.

77. Vernon Aspaturian, "Soviet Global Power and the Correlation of Forces," *Problems of Communism* (May–June 1980), p. 10.

78. Hannes Adomeit, *Soviet Risk-Taking and Crisis Behavior: A Theoretical and Empirical Analysis* (Boston: Allen & Unwin, 1982), p. 223.

79. William Odom, "Soviet Force Posture: Dilemmas and Directions," *Problems of Communism* (July–August 1985), p. 2.

80. Ibid.

81. R. Gaucher, *Les Terroristes* (Paris: 1965), p. 359. As quoted in Alex P. Schmid, *Political Terrorism: A Research Guide to Concepts, Theories, Data Bases and Literature* (Amsterdam: North Holland Publishing Co., 1983; Transactions Books, 1985), p. 206.

82. Hylke Tromp, "Politiek Terrorisme: De Derde Wereldoorlog in een Volstrekt Onverwachte Vorm?" *Universiteitskrant* (Groningen: 1978), p. 11. As quoted in Schmid, op. cit., p. 208.

# CHAPTER 5

# TERRORISM

■

## Introduction

This chapter introduces terrorism, providing a basic definition of the
phenomenon and describing how it employs force. Like warfare, terrorism is a highly specialized activity having unique characteristics
that can be isolated, studied, and understood. It is a recurring phenomenon consisting of individual events that are, nevertheless, based upon
the same basic patterns of activities and motives. This chapter identifies the consistencies and patterns that provide the foundation and
common denominator for all terrorist activities. This will provide, in
turn, a basic understanding of the various types of terrorism that will
be discussed in successive chapters. These are apolitical terrorism,
state terrorism, and revolutionary terrorism. In addition to explaining
the unique characteristics of each of the forms of terrorism introduced,
the successive chapters will also analyze each type from the perspective of the purpose and function of war introduced in the first three

chapters of this book. In this manner it will become possible to identify which of the various forms of terrorism are also forms of war.

## Defining Terrorism

Nearly every discussion of terrorism necessarily begins with wrestling
with the definition of terror and terrorism. The reason it is so difficult
to define these terms stems from cultural, professional, or political
biases that can strongly affect the definition formulated. Alex Schmid
suggests, "The question of definition of a term like terrorism cannot
be detached from the question of who is the defining agency."[1] J. Bowyer Bell supports this contention: "The very word [terrorism] becomes
a litmus test for dearly held beliefs, so that a brief conversation on
terrorist matters with almost anyone reveals a special world view, an
interpretation of the nature of man, and a glimpse into a desired future."[2] It often boils down to a normative question of whether one perceives terrorism to be a positive (good) force or a negative (bad) force.
For the political scientist, however, this is not the issue. The political
scientist seeks to understand the phenomenon, not justify it. Still,
there is an extremely wide range of "scientific" definitions of terror
and terrorism.

Nearly everyone will accept a dictionary definition of the word *terror*. But terror is a subjective phenomenon. As Grant Wardlaw notes,
"We all have different thresholds of fear and our personal and cultural
backgrounds make certain images, experiences, or fears more terrifying
to each of us than others."[3] This subjectiveness makes it extremely
difficult to scientifically operationalize the concept of terror. And,
since terror is an integral part of terrorism, it stands to reason that
terrorism is equally difficult to operationalize. Consequently, any definition of terror and terrorism is, of necessity, an arbitrary one—the
primary purpose of which is to establish a point of reference or departure for further discussion. It is with this caveat in mind that the following definitions are offered.

> *Terror* **is an intense paralyzing fear, or the dread of it.** *Terrorism* **is a
> deliberate attempt to create terror through a symbolic act involving the
> use or threat of abnormal lethal force for the purpose of influencing a
> target group or individual.**

The term *lethal force* is used in lieu of *lethal violence* due to the pejorative nature of the latter term. In conventional parlance *violence* connotes the illegitimate use of force, as in *criminal violence*. But even when coupled with a more "neutral" term such as *political violence* it still conjures images of force used against a legitimate, established authority. As observed by Hannah Arendt, "Violence can be justifiable, but it never will be legitimate."[4] Consequently, this book employs the more neutral term *force* to avoid to the greatest possible degree any normative concepts. Terrorism, as we seek to establish here, is an instrument of war. Like any instrument of war, terrorism may be used in a manner considered by those adhering to the ideological school as being "good" or "evil." Certainly the same Western democratic nations that today decry the use of terrorism as being evil, barbarous, or criminal would have warmly applauded the terrorist attack on Adolf Hitler and his Nazi regime in July 1944. And, to use a more contemporary example, were Kaddhafi to meet the same fate as Anwar Sadat, few in the Western democratic world would be likely to condemn such an act. Clearly, then, arguments of the legitimacy of the use of force in a terroristic manner are superfluous to understanding the utility of that force. Such arguments will therefore not be addressed in this book.

This is not to say, however, that this book analyzes only the objective and rejects the subjective aspects of terrorism. Not only is such objectivity impossible to achieve, it would be counterproductive. As mentioned in chapter 1, men adhere to certain feelings or beliefs, and this in turn affects how, when, and where they apply lethal force. The normative values of mankind inhibit, restrict, or channel the employment of lethal force. These normative values thereby become part of the power equation. As Andrew Schmookler observes,

> *Value may be defined as the basis for choice.* In the absence of values, any alternative is as good as any other. Indifference reigns. To be or not to be can be no question, for there is no basis for answering. Values are implicit in any choice, and choice is required for any action.[5]

Terrorism is called *terrorism* because it violates the normative values of the target entity regarding the employment of lethal force. The more horrifying the act the greater the psychological impact upon the target. According to Alex Schmid, this "extranormalness" is what sets terrorism apart from all other forms of force employment:

The adherence to social norms in human interactions makes behavior predictable and thereby contributes to a sense of security. . . . Even in wartime some minimal rules of conduct are observed most of the time by the belligerents. Deliberate attacks on civilians are not considered justified in war either as an end or a means to an end. Certain basic rights are granted to the enemy in war, such as humane treatment of prisoners and special consideration for women, children and old people. . . . All this is absent when we speak of terrorism. . . . No rule of combat is respected if the rule violation serves the terrorist's purpose.[6]

It is this factor of abnormality that separates terrorist force from other types of force employment. This of course invites the question of what is to be considered abnormal. Clearly, abnormality is at best a transitive phenomenon. As Schmid notes, when tanks and poison gas were first used in combat they were considered abnormal and caused panic and terror among those who initially faced them.[7] Today most people would probably agree that tanks are normal, legitimate instruments of war, while poison gas is not.

Perhaps the most widely accepted criterion used to define abnormal force in war is the killing of noncombatants—particularly civilians. Even this is not always considered abnormal, however. Indeed, killing civilians was considered commonplace until it went too far during the Thirty Years' War. The sack of Magdeburg in May 1631 was so complete and bloody that historian H. W. Koch calls it the Hiroshima of the Thirty Years' War.[8] Nearly all of Christendom was repelled at the horror of the wanton pillaging, slaughter, and destruction. The reaction to this and the terrible cost of the war in general resulted in the Peace of Westphalia, which, among other things, placed limitations on warfare and protected noncombatants from its scourges. As Gwynne Dyer notes, "It was a century and a half before there was another war in Europe that caused deaths on anything like the same scale, and fully three centuries . . . before civilian losses again outnumbered military casualties."[9] But by World War I and certainly by World War II killing civilians once again became less and less an abnormal element of warfare.

Clearly, then, abnormality is a transitory factor subject to the interpretations of those involved in the incident at the time. Rather than try to identify abnormality in terms of weapons or methods, this book will simply accept as abnormal anything identified as such by the most widely accepted cultural mores of the group receiving the lethal force.

For instance, for a soldier who enters combat for the first time, being shot at is an extremely unusual and probably unprecedented event, but it is hardly abnormal—providing the soldier is being shot at by an enemy soldier. Soldiers are trained and expected to shoot and be shot at. The same can be said for bombing cities. During World War II nearly every belligerent who could bomb enemy cities did so with the general concurrence of the civilian populations of the nations doing the bombing—particularly those populations that had already suffered under enemy bombing. Certainly by the time America entered the war, bombing cities and the incidental killing of civilians was considered simply another factor of modern warfare and definitely not an abnormal use of lethal force.

Abnormal force, by itself, is not sufficient to establish that an event is an act of terror, however. The perpetrator of the act must intend to terrorize the target for abnormal lethal force to be considered terrorism. For instance, the Soviet downing of a Korean civilian airliner in September 1983 was certainly an example of abnormal force, but in all probability it was not an act of terror. Indeed, there is considerable evidence to substantiate the Soviets' claim that they—or at least anyone who had the authority to countermand Soviet Air Defense Command (PVO) standing operating orders requiring all unidentified intruders be shot down—did not know the target was a civilian airliner.[10] While it was the intention of the Soviet Union to defend its airspace, Moscow apparently had no intention of terrorizing anyone through the employment of lethal force. Consequently, though it is inexcusable that Soviet command and control procedures were so rigid and cumbersome that 269 civilians were needlessly killed, the shooting down of the airliner was not an act of terror.

Lethal force is terrorism only when the force employed is considered abnormal by those receiving that force and when it is the intention of the perpetrator of the force to terrorize the target. Remove either factor and no matter how terrifying the deaths of the victims, what occurs is not terrorism.

It is also important to understand at the outset that terrorism does not equate to any particular ideology. It does not fall solely within the purview of communism, fascism, or jointly, totalitarianism. Nor is it strictly an instrument of anarchism. Terrorism was used by both loyalists and rebels in the southern colonies during the American Revolutionary War. During the American Civil War, Mosby's Rangers often conducted operations in which terrorism, as defined above, was employed. Moreover, both Nazi Germany and democratic Britain attempted to terrorize each other's populations during World War II by employing air power against civilian targets. So terrorism is an instrument capable of achieving the objectives of any group, regardless of ideology—although some are clearly more likely to employ a certain form of terrorism than another.

## How Terrorism Functions

Following nearly every terrorist attack, statesmen and journalists condemn the attack as being "barbaric," "criminal," "mindless," and so on. Depending upon one's definition of the terms, such attacks may indeed be barbaric or criminal. One thing is certain, however—such attacks are seldom, if ever, mindless. As Michael Stohl contends, the idea that political terrorism is the province of madmen is a myth, one "that finds a particularly warm reception in the American media and in government statements concerning terrorism. . . ."[11] As suggested by the definition of terrorism presented in the previous section, terrorism is not mindless violence, but the employment of lethal force to create certain conditions that, in turn, improve the probability of achieving a given end.

At the most basic level the purpose of all terrorism is to influence the behavior of some target entity. This normally, but not always, entails the creation of a state of fear or terror in a target collectivity that is so intense it renders that target helpless—unable or unwilling to resist. Precisely how this condition is achieved will vary from target to target and will depend to a great extent upon who is the terrorist and who is terrorized. Obviously the means employed would vary greatly between a government employing state terrorism on an unarmed populace and a small revolutionary band employing agitational or revolutionary terrorism against a state. Ultimately, the end sought is essentially the same—to undermine and destroy the cohesion of the target entity, reducing it to its smallest constituent part: the isolated, individual human being. As Grant Wardlaw contends, "The ultimate [expression] of the terrorization process occurs when the individual is so isolated as to be unable to draw strength from usual social supports and is cast entirely upon his or her own resources."[12] In such cases the very cohesion of society is in jeopardy, and resistance to the terrorist becomes increasingly difficult. The terrorized target becomes malleable or indifferent and, hence, no longer a factor in the power equation.

Eugene Walter, writing of the institutionalized terror of the nineteenth-century Zulu king Shaka, noted that terror was an effective tool for controlling the body politic. Terror effectively rendered resistance psychologically and behaviorally impossible for his subjects.

> The aim was to deny the people any resistance potential, that is, to deny their ability to participate in the power process, by withdrawing their empowering responses that would collapse the established order. . . . It is also interesting that over a period of time there was overt behavioral evidence that participation in maintaining terror arose to the point of offering no protest, or even of gladly welcoming one's own destruction; and this occurred at all levels in the body politic.[13]

Such examples are not restricted to institutionalized "terror from above." As the Nazis clearly established in the late 1920s and early 1930s in Weimar Germany, terrorism also had utility in combating the regime. Hitler employed terrorism to undermine and disrupt key elements of the German social base. Force was used by Nazi SA *(Sturm-abteilung)* storm troopers to alter certain conventions within German society to make a democratic form of government inappropriate to it. As Martin Oppenheimer observes in his book, *The Urban Guerrilla,*

> By the use of street brawling, beatings, and assassinations, the Nazi party discredited "argument and compromise as political means" and transferred political decision-making from the parliamentary environment to the streets.[14]

Under such conditions the average German citizen became politically malleable or withdrew from politics altogether. Hitler continued to employ terrorism once he gained power. As William S. Allen has noted, this terrorization clearly affected the cohesion of the targeted entity and broke down social mores, which could be measured through a concomitant rise in the crime rate.[15] He goes on to write that

> the evidence suggests some kind of social disorganization, resulting possibly from the effect of living the life of insincerity required by the Nazi regime. [There resulted] . . . a general breakdown of trust and . . . the destruction or perversion of hitherto unifying social organizations. The

response of the individual was generally withdrawal, sometimes aggression.[16]

Moreover, as recent events in Kentucky have shown, terrorism can be employed even in an open democracy and can yield precisely the same psychosocial results. For instance, Jules Loh has noted the effects of a small number of allegedly corrupt officials in a small, isolated Kentucky county. Sixteen persons, including the county judge and sheriff, were arrested for crimes including extortion, drug running, and larceny. Quoting the local newspaper editor, Loh writes,

> We've had murders go unsolved, burnings go unsolved, shootings go unsolved. The people feel betrayed and feel they can't trust the police and the courts. . . . When that happens, the whole structure of how people hold together their lives begins to wobble. When they ask themselves "Whom can I trust?" and the answer is "nobody," they tend to build a shell around themselves. There goes our sense of community.[17]

The end result in each of the above-cited cases is the destruction or at least disruption of the psychological ties that bind human beings to larger psychosocial organisms such as the local or state community. In short, its cohesion is shattered. According to Alexander Dallin and George Breslauer,

> Terrorism affects the social structure as well as the individual; it upsets the framework of the precepts and images which members of society depend on and trust. Since one no longer knows what sort of behavior to expect from other members of society, the system is disoriented. The formerly coherent community dissolves into a mass of anomic individuals, each concerned only with personal survival.[18]

Once the conventions of a given society are disrupted to such a degree, they may be relatively easily replaced by conventions provided by the terrorists. Grant Wardlaw suggests that the disoriented victim of terrorism often does not know what he fears, or the source of his fear lies outside his field of experience.

> [And] if the victim cannot obtain an understanding of the source of danger within a framework which he or she is able to construct from his or her own resources, it is likely he or she will turn to a leader who gives the appearance of wisdom [and has] the strength to interpret and control events.[19]

Gerald Holten would agree. He notes that "precipitous changes in the human condition stretch personal and historic memory beyond [ordinary] limits . . . leaving the psyche different, distorted, and ready to crystallize . . . in new ways."[20] The disoriented individual is in a mental state approaching neurosis and to relieve his anxiety the individual is ready to accept almost *any* structure promising to bring order out of the existing chaos. It is at this point the terrorists have achieved their first goal. They have created conditions amenable to achieving specific ends. The terrorized, target entity is likely to accept any alternate social conventions proffered by the terrorists so long as it promises restored order. The terrorists, in turn, may rebuild society in their own image and in a manner so as to achieve their own ends. Clearly the use of terrorism in such a manner cannot be described as "mindless."

What is important to understand is that terrorism can result in a multitude of reactions. There are varying degrees of "being terrorized." Thomas Thornton has identified four broad categories of responses to terrorism, shown in table 5. Depending upon the terrorists' goals, they will seek to create a level of response most likely to bring that end to pass.

Different forms of terrorism, then, may require different levels of response to achieve their ends. As noted earlier, terror from above, or *state terror,* can be used to control a population. In so doing, however, the terrorists cannot create despair (level 4) among the populace since it would result in a virtual loss of social cohesion. Should this occur, the state has, in essence, destroyed itself, since anomic individuals are almost totally psychologically isolated and incapable of forming or maintaining psychological bonds to a higher social structure. State terrorists would therefore seek only to frighten (level 2) the populace if the regime wanted to maintain status quo or to cause anxiety (level 3) if the regime sought to create a revolution from above by disorienting the target and causing it to "cast about for new guidance," like Stalin in the 1930s. Revolutionary terrorists, on the other hand, seek nothing less than the total destruction of the targeted regime and its forces of coercion. Thus, the revolutionary terrorist would attempt to cause despair (level 4) among members supporting the regime, hoping to utterly destroy its cohesion. Terrorists must therefore tailor how they employ force to achieve a specific desired end. Yet, at the most basic level, the process is essentially the same. The terrorists employ lethal force to destroy or weaken the cohesion of the target entity thereby destroying or weakening its willingness and/or ability to resist.

To this point the terms *terrorist victim* and *terrorist target* have

**TABLE 5**    Thornton's Four Levels of Response to Terror

*I. Enthusiasm*—The one positive response to be achieved is *enthusiasm* among the terrorists (and those they wish to garner as supporters.) This represents strictly a morale building function.

*II. Fright*—This is the lowest negative reaction in which the frightened person experiences a specific danger that is not quantitatively different from other dangers with which he is personally or vicariously familiar. Since the perceived danger fits into the pattern of his previous experience, his response will be meaningful in terms of familiar norms of action; it will be both subjectively and objectively logical and reasonably predictable.

*III. Anxiety*—This is the middle level response which is called forth by fear of the unknown and the unknowable. Traditional norms of behavior show no relevance to the new situation, and the victim becomes disoriented, casting about for guidance. The exact nature of response is unpredictable, but it is likely to lead to activity that is logical in terms of the new situation as perceived by the target.

*IV. Despair*—This is the most extreme level of response, which is is basically an intensified form of anxiety. The victim perceives the threat to be so great and unavoidable that there is no course of action open to him that is likely to bring relief. As a result the victim withdraws from the situation to the maximum possible extent.

SOURCE: Thomas P. Thornton, "Terror as a Weapon of Political Agitation." *Internal War: Problems and Approaches*, edited by Harry Eckstein (New York: The Free Press of Glencoe, 1964) pp. 80–81. As presented in Schmid, op. cit., p. 71.

been used interchangeably. But in many cases they are not equivalent. According to Brian Jenkins,

> Terrorism is violence for effect; not only, and sometimes not at all, for the effect on the actual victims of the terrorists. In fact the victims may be totally unrelated to the terrorists' cause. Terrorism is violence aimed at the people watching. Fear is the intended effect, not the byproduct of the [the force employment.][21]

In a classical terrorist scenario, the terrorists attack a specific "victim" to convey a message to a target group or individual who, in turn, experiences chronic fear or terror of the terrorists. As shown in table 6, there are three discrete elements in classical terrorist acts: (1) the terrorist, (2) the victim, and (3) the target.

From table 6 one may conclude that terrorism is a process having,

**TABLE 6**   How Terrorism Functions

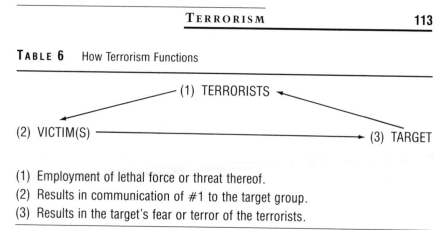

(1) Employment of lethal force or threat thereof.
(2) Results in communication of #1 to the target group.
(3) Results in the target's fear or terror of the terrorists.

SOURCE: Alex P. Schmid and J. de Graaf, *Violence as Communication* [London: Sage Publications, Ltd., 1982], p. 176. As quoted in Schmid, op. cit., p. 91.

as Eugene Walter suggests, "three elements: the act or threat of violence, the emotional reaction to extreme fear on the part of the ... potential (future) victims, and the social effects that follow the violence (or its threat) and the consequent fear."[22] The true product of the terroristic process, then, is not the *physical* attack on the victim, but the *psychological impact* upon the target. As a consequence, the terrorist's victims must be carefully selected to assure the maximum possible psychological impact upon the target. This is achieved by selecting victims having some sort of symbolic significance to the target entity. To again cite Thornton, "The optimum targets are clearly those that show the highest symbolic value and are dominated by symbols that are most vulnerable to attack."[23] Moreover, "Terrorism," writes Schmid, "is symbolic in the sense of 'you too might become a victim' ... because of some common quality, e.g., membership in the same class, party, creed, [or] race."[24]

This process is clearly seen in descriptions of the first terrorist-induced revolution in history; the revolt of the Jews against Roman rule in A.D. 132–135. As the Roman-Jewish chronicler Josephus clearly discloses in his history of this revolt, the terrorists, or *Sicarii* as they were then called, succeeded in creating conditions ripe for revolt against Rome through using terroristic force against Jewish leaders who opposed the revolution. Josephus writes of the Sicarii that

> Their favorite trick was to mingle with the festival crowds, concealing under their garments small daggers with which they stabbed their op-

ponents. When their victims fell, the assassins melted into the indignant crowd. . . . [And] more terrible than the crimes themselves was the fear they aroused, every man hourly expecting death as in war.[25]

By targeting these symbolic victims the Sicarii managed to silence most of those who openly sought to avoid war with the Romans. The terrorists assured that only their views took hold among the populace and, equally important, ensured that the Romans perceived all Jews as a threat since the only voices being heard consistently were those calling for revolt.

To this point only simple *triadic* terrorism has been addressed; that is, when the terrorist, target, and victim are separate entities and the target's behavior is influenced by the lethal force employed or threatened upon the victim. This is classical or *direct* terrorism. It is important to understand, however, that terrorism can also function in an *indirect* manner.

In direct terrorism the target of influence and the target of terror are one and the same. In indirect terrorism, however, the entity targeted to receive the terror and the entity targeted to be influenced are separate. Perhaps the classic example of this form of terrorism is revolutionary terrorism, wherein the target of terror is the members of the state's ruling apparatus and the target of influence is the population. As the government becomes increasingly paralyzed as its members are terrorized, the population is mobilized as they perceive the growing weakness of the state. Indirect terrorism, then, is more adequately presented in table 7.

Terrorists (1) commit an act of terror upon a carefully selected victim (2) causing terror in the target of terror (3). As this target begins to weaken and lose its cohesion, this is perceived by the target of influence (4), which in turn begins to act favorably toward the terrorists and their intentions.

Whether the terrorism is triadic or quadratic, however, it still relies upon the employment of lethal force to influence the behavior of a given target entity or entities. But is it war?

Although tables 6 and 7 were created to depict how all types of terrorism function, upon closer scrutiny it becomes apparent that they also provide an excellent model for how warfare operates. By substituting the word *soldier* or *combatant* for the word *terrorist* in these two tables, one can see how classical warfare truly functions at the most abstract level. In direct terrorism the combatant employs lethal

**TABLE 7** Indirect Terrorism

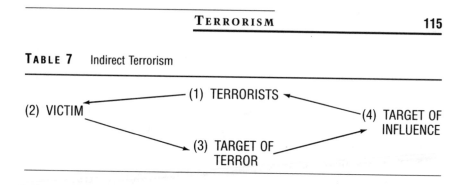

force against a victim with the aim of causing those who most closely identify with the victim—usually his comrades-in-arms—to become terrorized and much more interested in sparing themselves the same fate as the victim rather than to continue fighting. Indirect terrorism is seen in war when the combatant employs lethal force against a victim not only to terrorize the surviving members of the victim's group, but to influence the behavior of a nonterrorized entity, such as the victim's commander or national government. While not personally suffering the effects of terrorism, the commander of terrorized troops or the government of a terrorized populace clearly suffers indirect psychological pressure from the terrorization process. This only further reinforces Liddell Hart's comments, first presented in chapter 2, that the strategist should always think "in terms of paralyzing, not of killing" (see page 20).[26]

From this, one may conclude that, at the most basic level, both terrorism and the more classical forms of warfare function in the same manner. Both employ lethal force against a victim to affect the morale of the much larger target or targets. Force is employed not so much for its physical but its psychological capabilities—that is, its ability to affect the target's morale and thereby influence its decisions and actions directly, or those of its superiors indirectly. Thus the only significant difference between terrorism and the more classical forms of warfare is the aforementioned selection of abnormal means by the terrorists. This difference will be explored in greater detail when we examine terror as a weapon of war in chapter 8.

It is the ability to affect the enemy's moral force that makes terrorism such an efficient weapon of war. It takes a minimum amount of physical force and converts it into the maximum amount of power—thus becoming the ultimate expression of Luttwak's input-output model described in chapter 2. By applying a small amount of lethal force against a properly selected symbolic target, a single terrorist may affect the lives of thousands or even millions of people in a target entity. So long as the members of the target entity perceive that the terrorists may strike again with impunity, the political and military power of even the most powerful nation-state can be virtually neutralized. This was clearly established in the October 1983 bombing of the U.S. Marine barracks in Beirut. One man in a bomb-laden truck killed 241 American Marines and resulted in relatively major alterations in U.S. foreign policy in Lebanon, including the withdrawal of the U.S. forces there. According to Robert Kupperman, "In the minds of many people, the U.S.—a massive power with thousands of nuclear weapons, ships [and] tanks—was forced to leave Lebanon by a comparatively tiny proxy force."[27]

This disparate payback in political power for a minimal expenditure of lethal force makes terrorism the natural weapon for the very weak. It is quite interesting to note, for instance, that the British instigated "terror" bombing of German cities at the moment of England's greatest relative weakness to the Nazis during World War II. As Paskins and Dockrill point out, "There were times during World War II when Britain was powerless to do anything more in her fight against Germany [but bombing]. . . ."[28] Terror bombing was born of a desperate need to show both the British people and the rest of the world that Britain was still in the war and could still hurt the enemy.

Clearly, terrorism is also an effective tool for a weak, fledgling revolutionary organization that simply does not have the resources to engage the regime's armed forces head on. Using terrorist tactics—by employing lethal force against the regime's morale rather than against its physical forces—a revolutionary organization can maximize its extremely limited coercive capabilities. As Bard O'Neill contends:

> The long-term goal of [revolutionary] terrorism has not been so much the desire to deplete the government's physical resources as it has been to erode its psychological support by spreading fear among officials and their domestic and international supporters.[29]

Even when powerful states use terrorism to maintain internal control they often resort to this form of coercion due to its efficiency. A few acts of terror may often be enough to obviate the need of increasing the size of or diverting military and security forces from other endeavors. Adolf Hitler strongly believed in the utility of terrorism for maintaining internal control. In an interview Hitler reportly remarked: "These so-called atrocities save me hundreds of thousands of individual actions against the protesters and malcontents. Each one of them will think twice to oppose us when he learns what is awaiting him in the [concentration] camps."[30]

Employing force on the psychological plane is, then, the most efficient use of that force. And terrorism is the purest expression of this mode of force employment.

Of course it should be stressed that while terrorism is the most *efficient* use of lethal force it generally is not the most *effective*. A fully equipped army from nearly any modern nation-state enjoys far more raw power than any terrorist organization—as do most metropolitan police forces for that matter. Consequently, it is far more effective to employ conventional military forces to resolve interstate and intrastate conflicts due to the decisiveness and relative quickness of the outcome. Despite Adolf Hitler's obvious belief in the efficiency of terrorism, when it came time to resolve political differences with France, Hitler chose tanks over terrorists.

Finally, while terrorism represents the most efficient use of force, it does not necessarily mean it is the most efficient means of controlling the population. This is done not by force, but by the other elements of the power continuum, including *persuasion* and *influence*, which induce voluntary cooperation with the regime. Terrorism, on the other hand, is probably the least efficient means of governing a nation, since resources must be diverted to control the population, which in turn becomes an adversary rather than an asset of the regime. Force, as Edmund Burke noted, "may subdue for a moment; but it does not remove the necessity for subduing again; and a nation is not governed which is perpetually to be conquered."[31]

## Summation

Terrorism is a force employment process in which abnormal lethal force is used against a symbolic victim to affect the will of a target entity. It is not mindless violence but the rational selection of lethal force to effect a specific end—the submission of the target entity to the terrorists' will. Moreover, it is a dynamic process wherein the level of force and selection of a victim must be carefully orchestrated with the level of terror desired in the target entity. Once the target entity experiences the desired level of terror it becomes politically malleable, affording the terrorists the opportunity to create the political situation suitable to their needs. At one end of the spectrum of responses to terrorism is enthusiasm within the terrorists' own ranks providing and reinforcing group cohesion. At the other end of the spectrum is despair within the target entity resulting in the total atomization of society into its smallest constituent parts—individual persons. Despair represents an almost total shattering of group cohesion where each person relies almost exclusively upon himself for all of his own needs.

Due to its tremendous efficiency, terrorism is the natural tool for the very weak. It affords the absolute maximum amount of power for the minimum expenditure of physical force. Consequently, entities that are too weak to physically compel an enemy outright often choose to employ terrorist tactics to undermine and influence enemy morale and will to resist. By systematically and with seeming impunity attacking a given class of targets, the terrorists send a clear message to anyone who is a member of that target class—whether through race, creed, color, or political persuasion—that they are helpless and vulnerable. This results in the withdrawal, to the maximum degree possible, of the constituent members of that target class, resulting in its eventual destruction through loss of cohesion. Equally important, even elements that are not terrorized can be influenced to behave in a certain manner simply from the realization that the terrorized entity is rapidly being weakened and removed from any power equation.

At the most abstract level, then, terrorism meets the same basic criteria as war. It represents consciously selected force applied for a specific end. Moreover, it employs kinetic, physical force to influence the enemy psychologically through the erosion of his will to continue to resist. As in war, this is easily measured by the degree to which the cohesion of the targeted entity is affected. In this way, terrorism represents a clash of wills between two contending parties. If both parties employ force to resolve this clash of wills, and if both parties seek a political end through this conflict, then a state of war exists, and the terrorism used by either belligerent constitutes a form of war.

As will be seen in subsequent chapters, there are many types of terrorism. Each of these will be examined to ascertain which are forms of war. Some types of terrorism will be rejected because they employ force for nonpolitical purposes. Others will be rejected for violating principles of war. In the end, however, types of terrorism will be identified as forms of war because they employ force not only for the same ends, but in precisely the same manner and under the same principles as the classical forms of war.

## Notes

1. Alex P. Schmid, *Political Terrorism: A Research Guide to Concepts, Theories, Data Bases and Literature* (Amsterdam: North Holland Publishing Co., 1983; Transactions Books, 1985), p. 6.

2. J. Bowyer Bell, *A Time of Terror: How Democratic Societies Respond to Revolutionary Violence* (New York: Basic Books, 1978), p. x. As quoted in Schmid, op. cit., p. 6.

3. Grant Wardlaw, *Political Terrorism: Theory, Tactics and Countermeasures* (Cambridge: Cambridge University Press, 1984), p. 5.

4. Hannah Arendt, *On Violence* (New York: Harcourt, Brace, Jovanovich, 1970), p. 46. As quoted in Schmid, op. cit., p. 13.

5. Andrew Schmookler, *The Parable of the Tribes: The Problem of Power in Social Evolution* (Berkeley: University of California Press, 1984; Houghton Mifflin Co. paperback edition, 1986), p. 138. (Emphasis in orginal.)

6. Schmid, op. cit., p. 109.

7. Ibid., p. 107.

8. H. W. Koch, *The Rise of Modern Warfare: 1618–1858* (London: Hamly Publishing Group, Ltd., 1981), p. 32.

9. Gwynne Dyer, *War* (New York: Crown Publishers, Inc., 1985), p. 60.

10. See Alexander Dallin, *Black Box: KAL 007 and the Superpowers* (Berkeley: University of California Press, 1985), pp. 61–65.

11. Michael Stohl, "Myths and Realities of Political Terrorism," *The Politics of Terrorism*, edited by Michael Stohl (New York: Marcel Dekker, Inc., 1979), p. 5.

12. Wardlaw, op. cit., p. 34.

13. Harold D. Lasswell, "Terrorism and the Political Process," *Terrorism: An International Journal* 1, nos. 3/4 (1978), pp. 260–61. (Quoting Eugene Walter.)

14. Martin Oppenheimer, *The Urban Guerrilla* (Chicago: Quadrangle Books, 1969), p. 75.

15. William S. Allen, "The German People and National Socialism: The Ex-

perience of One Town," *Adolf Hitler and the Third Reich, 1933–1945*, edited by Robert E. Herzstein (Boston: Houghton Mifflin Co., 1971), pp. 20–21.

16. Ibid., p. 21.

17. Jules Loh, "Big-Time Crime Hits Kentucky Hill County," (Associated Press) *San Jose Mercury News* (July 20, 1986), p. 11A.

18. Alexander Dallin and George Breslauer, *Political Terror in Communist Systems* (Stanford: Stanford University Press, 1970), p. 2. As quoted in Schmid, op. cit., pp. 172–73.

19. Wardlaw, op. cit., p. 35.

20. Gerald Holten, "Reflections on Modern Terrorism," *Terrorism: An International Journal* 1, nos. 3/4 (1978): 271.

21. Brian Jenkins, *International Terrorism: A New Mode of Conflict* (Los Angeles: Crescent Publications, 1975), p. 1.

22. Eugene V. Walter, *Terror and Resistance: A Study of Political Violence with Case Studies of Some Primitive African Communities* (New York: Oxford University Press, 1969), p. 5. As quoted in Wardlaw, op. cit., p. 12.

23. Thomas P. Thornton, "Terror as a Weapon of Political Agitation," *Internal War: Problems and Approaches*, edited by Harry Eckstein (New York: The Free Press of Glencoe, 1961), p. 86.

24. Schmid, op. cit., p. 86.

25. Josephus, *The Jewish War*, translated by G. A. Williamson (New York: Dorset Press, 1985), p. 147.

26. Sir Basil Liddell Hart, *Strategy* (New York: Praeger Publishers, Inc., 1968), p. 25.

27. Robert M. Kupperman, "Terrorism and National Security," *Terrorism: An International Journal* 8, no. 3 (1985):25.

28. Barrie Paskins and Michael Dockrill, *The Ethics of War* (Minneapolis: The University of Minnesota Press, 1979), p. 43.

29. Bard E. O'Neill, William R. Heaton, and Donald J. Alberts, *Insurgency in the Modern World* (Boulder, Colo.: Westview Press, 1980), pp. 4–5. As quoted in L. C. Green, "Terrorism & Its Responses," *Terrorism: An International Journal* 8, no. 1 (1985).

30. Herman Rauschning, *Gesprache mit Hitler* (Vienna: 1940), p. 82. As quoted in Schmid, op. cit., p. 90.

31. Gehard Lenski, *Power and Privilege: A Theory of Social Stratification* (New York: McGraw-Hill Book Co., 1966), p. 51. (Quoting Edmund Burke.)

# 6

# APOLITICAL
# TERRORISM

■

## Introduction

As the name suggests, apolitical terrorism is the employment of lethal force in a terroristic manner but for nonpolitical ends. Based upon our definition of war, this lack of political purpose alone would seem sufficient to disqualify apolitical terrorism as a form of war. As will be seen, however, some people argue that psychotic and criminal terrorists are, in fact, unwitting political terrorists subconsciously reacting to their political and social environment. Given this, it is necessary to subject the apolitical forms of terrorism to a more rigorous examination before determining whether they are a form of war.

There are three main types of apolitical terrorism: psychotic, criminal, and mystical. Most psychotic and criminal acts, and many mystical acts, involving abnormal lethal force are clearly not terrorism due to the simple fact that no one is terrorized or influenced except the victim. But many such acts are in fact committed precisely for the purpose of terrorizing and influencing other entities through the employment of abnormal lethal force upon a symbolic victim. In such cases, that force is employed in a terroristic manner—and whether the perpetrator is psychotic, criminal, a member of a mystical sect, or all three together, he is also a terrorist.

From the outset it should be stressed that these three categories are by no means mutually exclusive and, indeed, quite often overlap. Moreover, all three types of apolitical terrorism are similar in that they are based upon achieving goals having no consistent, overt political purpose.

## Psychotic Terrorism

Psychotic terrorism develops from *abnormal behavior,* a psychological term that rests predominantly upon normative values and is therefore as difficult to define scientifically as the term *terrorism.* Those who engage in psychotic terrorism, however, are defined by J. Bowyer Bell as "those who attempt bizarre, ostensibly political actions with uncertain or irrational outward motives . . . for what are internal personal reasons."[1] Such terrorists are often confused and have no clear idea of their political aims. They frequently select their victims on a random basis and are given to spontaneous rather than systematic use of lethal force. Indeed, inconsistent behavior reflecting idiosyncratic values is the hallmark of the psychopathic criminal (or terrorist).[2]

A good example of this is Charles Manson and his "Helter Skelter" group. Espousing vague political goals including a desire to cause a black-white race war, Manson and his "family" brutally murdered actress Sharon Tate and her unborn baby and in another episode murdered the La Bianca couple. The total absurdity of the means by which they sought to initiate a race war, and the haphazard manner in which the murders were committed, belies the political motivation of the Manson group. (Manson and his group sought to cause a race war by killing whites and blaming it on the blacks. Once both sides were destroyed by the ensuing holocaust, Manson and his followers supposedly would then control whatever remained.) Still, it was terrorism. Manson and his followers, like most psychotic terrorists, employed lethal force in an extremely abnormal manner to bring attention to themselves by terrorizing the general public. Psychotic terrorists crave attention, and the terroristic method provides the correct tool. As Dr. Lawrence Freedman observes, by employing terrorism "the terrorist is recognized, and is negotiated with, and is able to prove his power to bring the most powerful and admired figure . . . to his knees."[3] Moreover, many psychotic terrorists are provided with other important feedback from the terrorist act—an intense feeling of thrill and pleasure in committing the act itself.

While Manson's terrorism was based upon dubious overt political rationale, there are some who would argue that it was, at least subconsciously, a product of sincere political motivations. For example, Emma Goldman, one of the leading twentieth-century anarchists, suggests that ideological (psychotic) terrorists are supersensitive to the wrongs and injustices of society causing them to "pay the toll of our social crimes."[4] She argues, for instance, that the assassin of President McKinley in 1901 "was not a depraved creature of low instincts [but] in reality 'supersensitive' [and] unable to bear up under the too great social stress."[5]

The stress of which Goldman is speaking manifests itself in the postindustrial world by three primary factors: (1) the dehumanization of man in his dealings with those who control his life, (2) his alienation from society, which is caused by his inability to reconcile his differences and conform to that society, and (3) the realization that nothing short of force can change the current sociopolitical environment. Karl Marx wrote extensively on the dehumanization of man in his work *Das Kapital*. He was particularly critical of the modern industrial process that converts man into "a mere appurtenance of the machine. . . ."[6] In such a society man is judged less upon his value as a human being than as an element of production. Moreover, man becomes a fragmented being. As Ralph Waldo Emerson observes,

> Man is not a farmer, or a professor, or an engineer, but he is all. Man is priest and scholar, and statesman, and producer, and soldier. In the *divided* or social state these functions are parceled out to individuals, each of whom aims to do his stint of the joint work, whilst each other performs his. . . . Unfortunately, this original unit, this fountain of power, has been so distributed to the multitudes, has been so minutely subdivided and peddled out, that it is spilled into drops, and cannot be gathered. The state of society is one in which the members have suffered amputation from the trunk, and strut about as so many walking monsters—a good finger, a neck, a stomach, but never a man.[7]

Such estranged and fragmented individuals eventually suffer from what Robert Taylor and Byong-Suh Kim identify as reification. This is a social process through which individuals begin to view themselves and others as impersonal objects or things, and thus lose their self-identity.[8]

These reified individuals are immediately confronted with the question of whether they and their fellow humans are doomed to be controlled by a soulless technocratic bureaucracy that requires absolute conformity or whether the system can be changed. Moreover, these same individuals generally experience an identity crisis. If they are not what the system says they are, then what are they? A particularly poignant example of this identity crisis was written by a Japanese student a few days before he was killed in a university riot:

> I came into existence 18 years and 10 days ago. What have I done to live during this period? I can feel no sense of responsibility, either for the present or for the future. I constantly find myself doubtful, if not indifferent, and I borrow others' words to defend myself. What on earth am I?[9]

During the 1960s, thousands of alienated people experiencing similar identity crises took to the streets in protest. By employing force these individuals sought two simultaneous objectives: to change the system and, equally important, to achieve some sort of self-identity by engaging in an action that was clearly independent of the system they sought to change. This can represent a political action. For instance, one is reminded here of Frantz Fanon's statement, "The colonial subject, by killing a white man, can regain a sense of manhood, a sense of power, a new image of himself."[10]

Clearly, the stresses of postindustrial societies create many people alienated by the dehumanization processes inherent in such societies. These people resort to the use of force both as a means to redress grievances and to provide a form of self-identity apart from that given to them by the system. For the majority of those who are "sane," the force selected tends to be nonlethal, such as protest marches and sit-ins. These people are generally quickly recoopted into society. For the psychotics, however, there is often no reconciliation with society. Not only have the psychotic terrorists rejected society, but they are unable to comprehend fully the moral principles espoused by that society. As a result, they all too often select lethal forms of force as a means of protest and self-identity. Consequently, they, as Emma Goldman notes, pay the ultimate price of being unable to conform to the sociopolitical environment in which they find themselves.

To the degree that the psychotic terrorist is motivated to take up arms by his sociopolitical environment, it may be concluded that his use of force is a political act. It is not, however, an act of war. As suggested in chapter 1, war exists when lethal force is employed to compel an enemy to conform to a given political end. Psychotic terrorists are generally incapable of such rationalization. Psychotic terrorists such as Charles Manson offer the target group, which is usually ill-defined, no consistent idea of how to avoid future terror. Under such conditions it is impossible to comply with the terrorists' will, even if such were deemed desirable.

In the final analysis, then, psychotic terrorists employ lethal force primarily to meet some inner, personal need or to satiate an emotional or psychological desire. As Walter Laquer has observed,

> The less clear the political purpose in terrorism, the greater its appeal to unbalanced persons. The motives of men fighting tyranny are quite different from those of rebels against a democratically elected government. Idealism, a social conscience or hatred of foreign oppression are powerful impulses, but so are free-floating aggression, boredom and mental confusion. Activism can give meaning to otherwise empty lives.[11]

For the psychotic terrorist, then, the act of terrorism is not so much a means to an end as an end in itself. The compulsion of others to submit to the psychotic terrorist's will is simply an incidental factor of the terrorist act. Although possibly caused by given sociopolitical conditions, psychotic terrorism at best only superficially attempts to affect the sociopolitical milieu. Equally important, the psychotic terrorist generally employs abnormal lethal force to satiate only his own personal psychological needs. Given that war is a sociological as well as a political phenomenon, this personalization of the use of lethal force clearly places psychotic terrorism outside the pale of war.

## Criminal Terrorism

Criminal terrorism is defined as "the systematic use of terror for ends of material gain."[12] It is not difficult to envisage this form of terrorism. The primary manifestations of force in this form of terrorism include kidnapping, extortion, gangland assassinations, and murders. Although such activity may actually result in political and/or social change, such change is usually incidental and a byproduct of the use of force.

Not all crime involving lethal force is, of course, terrorism since it generally involves only the criminal and the victim. On the other hand, certain criminal acts are by their very nature terrorism. One obvious example is kidnapping. The kidnappers threaten to kill the victim to terrorize the family into paying a ransom and to influence the authorities not to interfere.

As with psychotic terrorism, criminal terrorism is essentially the employment of lethal force for personal motives. Additionally the criminal terrorist may elect a life of crime for the same reasons as the psychotic terrorist, including alienation from society and a need to establish a self-identity. But here is where the parallel stops. While the actions and results of psychotic and criminal terrorists are the same, according to Frederick J. Hacker, they have fundamentally different attributes. In Hacker's opinion the psychotic, or to use his term, "crazy," terrorist is "predominately inward-directed, . . . suicidal, unstable and immature. [An] inept individual with a weak ego and overt behavior disturbances [and who is] unpredictable. . . ."[13] The criminal terrorist, on the other hand, is outward-directed and homicidal, having a seemingly intact ego and no overt behavioral disturbance. Most important the criminal terrorist is predictable, logical, determined, and ruthless.[14] Probably the only operational difference between the two is that it may be possible to reason with the criminal terrorist but generally not the psychotic terrorist. Moreover, being outward-directed, the criminal terrorist is far more likely to work with a group of other criminals whereas the psychotic tends to be a loner.

Some have argued that criminal terrorists, as with psychotic terrorists, are unwitting political actors. For instance Martin Oppenheimer suggests that certain criminals may be defined as "social bandits" who employ force without political goals or mass support but who, by resorting to force, affect the social milieu.[15] A social bandit is described by E. J. Hobsbawm as "a man [who] does something which is not regarded as criminal by his local conventions, but is so regarded by the state or local rulers."[16] Classical examples of these social bandits are Robin Hood or Jesse James.

These social bandits, as Oppenheimer points out, are capable of setting limits to state oppression by targeting and terrorizing the upper stratum of society and agents of the government.[17] But due to a lack of political ideology, social bandits are only local phenomenon and can only mitigate the oppression by the state, not solve its basic causes. Indeed the targets for the force used in criminal terrorism are selected based primarily upon considerations of personal, material gain and fall outside the political arena. If a member of the governing apparatus is targeted at all, it is either for direct personal gain or to reduce interference by governmental authorities in their efforts to interdict criminal activity. Any impact upon the social or political milieu is purely incidental to the criminal terrorists' main objective—personal gain. Indeed, the social impact of criminal terrorists may be purely ascriptive in nature; a search by the population for a deliverer from perceived oppression. Robin Hood, for example, is the archtypical social bandit, but he is merely a legend. And Jesse James was no more than a young man brutalized by war who continued to do what he did best when the war ended. There is no evidence that Jesse James perceived himself to be other than what he was after the war—a simple outlaw.

In the final analysis, then, criminal terrorism is not a form of war for precisely the same reasons psychotic terrorism is not. Not only is it the employment of lethal force for nonpolitical goals, but that force is also used primarily to satiate the personal desires of the terrorist. Any impact upon the sociopolitical milieu is for the most part purely incidental. It is not a form of war.

## Mystical Terrorism

Mystical terrorism involves the use of lethal force against a symbolic victim to influence or invoke supernatural powers. At the most basic level of analysis it is *quadratic* terrorism, where the people are the target of terror and the supernatural power the target of influence. Collectivities practicing this form of terrorism have political aspirations only insofar as they are interested in creating and maintaining a sociopolitical environment sufficient to assure their continued existence.

Although there have been very few purely mystical terrorist groups throughout history, mysticism has played a major role in many terrorist organizations. As Walter Laquer has noted, French and American anarchists, Rumanian fascists, nineteenth-century Russian terrorists, and contemporary Irish and Arab terrorists have embraced mysticism as a means of legitimizing both their cause and the sacrifices they ask of their membership.[18] He writes,

The parents, the brothers and sisters of Fascist terrorists were as convinced as the families of Russian revolutionaries that their dear ones
had died for a "holy cause." [Indeed] the last words of some of those
about to be executed . . . reveal that these men and women were deeply
convinced that upon them, as on Christ, rested the burden of deliver-
ance.[19]

In explaining why terrorism terrorizes, Dr. Lawrence Freedman
points to man's primal fear of becoming isolated and alone, a factor
modern terrorists play upon as a means of manipulating the target of
terror.[20] This is, according to Freedman, a continuation of the tradition
of mystical prophets and messiahs:

The prophet predicted and threatened: he predicted social justice and
God's grace with conformity to god's rules, but he threatened terrors
unless sin ended and propitiation of the gods was successful . . . . Only
behavior and feelings suitable to the injunctions of the god or the god's
designated messiahs and prophets could bring respite.[21]

Mysticism, therefore, plays a part in both the instigation of terrorism and the enhancement of its effect. Although mysticism is generally an adjunct to political terrorist movements, it can and has existed
in pure form. Perhaps the best example of purely mystical terrorism is
the Hindu thuggee movement of eighteenth- and nineteenth-century
India. The thuggees murdered thousands of Indians from all castes of
society as sacrifices to the goddess Kali. Though these terrorists generally selected their victims at random, they were also quick to move
against any Indian who jeopardized the thuggee movement. The thuggees were so effective and so terrorized the general Indian population
that the best efforts of the British Empire found it extremely difficult
to prevail in destroying the movement. The British historian V.A.
Smith described the thuggees in terms that could easily apply to a
modern criminal terrorist gang:

The gangs had little to fear, and enjoyed complete immunity. . . . The
moral feeling of the people had sunk so low that there were no signs of
[resistance to] . . . the cold-blooded crimes committed by the thugs.
They were accepted as part of the established order of things, and until
the secrets of the organization were given away . . . it was usually impossible to obtain evidence against even the most notorious thugs.[22]

The tremendous success of the thuggees can be attributed both to their effective use of lethal force to deter informants as well as the population's acceptance of the movement as a legitimate part of the social order. It is this latter factor that explains why mysticism attracts many modern terrorists.

As to the question of whether mystical terrorism, by itself, is a form of war, the answer must be no. To be sure, mystical terrorism does involve the use of lethal force to sustain a given sociopolitical environment and, to that limited extent, qualifies as a use of force for a political end. Upon closer scrutiny, however, it is quite clear that mystical terrorists are much less interested in political power than in social structures. Moreover, although the lethal force does facilitate achieving and maintaining a given sociopolitical environment and to that extent qualifies as the use of force as a means to an end, lethal force in mystical terrorism is also an end in itself. In classical warfare, the employment of force ceases when the enemy complies with the victor's will. In mystical terrorism, the employment of force continues ad infinitum—the people simply cannot alter their behavior to avoid future terror. Force employed as an end in itself is not a form of war.

One final element is absent in mystical terrorism as warfare, and that is, it fails to meet the preeminent principle of war—the *principle of engagement*. As emphasized in chapter 3, it is not enough for an entity to employ force for a political objective for that use of force to be considered a form of war; it must also involve a clash of arms—the employment of force by both sides. In mystical terrorism only the terrorists employ force. Force employed in this manner is not warfare.

## Summation

None of the three forms of apolitical terrorism qualifies as a form of warfare. Although Goldman, Oppenheimer, and Freedman suggest a certain politicalness for psychotic, criminal, and mystical terrorism respectively, for the most part any political impact of these types of terrorism is incidental and ancillary. Both criminal and psychotic terrorism involve the use of lethal force that is often justified on political grounds but clearly employed to achieve or satiate personal goals and desires. Moreover, psychotic terrorism employs force in a highly idiosyncratic fashion making it impossible for the target of terror—if identified at all—to modify its behavior to avoid future terror. This represents the use of lethal force as an end in itself, rather than a means to an end and clearly places psychotic, as well as mystical terrorism—which employs force in the same manner—outside the pale of war.

Criminal terrorism generally employs force in a more utilitarian fashion than the other two forms of apolitical terrorism by making it quite clear to the target of the terror how it must behave to avoid future terror. But again, it is for personal goals having at best ancillary political ramifications. Because the criminal terrorist has no mass support, no political ideology, and limited aims, he is generally only a local or regional figure having at best a cursory impact upon the sociopolitical environment. Consequently, while the criminal terrorist, like the psychotic terrorist, may be a product of the sociopolitical milieu, his aims are not so much to change that milieu as to personally capitalize upon its weaknesses—an apolitical goal. In this regard alone, then, criminal terrorism, like the other two, is not a form of war.

## Notes

1. J. Bowyer Bell, *Transnational Terror* (Washington, D.C.: American Enterprise Institute for Public Research, 1975), p. 10.

2. Alan F. Sewell, "Political Crime: A Psychologist's Perspective," *International Terrorism and Political Crime*, edited by M. Bassiouni (Springfield, Ill.: Charles C. Thomas, Publisher, 1975), pp. 20–21. As quoted in Alex P. Schmid, *Political Terrorism: A Research Guide to Concepts, Theories, Data Bases and Literature* (Amsterdam: North Holland Publishing Co., 1983; Transaction Books, 1985), p. 29.

3. Albert Parry, *Terrorism: From Robespierre to Arafat* (New York: Vanguard Press, Inc., 1976), p. 28.

4. Bernard K. Johnpoll, "Perspectives on Political Terrorism in the United States," *International Terrorism: National, Regional, and Global Perspectives* (New York: Praeger Publishers, 1976), p. 35.

5. Ibid.

6. Karl Marx, *Das Kapital*, translated by Eden and Cedar Paul (London: J. M. Dent & Sons, 1933), p. 713. As quoted in Robert C. Tucker, *The Marxian Revolutionary Idea* (New York: W. W. Norton & Co., 1969), pp. 23–24.

7. Ralph Waldo Emerson, "Nature" and "The American Scholar," *The Heart of Emerson's Essays*, edited by Perry Bliss (Boston: Houghton Mifflin & Co., 1933), pp. 56–57. As quoted in Andrew Schmookler, *Parable of the Tribes: The Problem of Power in Social Evolution* (Berkeley: University of California Press, 1984; Houghton-Mifflin Co., paperback edition, 1986), pp. 91–92.

8. Robert W. Taylor and Byong-Suh Kim, "Violence and Change in Post-industrial Societies: Student Protest in America and Japan in the 1960s," *International Terrorism in the Contemporary World*, edited by Marius H. Livingston (London: Greenwood Press, 1978), p. 10.

9. Ibid., p. 215.

10. Frantz Fanon, *The Wretched of the Earth* (New York: Grove Press, 1963), p. 117, as cited by Paul Wilkinson, *Political Terrorism* (London: Macmillan & Co., 1974), pp. 101–102. As quoted in Alex Schmid, op. cit., p. 93.

11. Walter Laquer, *Terrorism: A Study of National and International Political Violence* (Boston: Little, Brown & Co., Inc., 1977), p. 12.

12. Grant Wardlaw, *Political Terrorism: Theory, Tactics and Countermeasures* (Cambridge: Cambridge University Press, 1984), p. 12.

13. Frederick J. Hacker, *Crusaders, Criminals, Crazies: Terror and Terrorism in Our Time* (New York: Bantam Books, 1978), pp. 13–19. As quoted in Austin P. Turk, *Political Criminality: The Defiance and Defense of Authority* (London: Sage Publications, Ltd., 1982), p. 74.

14. Ibid.

15. Martin Oppenheimer, *The Urban Guerrilla* (Chicago: Quadrangle Books, 1969), p. 33.

16. E. J. Hobsbawm, *Primitive Rebels* (New York: Norton & Co., 1965), p. 15. As quoted in Oppenheimer, op. cit., pp. 33–34.

17. Oppenheimer, op. cit., p. 34.

18. Laquer, op. cit., pp. 126–27.

19. Ibid., p. 217.

20. Lawrence Z. Freedman, "Why Does Terrorism Terrorize?" *Terrorism: An International Journal* 6, no. 3 (1983), p. 391.

21. Ibid., p. 400.

22. V. A. Smith, *Oxford History of India* (Oxford: Oxford University Press, 1923), pp. 666–67. As quoted in Will Durant, *The Story of Civilization*, vol. 1, *Our Oriental Heritage* (New York: Simon & Schuster, Inc., 1954), p. 499.

# 7

# REVOLUTIONARY TERRORISM

■

## Introduction

Certainly one of the most sensationalized forms of political terrorism in the world today is revolutionary terrorism. Often called *agitational terrorism* or *terror from below,* its primary purpose is to destabilize and topple the incumbent regime, replacing it with a political apparatus more acceptable to the revolutionaries. As shall be quickly established, however, terrorism alone cannot achieve the ends sought by the revolutionaries. Terrorism is but a small part of an overall process.

Understanding the role of terrorism in the revolutionary process is the subject of the first section of this chapter. This entails examining terrorism's immediate objectives and the means it employs to achieve them. Particular emphasis will be placed upon the conditions the terrorists seek to create in the regime on the one hand, and the population on the other. While conducting this investigation it will become possible to determine whether revolutionary terrorism is a form of war.

## The Role of Terrorism in the Revolutionary Process

As mentioned above, the purpose of revolutionary terrorism is to destabilize and overthrow the incumbent regime. To emerge victorious, these terrorists must generate sufficient power to compel the incumbent governmental leaders to relinquish the reins of power. Given that revolutionary terrorists normally have only a small fraction of the total armed force available to the regime, the question immediately arises, how can the terrorists succeed in the face of their extreme military weakness?

The answer, of course, lies in the unique characteristics of revolutionary warfare. As the American Revolutionary and Vietnam wars have clearly shown, victory in revolutionary warfare is not entirely dependent upon military power. Indeed, according to William Friedland,

> revolutionary warfare is preeminently a question of political and social relationships and not merely a matter of technology and skill. In contrast to other forms of warfare, revolutionary warfare is always directed not only at defeating the enemy by military means, but at the mass movement of the people as a crucial part of the process.[1]

It is the mobilization of the populace against the regime, then, that is the critical factor in revolutionary wars. Without the support of the majority of the populace, the revolutionaries would remain too weak to defeat the regime and its instruments of coercion. It is therefore not in open combat with the regime's armed forces that terrorism plays its major role, but rather as an instrument of mobilization within the revolutionary process. Before delving into how revolutionary terrorism actually mobilizes the populace, however, it is helpful to have a better understanding of the revolutionary process per se.

The great revolutionary leader Mao Tse-Tung saw revolutions occurring in three major phases.[2] Phase I is devoted to organizing, establishing, and preserving the revolution. Phase II is one of progressive expansion, and Phase III is the decisive phase in which the regime is destroyed by the revolution. Careful analysis of these political objectives reveals that different levels of force having different military objectives are necessary in each phase.

In the initial phase of the revolution the revolutionaries are extremely weak vis-à-vis the regime. If they are going to organize the revolution, communicate its goals to the populace, and preserve the existence of the revolutionary organization in the face of the overwhelming military force possessed by the regime, the revolutionaries require armed forces capable of operating in extreme secrecy, able to attack symbolic targets, and at the same time evade the regime's main forces. Consequently, terrorism is the obvious choice of armed resistance during this phase.

In the progressive expansion of Phase II the primary military objective is to secure *liberated zones* in which bases for recruitment and training can be built. In addition to the earlier purpose of communication, the armed forces of the revolution must now begin to weaken the regime by direct attacks on the regime's armed forces while avoiding excessive losses. Consequently, during Phase II the hit-and-run tactics of terrorism must be retained, but the revolutionaries must also be capable of doing substantial physical damage to the regime's coercive forces. Clearly, guerrilla warfare has the greatest utility in such situations.

Phase III of the revolution, according to Mao, is the *strategic offensive* phase.[3] The primary military objective here is total victory, which in Clausewitzian terms means the destruction of the regime's armed forces, the occupation of its territory, and most important, the destruction of its will to resist. To accomplish these objectives the revolutionaries require conventional military forces capable of seizing and holding terrain as well as defeating the regime's main combat forces.

All of this is not to say, of course, that terrorism is *not* used in the latter stages of the revolutionary process. Guerrillas and even conventional military forces frequently employ terrorism not only in revolutionary but interstate wars as well. The main point here is that terrorism enjoys its greatest relative utility in the initial phase of revolutionary mobilization. This is perhaps most clearly depicted by Thomas Thornton in his famous five stages of insurrection. As is shown in table 8, each phase of the revolutionary process is characterized by a different level of force.

One thing that Thornton has overlooked in his depiction of the stages of the revolutionary process is that during the consolidation phase there is often—as occurred in France, Russia, China, Cuba, Vietnam, Kampuchea, and Nicaragua—a return to terrorism in order to consolidate the revolutionary's hold on the reins of power. The postviolent phase often does not begin until after this reign of terror. Moreover, each phase also has a specific political objective; the identifica-

**TABLE 8**   Thornton's Five Stages of Revolution

| Phase | Characteristic |
|-------|----------------|
| I.   Preparatory | Previolent |
| II.  Initial Violence | Terrorism |
| III. Expansion | Guerrilla Warfare |
| IV.  Victorious | Conventional Warfare |
| V.   Consolidation | Postviolent |

SOURCE: Thomas P. Thornton, "Terror as a Weapon of Political Agitation," *Internal War: Problems and Approaches*, edited by Harry Eckstein (New York: The Free Press of Glencoe, 1964), p. 92. As quoted in Alex Schmid, *Political Terrorism: A Research Guide to Concepts, Theories, Data Bases and Literature* (New Brunswick: Transaction Books, 1985), p. 41.

**TABLE 9**   Stages of Revolutionary Mobilization

| Phase | Characteristic | Objective |
|-------|----------------|-----------|
| 1. Preparatory | Previolent | Establish Cause |
| 2. Initial Violence | Terrorism | Morally Isolate |
| 3. Expansion | Guerrilla War | Physically Isolate |
| 4. Victorious | Conventional War | Physically Destroy |
| 5. Consolidation | Terrorism | Reprogram Populace |
| 6. Administrative | Postviolent | Maintain Regime |

tion of which will make it easier to determine the military objective(s) germane to a specific phase of the revolutionary process. This expanded version of Thornton's revolutionary phases is presented in table 9. The "objective" column represents the political objective of the revolutionaries against the incumbent regime in a given phase.

As will be seen, the political objective during the initial violence phase of the revolutionary mobilization process will be to initiate the moral isolation of the regime. Once this is sufficiently under way, and increasingly more people join the revolution, the objective can be expanded to include liberation of territory to physically isolate the regime. Once sufficient territory has been liberated, giving the revolutionaries control over larger and larger numbers of people and other necessary resources, the revolutionaries can launch a conventional war with the military objective of destroying the regime's forces of coercion. The process proceeds in this manner until the final phase in which the revolutionaries establish control of the government and maintain their revolutionary goals through peaceful, administrative processes.

It should be noted here that the *characteristic* drives the *phase*. That is to say the revolutionary mobilization process will never move into the next higher phase until the revolutionaries adopt the level of force germane to that higher phase. Thus if the revolutionaries continue to rely exclusively upon terrorism and are unable or unwilling to adopt guerrilla warfare, the revolution will never move into the *expansion* phase. Indeed, according to Thomas Greene, "an exclusive reliance on terror as a revolutionary technique . . . is a certain sign of the movement's weakness."[4] He goes on to say that

> Marx, Lenin and Regis Debray are among those proponents of revolution who have admitted that terror alone can never bring about revolutionary change, that having to rely primarily on terror reflects the impossibility of achieving revolutionary goals under prevailing circumstances.[5]

The ultimate danger under these circumstances is that the revolutionaries lose sight of their goals and get increasingly wrapped up in the tactics of terrorism. As Paul Wilkinson points out, these terrorists are no longer capable of "viewing terrorism in instrumental-rational terms, involving a realistic calculation of its political effectiveness and the possibilities of success, [and consequently] acts of violence become ends in themselves."[6]

Still, it is evident from the above that terrorism plays a significant role in the revolutionary mobilization process, particularly in its earliest phases. The question now becomes one of *how* terrorism mobilizes the populace to support the revolution.

According to William Friedland, revolutionary mobilization consists of four elements: (1) raising consciousness, (2) increasing participation, (3) undermining the system, and (4) building the revolutionary organization.[7] As will be seen, terrorism has considerable utility in achieving all four elements of mobilization but is probably best suited to raising the consciousness of the population.

Raising the consciousness of the population is clearly a necessary and critical step in the mobilization process. As Ted Gurr establishes in his great work *Why Men Rebel*, men will *not* rebel unless (1) they are deprived of some expected value, and (2) they are aware of this deprivation.[8] If nothing else, terrorism is certainly a very effective means of communicating and highlighting existing grievances. Indeed, some analysts consider communication to be the most important aspect of political terrorism. For instance, Martha Crenshaw contends that "the most basic reason for terrorism is to gain recognition or attention. . . ."[9]

It is possible for the terrorists to raise the consciousness of the population because, as was pointed out in chapter 5, terrorism can function in a quadratic as well as a triadic fashion. In quadratic terrorism there are two targets: the target of terror and the target of influence. Those that the terrorists seek to mobilize are the target of influence.

The terrorist has an impact upon the target of influence in two important ways. First, it emphasizes to the people repressed by the target of influence that they are not isolated individuals experiencing some form of deprivation due to personal inadequacies, but rather they are part of a larger collectivity of like-minded individuals suffering from, and wishing to be rid of, the same oppression. In this way, the individual begins to realize he is part of a larger group having similar experiences and common desires. Secondly, by choosing the correct symbolic target, the terrorists can also educate the target of influence as to the source of their deprivation. This is extremely important since, as Ted Gurr points out, "an angered person is not likely to strike out at any object in his environment, but only at targets he thinks are responsible."[10]

In this way, terrorism initiates and reinforces a psychological polarization of society through the process of raising the consciousness of the target of influence. Of course, nothing limits the target of influence to only one social class. Theda Skocpol notes, for instance, that successful social revolutions involve not only an alienation and mobilization of the lowest classes, but also of the landed upper classes that have sufficient political autonomy to hinder the state's ability to put down the revolt.[11] Those that are influenced clearly begin to think in terms of "we" and "they" with the latter ascribed to the incumbent regime and its instruments of coercion. But as Ted Gurr suggests, simply being aware that one is deprived due to actions and policies of the regime does not necessarily mean men will rebel. They must also believe that resorting to violence has some utility, that there is some chance of success.[12]

Establishing the feasibility and utility of resistance to the regime is central to the second element of revolutionary mobilization: *increasing participation*. Here it is necessary to expose the regime's weaknesses and emphasize the revolutionary movement's strengths. This, of course, is best achieved by launching attacks against symbolic targets, such as government or police officials, and is most effective when carried out on a frequent basis and with seeming impunity. Each attack drives home the point that the regime is not omnipotent and can be successfully resisted.

Of equal importance, of course, is the reaction of the incumbent regime. If the terrorists can induce the government to overreact by using ever-increasing doses of repression to try to stop the people from supporting the revolutionaries, then the regime can begin to lose legitimacy in the eyes of the repressed populace. If larger and larger segments of the population become alienated from the regime, the number of people who may be induced to join the revolution also grows. This, of course, is a classical terrorist stratagem popularized by the terrorist revolutionary Carlos Marighella. He wrote in his *Minimanual of the Urban Guerrilla*,

> It is necessary to turn political crisis into armed conflict by performing violent actions that will force those in power to transform the political situation of the country into a military situation. That will alienate the masses, who, from then on, will revolt against the army and police and blame them for the state of things.[13]

Such a reaction by the government also reinforces the trend toward polarizing the society in question. This is particularly true regarding the members of the regime's elements of coercion. As the police and soldiers begin to perceive the population as being, if not the enemy outright, at least sympathetic to the revolutionaries, it justifies in the minds of many in the regime's armed forces the use of increasingly heavy-handed tactics against the population itself. By creating such conditions the terrorists hope to establish their *moral credentials* while undermining those of the regime. In this way the terrorists, according to Marighella, are provided with their most important advantage: moral superiority over the regime. In his opinion this moral superiority devolves from the fact that the terrorist is "defending a just cause, the cause of the people—whereas [the regime's forces] are on the side of an enemy the people hate."[14] Thus, the terrorists increase participation of the target of influence in the revolutionary process by, as political analyst Eqbal Ahmad describes it, "activating and perpetuating the moral isolation of the regime until such isolation has become total and irreversible."[15]

To morally isolate the government and increase participation in the revolution, the revolutionaries must avoid at all costs the use of arbitrary, indiscriminate terrorism. Indeed, as Ahmad observes, "[it] is a myth that terror is the basis of civilian support for the [revolutionaries]."[16] He continues by stressing that revolutionary

> warfare requires highly committed but covert civilian support which cannot be obtained at gunpoint. . . . [Moreover, resorting] to indiscriminate terrorism indicates lack of broad support, without which the movement soon collapses.[17]

This is essentially an echo of Che Guevara's admonition in the early 1960s that indiscriminate terrorism "is generally ineffective . . . in its results, since it often makes victims of innocent people and destroys . . . lives that would be valuable to the revolution."[18] Consequently, the revolutionary terrorists create a situation wherein they employ discriminate terrorism against very specific targets and hope they can induce the government to overreact with indiscriminate terror against the population writ large.

It is here that the Vietnam War provides a clear example. Because the governmental authorities by necessity operated overtly, they were easily located, observed, and at the proper moment, assassinated by Viet Cong (VC) terrorists. In this manner, the VC was able to apply very discriminant—one might even say surgical—force against specific "enemies of the people."[19] But, because the VC operated clandestinely and easily hid among the populace, the governmental security forces had great difficulty locating their enemy. As a consequence, these security forces often directed lethal force in an indiscriminate manner against large segments of the population suspected of supporting the VC. Thus, while a person knew how to act to avoid VC terror, it was often impossible to avoid that of the regime's. Moreover, the sheer lethality of conventional warfare using modern technology made it far less discriminant to use than the more carefully applied and easily controlled force germane to guerrilla and terrorist warfare employed by the VC and the North Vietnamese. As Robert Asprey notes, "During [one] twelve-day battle . . . [American] gunners fired over 18,000 artillery rounds, tactical aircraft dropped 1,375 tons of bombs, and B-52 aircraft dropped [another] 1,750 tons. . . ."[20] Since the battle just described occurred in and around the inhabited town of Dak To, the employment of such heavy ordnance in such massive quantities invariably resulted in large numbers of civilian casualties. Even when the regime tried to limit civilian casualties by searching out the VC cadre and destroying them, it often, indeed usually, backfired. For instance, describing U.S. Marine operations in Vietnam, Asprey writes,

> As elsewhere in Vietnam, search and destroy tactics continued to antagonize people who had to be won over. Marines were operating in a vast sea of fear that could easily turn into hatred, and frequent firefights, no matter how carefully conducted, could not but exacerbate the situation—moving bullets are promiscuous. Marine bands could play, and Marines could distribute food and clothing, and doctors could help villagers, but these advantages paled when one, two or more villagers were killed in a fire-fight or by bombs, rockets, naval shells or napalm. . . . Marines could hold "county fairs" until doomsday, but, unless carried to fruition, they were not only meaningless but dangerous [since they exposed] . . . friendly or potentially friendly villagers . . . to VC wrath.[21]

To be effective, then, terrorism must use only discriminant force against the regime and its supporters. But every possible precaution should be taken not to employ force—particularly indiscriminate force—against the general population. In short, terrorists must not alienate the population they seek to mobilize for the revolution. Rather, terrorists should endeavor to shatter the *political* cohesion of society by driving a wedge between the regime and the populace. Terrorists should also attempt to destroy the cohesion of the regime's governmental apparatus and its armed forces, but the *social* cohesion of the population should remain relatively intact and disrupted only to the degree necessary to effect the other two objectives just mentioned. It should be noted here that the revolutionary terrorists do not seek the total destruction of the social cohesion of the populace because *the populace is not the enemy.* The enemy is the incumbent regime and its instruments of control. Consequently, the terrorists can and should employ all force possible to totally destroy the regime.

Still as Theda Skocpol has clearly established, raising the consciousness of the governed masses and inducing them to *want* to overthrow the regime is in itself insufficient. As she so clearly puts it in her book *States and Social Revolutions,* "This image suggests that the ultimate and sufficient condition for the revolution is the withdrawal of . . . consensual support [by the ruled] and, conversely, that no regime could survive if the masses were consciously disgruntled."[22] A few pages later she further reinforces her point by stating, "Even after great loss of legitimacy has occurred, a state can remain quite stable—and certainly invulnerable to internal mass-based revolts—especially if its coercive organizations remain coherent and effective."[23] It can be concluded from this that the regime's center of gravity is its forces of coercion.

There are literally hundreds of historical examples to support Skocpol's contention. Two instances Skocpol uses to underscore her thesis are the Japanese Meiji Restoration of 1868–73 and the Prussian Reform Movement following that kingdom's defeat by Napoleonic France in 1806. In both examples, the state's ability to maintain control of its forces of coercion enabled it to wield superior force. This proved a major factor in the regime not succumbing to social revolution. Of course, the ability to wield superior force is dependent upon many important factors beyond the regime's control of existing coercive forces. As Skocpol notes, the existence of a politically autonomous elite and/or the existence of a military crisis diverting coercive forces to face an external threat play a major role in determining whether the regime has sufficient coercive force to stave off a social revolution.[24]

Perhaps the most poignant twentieth-century example of the critical role played by the regime's forces of coercion in averting a social revolution can be found in comparing the Russian revolutions of 1905 and 1917. In both cases, Russia was engaged in a losing war, but it was only after the much longer and more costly First World War had bled Russia's armies white that a social revolution succeeded in toppling the regime. As W. Bruce Lincoln observes when comparing the 1905 and 1917 Russian revolutions,

> Only the cruel fact that Russia's peasant army remained willing to shoot their brethren in town and country enabled Nicholas II to survive the turbulence of 1905. Of all the lessons that Russia's ill-fated emperor failed to learn from his nation's revolutionary experiences that year, the extent to which his power depended upon the army's loyalty proved the most dangerous to ignore.[25]

It is therefore apparent that success in a mass-based revolution requires more than the mere willingness of the population to revolt. It is also dependent upon the revolution's ability to neutralize the regime's coercive organizations. It is here that Friedland's third element of revolutionary mobilization—*undermining the system*—comes into play. Although terrorism is less effective in achieving this element of mobilization than it is in raising the consciousness or increasing participation, terrorism can nevertheless positively influence this revolutionary goal.

One of the primary means of undermining the system has already been mentioned, moral isolation, which is the psychological separation of the regime from the mass of the populace and/or large portions of the elite. Without the support of the majority of the people, or substantial numbers of the elite classes, the government will find it increasingly difficult to raise taxes or find willing replacements for its armed forces. As more and more reluctant members of the population are coerced into joining the police and/or military, the loyalty of these instruments of coercion to the regime becomes questionable. As Jack Goldstone notes,

> When army officers come primarily from a landed elite, they may sympathize with their own class in a conflict with the central government and elites. Where troops are recently recruited and fraternize with the populace, their sympathy for their civilian fellows may override their allegiance to their officers. In either ... [case], the unreliability of the army increases the vulnerability of the state to the revolution.[26]

The regime begins to find it more and more difficult to find commanders and soldiers who are willing to apply the "whiff of grapeshot" necessary to disperse and neutralize the rebellious populace. In this way, the state begins to lose control of coherent and effective instruments of coercion that Skocpol has so rightly pointed out are necessary to maintain power. The terrorists can also neutralize popular support for the incumbent regime by terrorizing those elements of the population opposed to revolution. For this to occur quickly and effectively, however, the terrorists must be sufficiently strong to create a psychological environment that disrupts the cohesion of the regime's supporters. Moreover, as Martha Crenshaw points out, the populace must be in general favorable to the terrorists and their stated objectives for the revolution to have a chance of success.[27] If the population is indifferent to the terrorists, inciting a revolution is extremely difficult, and if the majority of the populace is hostile to the terrorists, inciting a revolution is probably impossible. Still, in a society in which the general populace is already hostile to the regime—as in a colonial situation—the terrorists can greatly increase the polarization of that society by assassinating elements of the population favoring compliance with the regime and/or its policies.

Another major method the terrorists may use, and one that complements the above objective, is to attack the cohesion of the regime directly. Fortunately for the terrorists, modern industrial societies are sufficiently complex that they provide an extremely target-rich environment. More important, these societies are highly dependent upon relatively fragile elements of cohesion that are easily disrupted. For instance, as David Carlton notes,

> The fact is that advanced democracies—and maybe advanced totalitarian states as well—are much more vulnerable than states . . . even half a century ago. Large-scale industrialization has steadily grown and sophisticated processes are commonplace. Any breakdown in communications or in the flow of components or the supply of electricity or in the working of computers can instantly render idle thousands of workers. . . .[28]

Consequently, the modern industrial powers are extremely vulnerable due to their intrinsic complexity. The fragility of the industrial system can be seen in the following description of the 1965 New York City power blackout:

> In the gathering darkness of a cold winter evening on 9 November 1965 . . . a small metal cup inside a black . . . box began to slowly turn. As it turned, a spindle set in its center and carrying a tiny arm also rotated, gradually moving the metal arm . . . to a metal contact. Only a handful of people knew the exact location of the cup, and none knew it had been triggered. At precisely eleven seconds past the minute the two tiny objects made contact, and . . . set in motion a sequence of events that would lead, in twelve minutes, to chaos. During that time life in 80,000 square miles of one of the richest, most highly industrialized, most densely populated areas in the Western world would come to a virtual standstill. Over thirty million people would be affected . . . [and] as a result some of them would die. For all of them, life would never be quite the same again.[29]

The impact of this man-made yet freak accident is easy to see. The damage was undone within thirteen hours because the infrastructure of the power grid was undamaged, and power was easily restored. One can only imagine the chaos created if the damage had been irreparable for several days or weeks. As Richard Rubenstein notes,

> Even the richest, most powerful city can only survive as long as the umbilical cord to the countryside is not cut. One of the frightful images of the death of civilization envisages a time when the city, deprived of the countryside's surplus population, feeds upon its own ever-diminishing self and finally collapses.[30]

Clearly political cohesion would be virtually impossible under such a situation. Luckily for the regime, even the most dedicated and highly skilled terrorists would probably be too weak to bring about such a level of chaos by themselves. Yet disruption to the degree described by Rubenstein may not be really necessary. The mere threat of such chaos and loss of control can undermine the regime and weaken its forces of coercion.

To retain absolute political control, the regime must counter every terrorist attack and/or must undo all damage done. Given the complexity and vulnerability of the system, protecting everything would be cost-prohibitive. As Thomas Greene notes, "Not knowing where the terrorists will strike next can immobilize thousands of government troops, constrained to take up a defensive posture by guarding officials, residences, offices, and utilities and communication facilities."[31] Thus the government's expenditure of effort far outweighs that of the revolutionaries. The revolutionaries conserve their strength while the regime grows continuously weaker. As the nineteenth-century Russian terrorist Stepniak-Kravchinsky puts it, "In the struggle against an invisible, impalpable, omnipresent enemy, the strong is vanquished, not by the arms of his adversary, but by the continuous tension of his own strength, which exhausts him, at last, more than he would be exhausted by defeats."[32] This, of course, is a return to Sun Tzu's simple admonition that the enemy should always be kept under strain and gradually worn down.[33]

The objective here is to create conditions wherein the regime's armed forces become an occupying army in their own country. Here again, the Vietnam War provides a classic example of this situation. The Viet Cong, by launching a series of terrorist attacks, caused the governmental forces to begin to perceive that they were in a state of war. By 1961, according to Stanley Karnow, the South Vietnamese Army (SVA) had been converted from a national army representing the people into an army of occupation that represented a far-off regime increasingly under the influence of a foreign power. Karnow, writing of the South Vietnamese Army, states,

> Not only did they neglect the economic and social needs of the local population, they operated as if they were in enemy territory—living in fortified garrisons protected by blockhouses and barbed wire, venturing into the countryside only under heavy guard, often accompanied by American advisers whose presence lent substance to the Viet Cong denunciations of . . . the "neocolonial" collaboration between American and [South Vietnamese President] Diem. . . . One of Diem's aides confessed at the time: "Except for the color of our skin, we are no different from the French."[34]

Although morally isolating the regime and gradually wearing down and exhausting its armed forces are crucial parts to successful revolution, they are by no means sufficient in and by themselves. There must be more than a moral and physical break by the people from the regime. There must be a psychological break as well. Friedland, for instance, points out that "seizing the state is not a simple physical activity; post offices, radio stations, governmental buildings, workplaces, and corporate offices may be occupied, but the ideological assumptions and habitual behavior that underlie the manner in which these institutions operate are more difficult to uproot."[35] Thus, the habitual behavior of the people must be transformed for the revolution to be successful. Old loyalties and behavior patterns must be replaced by those supplied by the revolutionaries. Here again, terrorism can play a significant role.

As was noted in chapter 5, terrorism can disrupt the cohesion of society to the point of total despair—a level in which society is reduced to a conglomeration of anomic individuals. This would clearly be counterproductive for the revolutionary terrorist who was trying to mobilize that population. But if the terrorists are able to create a level of *anxiety* in the population sufficient to disrupt previous patterns of social intercourse but not to the degree of total isolation and despair, then as Thomas Thornton suggests, the people will begin to cast about for new guidance. That guidance, of course, is provided by the revolutionaries themselves.

The terrorists create this anxiety by disrupting previous social patterns through the neutralization of the regime's normal socialization and service mechanics. In this way they physically isolate the regime. This proved extremely effective in South Vietnam. By targeting local officials at the village and hamlet level, the terrorists were able to disrupt much of Saigon's presence and influence among the populace. Nor was this assassination campaign limited to government officials and agents. Schoolteachers, doctors, missionaries, and anyone else advocating compliance with the regime were targeted as well. According to James Harrison, the Viet Cong, by using terrorist tactics, had virtual control of An Loc province by 1960, "since the Communist assassinations were sufficient to cripple the government apparatus at the hamlet and village level. . . ."[36] Only the massive influx of U.S. military power in 1965 was able to turn the tide against the VC. Without U.S. aid, Saigon's ability to retain political control and ultimately defeat the revolution is extremely questionable.

By physically isolating the people from the government's influence, the revolutionaries could then embark upon a reeducation program. The population was introduced to new ways of thinking and living. Those who would not or could not conform were eliminated. But this required the establishment of liberated zones where a microcosm of the revolutionary state could be set up and operated. Hence, this level can only be achieved when the revolution has reached the expansion phase and the revolutionary's primary means of force employment is guerrilla warfare. Since this is beyond the scope of this book, it is sufficient to note that terrorism has utility in the physical isolation of the people from the regime and that this, in turn, can be converted into psychological isolation.

Undermining the system is only useful, of course, if the revolutionaries can offer a suitable alternative; a goal that the population prefers over anything the regime can credibly offer. This is where Friedland's fourth, and in many ways most important, element of revolutionary mobilization comes into play—building the revolutionary organization.

It would be difficult to overemphasize the importance of the revolutionary organization. It is the common denominator for the other three elements of revolutionary mobilization. The revolutionary organization guides the revolution through the mobilization process, selecting the best means of raising the consciousness and increasing the participation of the revolutionary's reference group. The revolutionary organization also develops and ensures the correct implementation of an action strategy that ultimately results in the undermining of the incumbent regime. Finally, the revolutionary organization establishes new institutions to take the place of those of the crumbling regime, ensuring the postrevolutionary society is created in the image of the revolution.

The revolutionary organization, then, sets the goals or objectives of the revolution and creates and implements a strategy in which to bring these goals about. But the revolutionary organization performs another very critical function in the revolutionary process, namely, maintaining the political and military cohesion of the revolution. It is here that terrorism can also play an important role.

The importance of maintaining the cohesion of the revolution is self-evident. Without a cohesive political and military infrastructure there can be no revolution. It is helpful, therefore, to briefly examine how revolutionary organizations effect and maintain political and military cohesion within their ranks in the face of the overwhelming armed force usually enjoyed by the incumbent regime.

To begin with, it is interesting to note that revolutionary organizations must perform precisely the same basic functions as the nation-state in wartime to create and maintain political and military cohesion. Both entities must create a situation in which the individual, autonomous human being totally subordinates his will to that of the established hierarchy, even to the point of willingly sacrificing his or her life if necessary. As suggested in chapter 2, the armed forces of nation-states create such a condition by employing four overlapping and mutually supporting elements: (1) *leadership*, (2) *organizational compulsion*, (3) *group pressure*, and (4) the *survival instinct*. As shall be seen shortly, these four factors are also operational in creating and maintaining cohesion within revolutions as well.

That the revolutionary organization provides a leadership component is readily apparent and needs little elaboration here. As stated above, this organization establishes the goals and strategies of the revolution and, germane to this function, must mobilize resources, coordinate actions, establish acceptable patterns of behavior, and punish errant members.

Group or peer pressure is an effective tool for establishing and sustaining acceptable patterns of behavior. Recalling the citations from Ardant Du Picq, Morris Janowitz, and S. L. A. Marshall presented in chapter 2, men who are not totally accepted as part of a primary group are much less likely to subordinate their will and personal well-being to that group than men who are integral members of the group. Moreover, what the group perceives to be acceptable behavior governs how each member of the group behaves, providing they have been fully socialized within that group. The importance of this has not been lost upon revolutionary organizations, which endeavor to create small, closely knit cells of individuals who are all socialized in the same manner.

This socialization is critical to the success of the revolution because, as Paul Wilkinson points out, early in the revolutionary mobilization process the only advantage the terrorist can hope to generate is superior morale and political will.[37] This must be sufficient to compensate for their extreme weakness in military and political resources. It should come as no surprise, therefore, that the revolutionary organization places so much emphasis on properly indoctrinating new recruits to the movement. This indoctrination, according to Peter Watson, rests upon two psychological principles: (1) conformity comes from absolute control, and (2) behavior shapes attitudes.[38]

Behind the principle that conformity comes from absolute control is the idea of totally resocializing the individual. This entails at least the partial disruption of former patterns of behavior and social bonds. It is a concept with which military training systems throughout the world are familiar. Writing of military boot camp Gwynne Dyer says,

> Basic training is not really about teaching people skills; it's about changing them, so that they can do things they would not dream of otherwise. It works by applying enormous physical and mental pressure to men who have been isolated from their normal civilian environment and placed in one where the only right way to think and behave is the way the [military] wants them to.[39]

At the most basic level this is precisely how terrorist organizations train their combatants as well. Of course, revolutionary terrorists endeavor to change their recruits to a much larger degree than do most military organizations, consequently their methods are much more extensive, harsh, and unyielding. And terroristic force is an extremely effective tool in this reorientation process. Again as Dyer notes, "The first stage in any conversion process is the destruction of an individual's former beliefs and confidence, and his reduction to a position of helplessness and need."[40] In the individual's extreme anxiety he becomes more malleable and often readily accepts any positive feedback from his new environment, even if it means behaving in a manner he would have considered unacceptable a short time before. This behavior can range from driving a bayonet into a human being to placing a bomb in a crowded airport. The difference is merely one of degree. Of course, the stronger one's prior beliefs and the more radical the action the controlling agency expects to be performed, the less chance the resocialization will be completely successful. But revolutionary terrorist socialization processes are often quite effective. This process involves the complete isolation of the new recruit from his normal life, and through a long series of indoctrination sessions, which include heavy doses of self-criticism and high levels of anxiety, the individual becomes psychologically changed. Watson notes that new revolutionary terrorist recruits are often required to criticize themselves in public or in mass meetings where they admit to some deviation from the ideology of the revolution. Moreover, the recruits are also exposed to long discussions on ambiguous topics, since their attitudes on these have yet to be fully formed and the recruits are likely to be more malleable and easily persuaded than in discussions in areas with which the recruits already have formed strong opinions. These discussions then go on for many hours, ensuring the recruit becomes exhausted and, thereby, more susceptible to change. Finally, the recruit is often isolated from outside sources of information and support, which further reduces the ability to resist indoctrination.[41] A practical example of this technique is provided by William Henderson in his study of Viet Cong cohesion:

> Those individuals identified as "lazy," "lacking in commitment," or guilty of "rightest thoughts," or "a lack of an objective point of view," and so on, were subjected to criticism sessions of varying severity, depending upon the gravity of their deviation. Criticism was a psychological technique designed to bring anxiety to the [VC] soldier, who was culturally dependent for security upon his relationship with the group. The relief from anxiety produced by the individual's reaffirmation of his intent to comply with group expectations was a strong force for cohesion.[42]

Although most terrorist recruits are predisposed to such a lifestyle, even initially hostile persons can be susceptible to resocialization. Perhaps the most famous case is Patricia Hearst who, within eight weeks of being kidnapped, participated in a bank robbery for the Symbionese Liberation Army.

The commission of a crime also enhances the recruit's dependence upon the group by further isolating him from the rest of society. This is the second element of the resocialization process—behavior shapes attitude. As Watson points out,

> When you do something you have to rationalize why you have done it, so you change your attitudes [so that they are] in line with your behavior. . . . Not only do these [criminal acts] provide the opportunity for blackmail . . . they also help persuade the recruit that he is a member of something that matters, that is worth breaking the law for.[43]

Once an individual is socialized into the group, group pressure tends to keep that individual in the group. The group becomes that individual's main source of self-esteem—particularly when the revolutionary terrorist becomes a wanted man and cannot return to his old way of life. According to Paul Wilkinson, "It is partly for this reason that the classic exponents of revolutionary terrorism, such as Sergei Nechayev and Johann Most, have insisted on the need for the individual terrorist to utterly sever his ties of affection with his family and friends."[44] As Sergei Nechayev admonishes in his *Catechism of the Revolutionist*, "The revolutionary considers his friend and holds dear only a person who has shown himself in practice to be as much a revolutionary as he himself."[45]

It is here that group pressure gives over to the survival instinct. Not only do soldiers perceive their primary group to be their main source of self-esteem, but it also becomes their primary source of security as well. If the integrity of the group is threatened, then so are the individual members. Consequently, it is critical for each member of the group to be trusted by and to trust in return all of the other members of the group. The means the revolutionary terrorists employ to ensure this trust is quite simple. It is to make each new recruit an accomplice of terror—a wanted person. Frantz Fanon has pointed out that this is critical in ensuring the cohesion of the terrorist group:

> The group requires that each individual perform an irrevocable action. In Algeria, for example, where almost all the men who called on the people to join the national struggle were condemned to death or [were] searched for the French police, confidence was proportional to the hopelessness of each case. You could be sure of a new recruit [only] when he could no longer go back into the colonial system.[46]

Military and revolutionary organizations alike understand the importance to group cohesion of creating conditions wherein the incumbent members of the group associate security with that group. In such conditions, threatening situations only serve to increase rather than decrease the cohesion of the group.

This goes far in explaining how individuals socialized to society's norms can violate them to such a degree once they join a terrorist group. Jerrold Post in a study on the psychodynamic theory of terrorist behavior suggests the answer might be found in studying the Unification Church. In this study he notes that American young people willingly accepted a totally new system of norms when joining the church, even to the point of having their spouses chosen for them by the Reverend Moon.[47] It is suggested in another study by M. Galanter that those who found the greatest degree of security from the Unification Church were most likely to accept its mores and least likely to tolerate dissidence within the group.[48] As Post writes,

> In effect, to question the ethos of the group was to threaten the basis for their security. . . . [This] relationship between loneliness and psychological distress and staying in the group and the unquestioning acceptance of the group's standards probably apply to Terrorist groups as well. . . . For the Moonies, maintaining the boundary of the group is critical, for if it is breached, the [cohesion] of the group is threatened, [and] members might be influenced to return to the society from which they came. With the Terrorist group, the threat is even more extreme [since] transgressing the boundary may lead to death or imprisonment.[49]

Survival instinct, then, is operative in the maintenance of the cohesion of the terrorist group. Still, there are no doubt many who, once they get in, wish to return to society. Because this is such a grave risk to the revolution, few if any are ever allowed to return. It is here that the first of the four elements of cohesion come into play—organizational compulsion.

Like any military organization, revolutionary terrorists must instill order and discipline in its combatants. This is achieved through the development of special elements whose primary purpose is the enforcement of internal discipline. As John Wolf has noted,

> A terrorist organization of the FLN or Tupamaro variety establish . . . specialized enforcement units and attach them to their command coun-

cils for the purpose of executing sentences pronounced by a "revolutionary judiciary" upon those who attempt to leave the organization or others who were found guilty of some other serious breach of discipline.[50]

Moreover, Paul Wilkinson has observed, "some of the most savage acts of repressive terror are imposed on the members of the organization to impose an iron discipline of fear on the whole organization."[51] One particularly stark example is provided to us by Walter Laquer:

> In February 1972, a United Red Army hideout was discovered in Karuizawa, a mountain spa some eighty miles from Tokyo. There fourteen mangled and tortured bodies were found; one half of the group had liquidated the others for antirevolutionary failings, a few had been buried alive.[52]

Certainly there are many other equally graphic examples. The important point here is that the revolutionary organization must be willing and able to apply coercion and, if necessary, lethal force against its own members to maintain strict internal discipline. As the previously cited example of the U.S. Army in Vietnam clearly shows, without discipline the cohesion of the military organization begins to wane when facing combat conditions. This is critical for revolutionaries, especially in the early phases of the revolutionary mobilization process, since it is only in moral force that they are likely to generate any superiority over the incumbent regime. In so doing, the revolutionaries are likely to rely heavily upon organizational compulsion to maintain absolute control over those who may begin to waiver in the face of the regime's overwhelming political and military superiority. Moreover, this organizational compulsion may often include the use of terroristic force. As with the British NCOs at Waterloo or the Somme, it is often necessary to employ lethal force against a symbolic few to keep the remainder in line.

In mobilizing the revolution the revolutionary organization not only establishes the goals and strategies for the revolution but, most important, ensures the revolution remains a cohesive entity. In so doing, it employs the same group dynamics as military organizations the world over, both to socialize and maintain control of its constituent members. So long as the revolutionary organization is able to sustain its cohesion in the face of the superior armed forces of the regime, the revolution has a chance for success.

Revolutionary terrorism, then, not only plays a significant role in the mobilization of the revolution, but in the preservation of the revolution as well. Terrorism is instrumental in raising the consciousness of the target populace, inducing many to join the revolution, contributing to the undermining of the regime, and helping maintain the cohesion of the revolutionary organization. These are clearly integral elements of the revolutionary mobilization. The question now becomes, are these activities by the revolutionary terrorist acts of warfare? It is this question that we now address.

## Revolutionary Terrorism—A Form of War?

For revolutionary terrorism to qualify as a form of war it must meet the three basic criteria outlined in the first three chapters of this book. It must involve the employment of lethal force (1) for a political objective and (2) in a manner that seeks to destroy the enemy's will to resist. Moreover, to be a form of war, revolutionary terrorism must (3) also involve armed engagements between contending political entities that are seeking to physically compel each other.

The first two criteria have been adequately dealt with in the preceding section and require little further discussion here. From the above, it is apparent that revolutionary terrorism can help mobilize the revolution: a political objective. Additionally, the will to resist is also targeted since the primary method employed by revolutionary terrorists is the moral isolation of the incumbent regime from the general populace. This increasing isolation ultimately shatters the political cohesion of the state and undermines the willingness of the regime's armed forces to continue to support the crumbling and isolated regime. The question remains, however, does revolutionary terrorism meet the last criterion: does this form of lethal force involve armed engagements with the regime?

As will be recalled from chapter 3, the principle of engagement requires that both political entities employ lethal force to compel the other to do its will. Upon initial reflection, it would appear that not only does revolutionary terrorism *not* involve such armed engagements, but the terrorists do everything in their power to avoid such clashes. Indeed, the targets most often attacked by revolutionary terrorists are rarely armed, and in a majority of the cases where such targets do have a means to resist, terrorists usually employ force unilaterally. From this, it is easy to conclude that revolutionary terrorism violates this, von Clausewitz's preeminent principle of war, and therefore cannot be considered a form of war.

Upon closer inspection, however, it becomes apparent that this is an overly narrow interpretation of the principle of engagement. To be sure this principle normally manifests itself in the form of a battle—i.e., the simultaneous and reciprocal employment of lethal force on both sides—but nothing limits this principle to only this manifestation of force. Often, even in conventional warfare, lethal force is emplolyed unilaterally. This is particularly true at the tactical level. For instance, to name just a few examples, submarines torpedoed unarmed merchant ships during World Wars I and II; fighter planes strafed unarmed trains and barges; and bombers and artillery bombarded cities, ports, and factories that had no means with which to reply.

Von Clausewitz's principle of engagement is therefore not restricting warfare only to those instances, as in a duel, where both sides are equally capable of inflicting lethal force on each other. Otherwise, such time-honored military tactics as the surprise attack and the ambush would fall outside the pale of warfare. As von Clausewitz observes, "[When] the preservation of one's own fighting forces [is] the dominant consideration . . . the attacker will attempt destructive action only under favorable circumstances. . . ."[53] Von Clausewitz acknowledges that engagements could occur without battles, but he cautions,

> These means are generally overrated; they seldom achieve so much as a battle, and involve the risk of drawbacks that may have been overlooked. They are tempting because they cost so little. [But] they should always be looked upon as minor investments that can yield only minor dividends, appropriate to limited circumstances and weaker motives. But they are obviously preferable to pointless battles—victories that cannot be fully exploited.[54]

Clearly, then, von Clausewitz understood that when one side is considerably weaker than the other, it will avoid open confrontations with the enemy's armed forces to the greatest degree possible, and military operations will be restricted to hit and run or other such tactics where damage can be done to the enemy without further weakening the attacker. Sun Tzu puts it another way, "Now an army may be likened to water, for just as flowing water avoids heights and hastens to the lowlands, so an army avoids strength and strikes weakness."[55] These ideas were "rediscovered" and implemented by T. E. Lawrence as he strove to turn the fledgling Arab national rebellion into a viable military threat to the Ottoman Empire during World War I. According to Lawrence,

> Battles in Arabia were a mistake, since we profited in them only by the ammunition the enemy fired off. . . . [Marshal Maurice de] Saxe told us that irrational battles were the refuges of fools: rather they seemed to me impositions on the side which believed itself weaker, hazards made unavoidable either by lack of land room or by the need to defend material property dearer than the lives of soldiers. We had nothing material to lose, so our best line was to defend nothing. . . .[56]

Revolutionary terrorism is the ultimate expression of this idea. When the Chinese People's Army or Viet Cong went into a village and assassinated the village chief or informant, it was a blow to the central government's power structure. Although no battle occurred, the terrorists did conduct a "destructive action" for a political end. Likewise, when the government forces entered that same village and "executed" suspected revolutionaries or their sympathizers, so, too, did they conduct a destructive act for a political end.

Engagements, therefore, do not have to involve open battles. It is sufficient that both sides employ lethal force to weaken their opponent morally and materially. The means each side employs, however, will rest upon the political-military situation and the objectives sought. For instance, the regime is generally waging a total war of position and annihilation against the revolution. Thus the regime seeks open conflicts with the revolutionaries where the former's superior combat power can be brought to bear. The revolutionary terrorists, however, are most often waging a total war of evasion and attrition. Their political objective is the absolute destruction of the regime, which in Clausewitzian terms means the destruction of the enemy's armed forces, occupation of his territory, and destruction of his will to resist. But because of their extreme weakness, revolutionary terrorists cannot achieve this by direct means and must therefore employ operational objectives commensurate with their limited strength. This requires them, particularly in the earliest phases of the revolutionary mobilization process, to adopt strategies and tactics permitting the terrorists to attack the enemy and begin wearing him down through attrition, without getting hit in return. Clearly this calls for a special form of engagement on the part of the revolutionary terrorists.

Revolutionaries can also find themselves waging a limited war, that is, a war in which the political objective is not necessarily to totally destroy the governing entity but merely exhaust its willingness to continue the conflict. This is the classical colonial situation wherein the insurgents do not wish or seek the total destruction of the colonial regime, but simply want the regime to tire of the conflict, cut its losses, and withdraw. As in the case of the Viet Cong, the insurgents were fighting two wars simultaneously: a total war against Saigon and a limited war against Washington.

Like all military organizations, terrorists have two basic weapon-types available to them: shock and fire. As pointed out in chapter 2, shock weapons are generally more effective—that is, they are more decisive since they result in the capture of territory and/or prisoners—but are also the most expensive to the users in terms of potential friendly casualties. This is due to the fact that the employment of shock weaponry requires the user to expose himself to the enemy.

Revolutionary terrorists employ shock to seize banks, hijack aircraft, or attack airports. But as the 1972 Japanese Red Army attack at Lod airport and the 1985 Palestinian attack at the Rome international airport clearly underscore, shock attacks are often *very* costly for the attackers. The terrorists must therefore adopt special tactics to mitigate the enemy's superior combat power. This is normally done by seizing hostages, the safety of which normally prevents the regime from bringing its overwhelming combat power to bear. Even so, such operations are extremely risky for the terrorists, and should a fire fight break out, as in Munich in 1972, the terrorist casualties—killed, wounded, and captured—are invariably 100 percent.

Fire weapons afford a much less risky, if less effective, means of hitting the enemy. The standard fire weapon of the terrorist is, of course, the time bomb, and like all fire weapons, this permits the attacker to strike the enemy with minimum exposure and risk. The primary drawback is that, in most cases, it lacks the decisiveness and effectiveness of a shock attack. Whereas a shock attack can result in the seizure of hostages who can afford the terrorists hundreds of days of press coverage, a bomb attack is often quickly forgotten. Yet the time bomb permits even the weakest terrorist organization to strike the enemy without unduly risking any casualties.

The question still remains, however, do these operations truly constitute a military engagement? This is where the seven principles of combat come into play. Since all military engagements are governed by these principles, it is reasonable to assume that if these seven principles are present in a terrorist attack, it is a military engagement. A few examples should be sufficient to establish this.

One of the most dramatic and successful examples of a terrorist organization overcoming superior combat power through the proper application of the principles of combat is the 1983 bombing of the Marine barracks in Beirut, Lebanon. By effectively using mass, maneuver, economy of force, unity of command, security, surprise, and simplicity, a single terrorist "overcame the theoretical military advantage of a Marine amphibious unit supported by aircraft carriers, a battleship and the nation's combined intelligence capability to gain a major political victory."[57] The *mass* of a 12,000-pound bomb was sufficient to destroy the designated target. One driver in one truck ensured *economy of force* since both the truck and the driver were already deemed expendable to the terrorists. *Maneuver* allowed the terrorists to place the weapon where it would be most decisive. *Unity of command* and *simplicity* were apparent in that the few elements involved required very limited command and control and achieved the planned results. It is also evident that all intelligence, logistics, planning, and operational execution were well coordinated, resulting in the application of force in the precise place and manner to achieve the desired political objective. Finally, and perhaps most important, the terrorists achieved *surprise* and maintained their *security* up until the moment of the attack. The attack occurred at a time, place, and manner for which the Marine commander was unprepared. Above all other factors, it was *security* and *surprise* that enabled the terrorists to achieve the force multiplication necessary so that one man in a truck could kill 241 enemy soldiers and force the United States to modify its political objectives in the region. It also ensured, at least for the near term, greater Islamic participation in the Lebanese government.

When revolutionary terrorist organizations ignore these principles of combat they are invariably defeated, often with catastrophic results. Indeed, according to Abraham Guillen, it was the loss of mobility— i.e., the ability to *maneuver*—and *security* that ultimately caused the collapse of the Tupamaros. He writes,

> By tying themselves to fixed terrain . . . the Tupamaros . . . lost both mobility and security. . . . In order to avoid encirclement and annihila-

tion through house-to-house searches, the guerrillas can best survive not by establishing fixed urban bases, but by living apart and fighting together. . . . Because the Tupamaros immobilized many of their commandos in fixed quarters, they were exposed in 1972 to mass detentions, they lost a large part of their armaments and related equipment and were compelled to transfer military supplies to the countryside for hiding.[58]

The Tupamaros' lack of security meant that the regime's forces could find their bases of operations and mass sufficient forces against them to destroy them. Moreover, by losing the ability to maneuver, the Tupamaros could not avoid the coming blow and were thereby doomed to defeat. Their last-ditch effort to move to the countryside proved illusory when the leadership brought along the same encumbrances that tied them down in the cities and at the same time robbed them of any remaining security they could have derived by hiding among the populace in a large city.

In another example, the Marxist revolutionary terrorist group that operated in Argentina during the 1970s known as the ERP suffered a devastating setback in December 1975 when it failed to achieve surprise or sufficient mass in an attack on a military stronghold at Monte Chingolo, a few miles south of Buenos Aires. According to Christopher Dobson and Ronald Payne,

> The garrison seems to have been forewarned and was ready for the attacking party. The fighting went on all night and in the end six civilians, nine soldiers and 85 guerrillas lay dead. It was a devastating blow and followed a series of defeats in the guerrillas' attempts to occupy a "liberated area" in the rugged mountains and jungle of Tucman. They lost an estimated 600 men in this campaign. . . .[59]

Poor security caused the Symbionese Liberation Army to give up the principles of mass, surprise, maneuver, and economy of force when their hideout was discovered and overwhelmed by 150 Los Angeles policemen and 100 FBI agents.[60] Lack of maneuver and poor security also resulted in the annihilation of the pro-Palestinian terrorists at Entebbe airport in July 1976. Moreover, lack of unity of command has drastically reduced the combat power of the Palestine Liberation Organization (PLO), which, according to Abu Iyad, has reduced that organization's cohesion and effectiveness.[61] Clearly, then, the principles of combat are critical to victory by revolutionary terrorists at both the tactical and strategic levels. From this, it may also be concluded that revolutionary terrorist operations are military operations from the most basic level of analysis. What is of greater importance to this book is that the presence and necessity of adherence to the seven principles of combat provide sufficient evidence to conclude that revolutionary terrorist operations constitute the element of armed engagement to establish that this form of terrorism is indeed a form of war.

## Summation

Revolutionary terrorism is clearly a form of war. The employment of lethal force for a political objective is readily seen in terrorism's integral function within the revolutionary mobilization process. Its employment of lethal force on the moral plane is also apparent, both to shatter the cohesion of the enemy and to sustain its own. Finally, revolutionary terrorism qualifies as the employment of force against force since revolutionary terrorist operations meet the basic definition of armed engagements.

The political objective of the revolutionary terrorists is to overthrow the incumbent regime. Because of their extreme weakness, this can only be brought about by indirect means. In this case, these indirect means involve the mobilization of the revolution, taking the revolutionary mobilization process from the preparatory phase to the expansion phase. In this process the terrorists must carefully apply force to raise the consciousness of the target of influence, increase their participation, undermine the regime, and assist in the building and maintenance of the revolutionary organization. All four of these are clearly political objectives that are within the capabilities of the terrorists.

Due to their extreme weakness, revolutionary terrorists rely very heavily upon the employment of force on the moral plane. In this way, the miniscule physical force available to the terrorists is converted to considerable power as it influences an increasing number of people, both in terms of terrorizing members of the regime and positively influencing the general populace. Equally important, revolutionary terrorism is instrumental in sustaining the cohesion of the revolutionary organization in the face of overwhelming odds. By providing leadership and creating conditions where group pressure, organizational compulsion and survival instinct become operative, revolutionary terrorists—

in precisely the same manner as military organizations the world over—ensure the maximum cohesion possible even under extremely adverse circumstances.

Finally, revolutionary terrorism involves the use of force on the physical plane. This is manifested in armed engagements that rest solidly upon the principles of combat espoused by Karl von Clausewitz. By focusing that force on the moral isolation of the regime, the government finds it increasingly difficult to maintain its forces of coercion. These forces of coercion are the center of gravity for the regime, and as Skocpol and others have clearly established, the loss of these forces is catastrophic for the incumbents. Although it is apparent that both the regime and the revolutionary terrorists are applying physical force to compel each other at the strategic level, it is less so at the tactical. Yet, as the Beirut bombing, Tupamaros, Symbionese Liberation Army, and Entebbe examples illustrate, the seven principles of combat are critical to success and are operative even when only one side is employing lethal force at a specific moment.

Revolutionary terrorism, then, involves the three grand elements of warfare: (1) the use of force for a political objective, (2) the use of force on the moral plane, and (3) the use of force against force on the physical plane. It is safe to conclude, therefore, that revolutionary terrorism is a form of war.

## Notes

1. William Friedland, *Revolutionary Theory* (Totowa, N.J.: Rowman & Allanheld Publishers Inc., 1982), p. 169.

2. Mao Tse-Tung, *On Guerrilla Warfare*, translated and edited by Samuel B. Griffith (New York: Praeger Publishers, 1961), pp. 20–22.

3. Ibid.

4. Thomas H. Greene, *Comparative Revolutionary Movements: Search for Theory and Justice* (Englewood Cliffs, N.J.: Prentice-Hall, Inc., 1984), p. 131.

5. Ibid.

6. Paul Wilkinson, "Terrorist Movements," *Terrorism: Theory and Practice*, edited by Yonah Alexander, David Carlton, and Paul Wilkinson (Boulder, Colo.: Westview Press, 1979), p. 107.

7. Friedland, op. cit., p. 155.

8. Ted Robert Gurr, *Why Men Rebel*, 4th ed. (Princeton: Princeton University Press, 1974), p. 24.

9. Martha Crenshaw, "The Causes of Terrorism," *Comparative Politics* (July 1981), p. 386. As quoted in Alex P. Schmid, *Political Terrorism: A Research Guide to Concepts, Theories, Data Bases, and Literature* (Amsterdam: North Holland Publishing Co., 1983; Transaction Books, 1985), p. 219.

10. Gurr, op. cit., p. 34.

11. Theda Skocpol, *States and Social Revolutions: A Comparative Analysis of France, Russia and China* (New York: Cambridge University Press, 1983), p. 110.

12. Ibid., p. 157.

13. Carlos Marighella, *Minimanual of the Urban Guerrilla* (Havana: Tricontinental Congress, no date). As quoted in Robert Moss, *Urban Guerrillas* (London: Temple Smith, 1972), p. 198.

14. Christopher Dobson and Ronald Payne, *The Terrorists: Their Weapons, Leaders, and Tactics* (New York: Facts on File, Inc., 1982), p. 13. Quoting Marighella from his *Minimanual of the Urban Guerrilla*.

15. Eqbal Ahmad, "Revolutionary Warfare and Counterinsurgency," *Guerrilla Strategies: An Historical Anthology from the Long March to Afghanistan*, edited by Gerard Chaliand (Berkeley: University of California Press, 1982), p. 245.

16. Ibid., p. 249.

17. Ibid.

18. Che Guevara, *Guerrilla Warfare* (New York: Monthly Review Press, 1961), p. 26.

19. James Pinckney Harrison, *The Endless War: Vietnam's Struggle for Independence* (New York: McGraw-Hill Book Co., 1982; McGraw-Hill Book Co., paperback edition, 1983), p. 190.

20. Robert Asprey, *War in the Shadows: The Guerrilla in History*, vol. 2. (Garden City, N.Y.: Doubleday Co., Inc., 1975), p. 1194.

21. Ibid., p. 1197.

22. Skocpol, op. cit., p. 16.

23. Ibid., p. 32.

24. Ibid., pp. 100–111.

25. W. Bruce Lincoln, *Passage Through Armageddon: The Russians in War and Revolution* (New York: Simon & Schuster Inc., 1986), p. 21.

26. Jack Goldstone, ed., *Revolutions: Theoretical, Comparative, and Historical Studies* (New York: Harcourt, Brace, Jovanovich, Inc., 1986), p. 8.

27. Martha Crenshaw, *Terrorism, Legitimacy and Power: The Consequences of Political Violence* (Middletown: Wesleyan University Press, 1984), p. 27.

28. David Carlton, "The Future of Political Substate Violence," *Terrorism: Theory and Practice*, op. cit., p. 207.

29. James Burke, *Connections* (Boston: Little, Brown & Co., Inc., 1978), p. 1.

30. Richard Rubenstein, *The Cunning of History: The Holocaust and the American Future* (New York: Harper & Row Publishers, Inc., 1978), p. 95.

31. Greene, op. cit., p. 132.

32. Serge Stepniak-Kravchinsky, "Underground Russia" (London: 1883), in Walter Laquer, ed. *The Terrorism Reader: A Historical Anthology* (New York: New American Library, 1978; Meridian Books, 1978), p. 87.

33. Sun Tzu, *The Art of War*, edited and translated by Samuel B. Griffith (London: Oxford University Press, 1963; Oxford University Press paperback, 1971), p. 68.

34. Stanley Karnow, *Vietnam: A History* (New York: Viking Press, 1983), p. 238.

35. Friedland, op. cit., p. 128.

36. Harrison, op. cit., p. 190.

37. Wilkinson, op. cit., p. 110.

38. Peter Watson, *War on the Mind: The Military Uses and Abuses of Psychology* (New York: Basic Books, Inc., Publishers, 1978), pp. 344–45.

39. Gwynne Dyer, *War* (New York: Crown Publishers, Inc., 1985), pp. 109–110.

40. Ibid., p. 111.

41. Watson, op. cit., pp. 344–45.

42. William D. Henderson, *Why the Viet Cong Fought: A Study of Motivation and Control in a Modern Army in Combat* (Westport, Conn.: Greenwood Press, Inc., 1979), p. 89.

43. Watson, op. cit., p. 344.

44. Wilkinson, op. cit., p. 113.

45. Sergei Nechayev, "Catechism of the Revolutionist," *The Terrorism Reader: A Historical Anthology*, edited by Walter Laquer, op. cit., p. 69.

46. Frantz Fanon, *The Wretched of the Earth* (London: Hammandsworth, 1967), p. 67. As quoted in Wilkinson, op. cit., p. 113.

47. Jerrold M. Post, "Notes on Psychodynamic Theory of Terrorist Behavior," *Terrorism: An International Journal* 7, no. 3 (1984), pp. 252–53.

48. M. Galanter, "Engaged Members of the Unification Church: Impact of a Charismatic Large Group on Adaptation and Behavior," *Archives of General Psychiatry* (in press). As quoted in Post, op. cit., p. 253.

49. Post, op. cit., pp. 252–53.

50. John B. Wolf, "Organization and Management Practices of Urban Terrorist Groups," *Terrorism: An International Journal* 1, no. 2 (1978): 177.

51. Wilkinson, op. cit., p. 114.

52. Laquer, *Terrorism: A Study of National and International Political Violence* (Boston: Little Brown & Co., Inc., 1977), p. 125.

53. Karl von Clausewitz, *On War*, edited and translated by Michael Howard and Peter Paret (Princeton: Princeton University Press, 1976), p. 529.

54. Ibid.

55. Sun Tzu, op. cit., p. 101.

56. T. E. Lawrence, *Seven Pillars of Wisdom* (New York: Doubleday & Co., Inc., 1935; Penguin Books, 1985), p. 201.

57. Jefferey W. Wright, "Terrorism: A Mode of Warfare," *Military Review* (Ft. Leavenworth, Kan.: U.S. Army Command and General Staff College, October 1984), p. 38.

58. Abraham Guillen, "Urban Guerrilla Strategy," *Guerrilla Strategies*, edited by Gerard Chaliand, op. cit., pp. 317–19.

59. Dobson and Payne, op. cit., p. 203.

60. Bernard K. Johnpoll, "Perspectives on Political Terrorism in the United States," *International Terrorism: National, Regional and Global Perspectives* (New York: Praeger Publishers, 1976), p. 41.

61. Abu Iyad, "Al Fatah's Autocriticism," *Guerrilla Strategies*, edited by Gerard Chaliand, op. cit., p. 326.

# CHAPTER 8

# STATE TERRORISM

■

## Introduction

State terrorism involves the employment of lethal force by state governments upon civilian populations for the express purpose of weakening or destroying their will to resist. This form of terrorism can be divided into two general categories: internal and external. Internal state terrorism is the use of lethal force by a state government against its own civilian population and can have two purposes: (1) to repress the people, making them apolitical or politically malleable, and/or (2) to weaken the population's willingness to support revolutionary or other antigovernment movements. This type of terrorism will hereafter be referred to as *repression terrorism*. External state terrorism involves the use of lethal force by a state government against a foreign civilian population ostensibly to weaken or destroy that population's morale and willingness to support its own government. This can be of two types depending upon the method employed: (1) *military terror-*

*ism* and (2) *state-sponsored terrorism*. As the name suggests, military terrorism involves the employment of terroristic force by elements of a given state's military forces against a symbolic target within the targeted entity. In state-sponsored terrorism the terroristic force is employed by surrogate terrorist forces usually having only clandestine ties to the supporting state.

This chapter will examine each of these forms of state terrorism to determine which qualify as war. The first to be examined is repression terrorism. In this section we will analyze the rulers' relationship to the ruled as well as the methods by which the rulers employ terrorism against the populace. In the next section we will analyze military terrorism, examining how this form of terrorism functions and the purposes for which it has been used by sovereign political entities. Third, we will examine state-sponsored terrorism, analyzing how this form of terrorism functions and to what ends it may be employed. In each section we will ascertain whether the type of terrorism being examined qualifies as a form of war.

## Repression Terrorism

All modern nation-states are heavily dependent upon power and coercion to command and control their resources—particularly their populations. As Andrew Schmookler points out in his book *The Parable of the Tribes*, the evolution of civilization is, quite simply, the story of ever-increasing social inequalities culminating in modern societies in which a highly centralized state bureaucracy has a virtual monopoly on power and most forms of coercion. Schmookler writes,

> A system has effective central control to the extent that there exists within it a part that can direct and coordinate all parts of the system. The evolution of civilization has manifested a broad trend toward the creation of such control. This has entailed first a differentiation of power among the members of society and second an elaboration of the organizational means by which the powerful parts can control society as a whole.[1]

This command and control by the powerful parts is, of course, highly dependent upon coercion to varying degrees. Examples are legion, ranging from traffic tickets, to IRS audits, to capital punishment. Certainly, many would consider capital punishment to be terrorism. Inasmuch as the state seeks to employ lethal force to "terrorize" or deter others from committing similar crimes, and to the degree that many, if not most, death-row inmates consider such punishment abnormal, capital punishment is "terroristic" as defined in this book. Still, it would be incorrect to label such states as terroristic based upon the use of capital punishment alone. For instance one could easily argue that the target population is not death-row inmates, but the general populace, the majority of which (particularly in democratic societies that elect the officials that make the laws) clearly see capital punishment as *not* being an abnormal use of force. And, since the majority of those subject to that force do not perceive it to be abnormal, it cannot be terrorism.

A terrorist regime is one that engages in repression terrorism against elements of its own population to create conditions sufficient for that regime to remain in political control. In other words, repression terrorism is the systematic use of lethal force by a state apparatus for the purpose of suppressing, quelling, or restraining political opponents within the population.[2] To the extent that maintaining political control over the population is a political objective, repression terrorism can be considered the employment of lethal force for a political end. As shall be seen, however, this alone does not qualify repression terrorism as a form of war.

As Alex Schmid observes, repression terrorism has clearly had a longer history than other forms of political terrorism.[3] Regimes throughout history have employed lethal force against symbolic victims as a means of terrorizing and neutralizing potential resistance within their respective populations. The moment humanity moved away from the egalitarian hunter-gathering society toward more complex social systems involving a hierarchy of command and control mechanisms the rulers began to employ force to maintain control of the ruled. That such a technique has survived down through the ages is a testament to its utility. According to Ted Gurr, "So long as men anticipate severe and certain retribution for prescribed actions they are likely to restrain their anger [against the regime]."[4] Theda Skocpol would agree. She writes, "Even after great loss of legitimacy has occurred, a state can remain quite stable . . . [provided] its coercive organizations remain coherent and effective."[5] But there is a price.

As was mentioned in chapter 5, coercive measures may be an effective and efficient means of *controlling* a population, but it is not an efficient means to *govern*. Clearly the most efficient way to govern a population is by the consent of the people. In this way resources are not wasted on maintaining internal controls. As Schmookler has noted, "The ruler who relies on brute force needs more power to conquer and hold the same territory. Therefore the value of consent must be part of the calculus of power."[6]

From this, it may be inferred that leaders who employ repressive terrorism normally do so not out of preference, but because they are compelled to do so. Indeed, according to Alexander Dallin and George Breslauer, repression terrorism is generally employed by those states that do not enjoy widespread legitimacy among the populace.[7] Although this situation is possible in long-standing regimes, lack of legitimacy is normally a factor of fledgling regimes that have recently acquired power through a coup d'état or revolution. Classic examples, of course, are the Red Terrors following the French and Russian revolutions.

To be sure, the Red Terror of the French Revolution was to become the archetypal expression of this form of terrorism. Although later "terrors" would claim far more victims, they would still not surpass the utter horror nor result in any more effective political control than the French Red Terror. Owen Connelly writes,

> The guillotine still appears to represent in the Western mind the ultimate in political repression, bloodletting, and misuse of power. Its some 2600 victims in Paris seem an insignificant number when compared to the millions executed by the Nazis during World War II or the five to ten million who died during Stalin's collectivization of farms in the Soviet Union. Yet the guillotine retains its horrible image. . . . Nothing before had created such horror abroad or so effectively intimidated a domestic population as did the Terror.[8]

The Soviets followed suit immediately after coming to power in Russia. One of the very first organizations Lenin created upon coming to power was his secret state police, or CHEKA. The CHEKA's primary function was to neutralize enemies of the revolution and to permit the fledgling Soviet government to consolidate its power. It was an organization of coercion born of necessity, and terrorism was its primary instrument. As Felix Dzerzhinsky, the first chief of the CHEKA, reportedly commented, "We don't need justice now. We must fight to the utmost. We need a revolutionary sword to destroy all counterrevolutionaries."[9] And as William H. Chamberlin points out,

No government could have survived in Russia in those years without the use of Terrorism. . . . The national morale was completely shattered by the World War. No one, except under extreme compulsion, was willing to perform any state obligation. The older order had simply crumbled away; a new order, with new habits and standards of conduct, had not yet formed; very often the only way in which a governmental representative, whether he was a Bolshevik or a White officer, could get his orders obeyed was by flourishing a revolver.[10]

Of course, repression terrorism is not limited to postrevolutionary situations. Peter the Great and Stalin employed repression terrorism in situations wherein their governments were *relatively* secure from any overthrow attempt. These leaders simply selected repression terrorism as the most efficient means not of governing but of effecting social change. The question remains, however, regardless of the conditions in which it is employed, is repression terrorism a form of war?

Based upon the first two of the three elements of war identified previously, it appears repression terrorism could be a form of war. It involves the use of lethal force (1) for a political objective and (2) for the purpose of destroying the target entity's will to resist. But as shall be quickly established, the target entity cannot be considered to be the enemy, and moreover, repression terrorism clearly violates von Clausewitz's most important principle of war—*the engagement*—since there is no armed clash between contending political parties. This being the case, repression terrorism clearly cannot be considered a form of war.

As was stated in chapter 2, war entails the employment of lethal force for the purpose of destroying the enemy's will to resist. Given that repression terrorism is lethal force employed by a state government against its own population, the amount of force employed must be carefully regulated, or the state will wind up destroying itself by destroying the cohesion of its own population. Clearly a state whose population is "reduced to a mass of anomic individuals" cannot, by definition, be a state at all. This careful orchestration in the amount of force used and the level of damage done is presented by Eugene Walter in his landmark work that analyzed repression terrorism employed by Zulu kings in the nineteenth century. He notes that there are

five conditions necessary for the maintenance of a terroristic regime, which may also be understood as functional prerequisites: 1) A shared ideology that justifies violence. . . . [since] legitimacy suppresses outrage. 2) The victims in the process of terror must be expendable. . . . If the violence liquidates persons who are needed for essential tasks, or if replacements cannot be found for their roles, the system of cooperation breaks down. 3) Disassociation of the agents of violence and of the victims from ordinary social life. . . . 4) Terror must be balanced by working incentives that induce cooperation. . . . 5) Cooperative relationships must survive the effect of the terror.[11]

From these characteristics, particularly characteristics number four and five, it is easy to see that the regime does not intend to *destroy* or defeat an *enemy*, but simply *control a friendly* population from which may be expected a certain level of consent to be governed in such a manner. Moreover, as Martha Crenshaw points out, terrorism of any kind can only be successfully employed so long as it is perceived to be morally justifiable in the eyes of the target of influence.[12] And as Lyford P. Edwards suggests,

> The terror is not so bloody as is often assumed. . . . [Indeed], the terror is the least bloody of all phases of the revolution . . . it is not a horrible series of atrocities perpetrated by a savage mob upon innocent and helpless victims. . . . [Rather] a reign of terror is just what the name implies. It is a *reign,* not an anarchy. It is an organized, governmental regime set up with a calculated purpose of social control.[13]

Admittedly Edwards wrote the above words in 1927, before Stalin's reign of terror in the USSR during the 1930s. Clearly the death of eight million to ten million Russian peasants during this terror was far greater than anything that occurred during the revolution proper. Still, despite the fact that Stalin's main purpose in employing state-terror against the peasants was to *neutralize* them as an autonomous political collectivity, it would have been not only counterproductive but dangerous for the Soviet Union if he had destroyed them completely. He needed their support for his regime, and he needed their labor. Thus, he only created a condition of *anxiety* among the targeted group—not *despair.* As Skocpol notes, "general fear of arrest and imprisonment among the Soviet population only served to reinforce labor discipline among those who remained out of prison."[14] Although it is true that Stalin went much further than necessary if his goal was simply to neutralize the peasants—the well-publicized execution of a few hundred, or at most, a few thousand resisters would probably have been sufficient—it is also true that the vast majority of those who died were *not* victims of the terror per se. Many, if not most, simply died of starvation due to the famine caused by the collectivization of the peasant farms. Indeed, Adam Ulam estimates that the Soviet standards of living fell by as much as 25 percent during this period of collectivization.[15]

Consequently, the regime employing repression terrorism must be very careful in the level of terror it creates. It must be strong enough to destroy or neutralize the population's will to resist but not be so great as to destroy that population's cohesion and thereby undermine the regime's own power structure. This introduces a factor of moderation into the equation that von Clausewitz categorically rejects in the first chapter of his great work. As he succinctly puts it, "To introduce the principle of moderation into the theory of war . . . would always lead to logical absurdity."[16] Thus, with its built-in structure of moderation, repression terrorism cannot be a form of war.

The final and perhaps most important reason repression terrorism is not a form of war pertains to von Clausewitz's primary principle of war, the principle of engagement. In repression terrorism there is no clash of arms between contending political entities as they try to compel each other to abandon political goals. The population has no armed forces, no political structure, and no territory. Under such conditions, the only resistance open to the populace is passive resistance.

Perhaps the ultimate example of this is the aforementioned Nazi extermination of the Jews. Clearly this event represented the employment of lethal force to achieve a political goal. But it is equally clear that this event entailed almost exclusively the unilateral employment of lethal force by the regime, and any resistance encountered was generally spontaneous and most often limited to one or two isolated individuals acting on their own. Indeed, as Richard Rubenstein has noted, the ultimate irony of the Nazi genocide campaign is that it would not have been so effective or efficient had the Nazis not been able to incorporate existing Jewish bureaucracies into their own. According to Rubenstein,

> The process of taking over the Jewish communal bureaucracies and transforming them into components of the extermination process was one of the organizational triumphs of the Nazis. . . . In addition to the cultural conditioning that affected even the most assimilated Jews, the organized Jewish community was a factor in preventing effective resistance. Wherever the extermination process was put into effect, the Germans utilized the *existing leadership and organizations* of the Jewish community to assist them. . . . [Indeed] in the Warsaw Ghetto and in

Lodz, Poland, the Jewish council, or *Judenrat,* did not resist German directives even when the Germans demanded the "selection" of 10,000 Jews a day for deportation. Jewish bureaucrats made the selection; Jewish police rounded up the victims.[17]

Clearly, this is not warfare. There was no counterforce involved on the part of the Jewish community—although there were isolated uprisings such as that in Warsaw. Moreover, as Eugene Walter has suggested, this form of terrorism is only possible as long as the victims are superfluous to the maintenance of the state's power, and as long as the cohesion of the civil population is not threatened. Since the holocaust directed lethal force against a portion of the populace that was deemed superfluous both by the regime and the majority of the German people, their destruction threatened neither the cohesion of the German populace nor the power structure of the Nazi regime; it could continue unabated until it achieved its end or the process was interrupted by outside forces. In short, the Jews were *in,* but not *of* the German population.

Of course, it is possible that members of a regime's population might coalesce into armed bands and employ lethal force to resist the regime. This is a revolutionary situation in which totally new and different criteria apply. As described in the previous chapter, the regime can view the revolutionaries as enemies and can wage war against them. Moreover, the regime may engage in repressive terrorism and revolutionary warfare simultaneously, but this does not make repression terrorism a form of war. Those members of the populace who do not join the revolutionaries are *not* enemies of the regime, and the regime must treat them accordingly. The regime may still subject them to terror to a degree necessary to control them but not to the degree that their social cohesion collapses and they are effectively destroyed. For this, and other reasons iterated above, repression terrorism is not a form of war.

## Military Terrorism

No study on terrorism as a form of war would be complete without examining the employment of terror by the military. Military terrorism is an ancient art that has become increasingly effective with the advances in technology and increased complexity of the sociopolitical infrastructures found in modern societies. Simply put, military terrorism is the employment of terrorism by a nation's military instrument against the civilian population of an enemy nation for the purpose of (1) undermining that population's *will* to support its own government, or (2) shattering the cohesion of the population making it *unable* to support its government. Thus, where repression terrorism sought to control the population, military terrorism seeks to make that target population unmanageable.

Terrorism, as defined in this book, is the employment of abnormal lethal force against a symbolic victim for the purpose of causing chronic fear or terror in a target collectivity identifying with that symbolic victim. As was previously mentioned, at the most abstract level, war functions in much the same way as terrorism. Whenever one combatant shoots another he not only hopes to remove the man he shot from the power equation, but he also desires that the victim's comrades will lose heart and cease fighting. In short, he wants to terrorize them. Still, despite the similarities, this is not terrorism. It is not terrorism because the force employed is not considered abnormal, either by the perpetrator or the recipient. Because this concept is so crucial to this book it needs to be examined further.

First, of course, it is necessary to operationalize "abnormal" force. As was mentioned in chapter 5, what qualifies as being abnormal depends upon the defining agency. It is, at best, a highly subjective concept that varies over time and place. Still, it is a factor in force employment and therefore must be clearly identified.

In chapter 5 it was suggested that what is abnormal is what the target entity perceives to be abnormal. This can be operationalized by two criteria: (1) the target entity clearly identifies the force being employed against it as being abnormal, and (2) the target entity either refrains from using the same methods in its own force employment or, if it uses such force, admits that it, too, is employing abnormal force.

It must be stressed, of course, that what is being addressed here is the general methods of force employment, not the means. It would be ludicrous, for example, to accept an argument by the Palestine Liberation Organization that aerial bombardment by fighter-bombers is terrorism and therefore they will refrain from using such means in their struggle against Israel. What is at issue is not what weapon system or piece of hardware is used but how it is used and against whom.

The central issue around abnormal force, at least since the Peace of Westphalia in 1648, has been the application of lethal force against noncombatants. Indeed, perhaps the most universally accepted element in any discussion of terrorism is its targeting noncombatants. As Alex Schmid notes, "A terrorist act lacks the symmetry of a duel or the preparedness of both parties for the fight of a battle."[18] He continues,

> In regular warfare the deliberate killing of noncombatants is not permitted and is considered a "war crime." Soldiers taken prisoner during hostilities are treated humanely according to conventions which protect their rights. By becoming nonbelligerent through capitulation, surrender or capture, soldiers can be reasonably certain that their lives will be saved. The prisoners of . . . terrorists, however, either as kidnapped [or disappeared] individuals or as a group of trapped hostages, cannot affect their own fate by handing in their weapons and [or] promising nonresistance.[19]

The primary difference between a terrorist and a soldier, then, is that the latter is willing *and able* to recognize the noncombatant status of persons in the enemy camp. Civilians, particularly women and children, are normally granted noncombatant status. Moreover, the enemy soldier can become a noncombatant, if he so chooses, simply by laying aside his weapon and surrendering. The terrorist, on the other hand, does not, and in most cases cannot, recognize noncombatant status. He takes no prisoners, but hostages. He does not merely inflict casualties to weaken enemy combat power, but kills the helpless and infirm, even when it is within his power not to do so. The soldier and the terrorist are therefore *not equivalent*. It is a fact that cannot be stressed too strongly.

Still, soldiers do frequently kill noncombatants in wartime. This, of course, gives rise to the question, when this occurs are these soldiers terrorists?* To answer this question it is necessary to go back to the definition of terrorism presented in chapter 5. It *is* terrorism if the soldiers deliberately use lethal force against noncombatants for the express purpose of terrorizing them *and* if those noncombatants perceive such force to be abnormal. Classic examples are provided by the Bataan Death March in 1942 and the Tulle and Oradour massacres by the 2d SS Panzer Division in June 1944.[20]

---

*The term *soldier* is used here to represent military service personnel from all services—airmen, sailors, etc.

Most noncombatant deaths cannot be so easily categorized as acts of terrorism, however. To begin with, the nature of modern warfare with its weapons of mass destruction has made it virtually impossible to avoid noncombatant casualties. This is particularly true when military targets are located near major metropolitan areas having large populations. Although the employment of lethal force in such areas is generally not meant to kill noncombatants, hundreds or even thousands are maimed or killed. Such unintentional casualties are euphemistically referred to by military planners as "collateral damage." But, regardless of how they are labeled, the killing of noncombatants in such situations is not terrorism. Indeed, according to William O'Brien,

> It should be noted that the law-of-war principle of discrimination or noncombatant immunity from direct attack prohibits targeting of noncombatants and nonmilitary targets as such. However, collateral damage proportionate to the military damage done is permitted by the principle of discrimination.[21]

Another major factor in modern warfare is the increasing fuzziness between combatant and noncombatant. Beginning with the American Revolutionary and Napoleonic wars the concept of total war began to take shape. Within 100 years no modern army could sustain itself in the field without a well-organized and motivated home front. Thus, the civilian munitions worker, scientist, or farmer became an increasingly important factor in a nation's overall power equation. If that civilian were to become unwilling or unable to provide the necessary support to the armed forces, then that nation's military power would be reduced. Clearly, then, the civilian is a major element in a belligerent nation's war-making capacity, and consequently any claim he might have to noncombatant status is severely compromised.

Even before the advent of industrialized societies, however, military terrorism was employed with good effect against civilian populations. This form of force employment was chosen, then as now, because of its extreme efficiency. There are many historical examples of this, but perhaps the best-known, preindustrial use of military terrorism in the modern epoch is that of Oliver Cromwell against the Irish rebellion in 1650. That Cromwell's campaign of terror was both successful in neutralizing the Irish population's will to resist, as well as represented the most efficient use of lethal force, can be readily seen in Lyford Edward's description of this campaign:

The massacres and reign of terror instituted in Ireland by Oliver Cromwell during the Puritan Revolution stand out clearly even in the blood-
stained history of that country.... The statistical evidence shows beyond doubt that Cromwell's conquest of Ireland was the least bloody of
any in its long history. His whole procedure, as his letter to Parliament
shows, was a scheme to terrify the Irish people so that they would not
dare to resist him.... At the very beginning of the war he ordered two
massacres, which he carried out in the most spectacular manner possible. He accompanied these massacres with the most dreadful threats
against all who should dare oppose him.... [Moreover] it was necessary
for him also to save his troops as much as possible for the war in Scotland, which had already begun, and which was more dangerous to his
power.... The deliberate massacre of 4200 men ... was his solution of
the problem. By that action he subdued the island in less than nine
months ... lost only a few hundred of his own troops, [while] ... three
large Irish armies, then in the field, dissolved from mere terror as soon
as the Puritan army approached....[22]

The first war in the early industrial era in which the morale of the
civilian population was specifically targeted is the American Civil
War, and certainly the most famous episode of this type of warfare is
Sherman's march to the sea in 1864. According to this Union general,
the Confederacy had begun the conflict and was therefore responsible
for all subsequent bloodshed. Prior to the burning of Atlanta General
Sherman told its mayor,

War is cruelty and you cannot refine it; and those who brought war into
our country deserve all the curses and maledictions a people can pour
out. [One might as well] appeal against the thunderstorm as against
these terrible hardships of war. They are inevitable, and the only way
the people of Atlanta can hope once more to live in peace and quiet at
home is to stop the war.[23]

By later standards Sherman's "harshness" would seem to be merely
child's play. Despite its reputation, the burning of Atlanta was not as
complete as many would later contend. Only approximately 37 percent
of the city was destroyed, mostly in the industrial and business districts, while most of the homes and nearly all of the churches were
spared the torch.[24] Still, the target and the lesson were clear; so long as
the southern civilian population supported the Confederate war effort,
it would be subjected to such harshness. Although lethal force was

rarely used against noncombatants, Sherman cut a 50-mile-wide swath of scorched earth as he marched to the sea. His objective, writes Dupuy and Dupuy, "was [to] deliberately make 'Georgia howl' as he devastated crops and the war-supporting economy of central Georgia."[25] Russell Weigley openly calls Sherman's strategy a strategy of terror:

> Sherman came to believe that if the terror and destruction of war could be carried straight to the enemy people, then they would lose their zest for war, and lacking the people's support, the enemy armies would collapse of their own weight. So he made his marches campaigns of terror and destruction. . . .[26]

Sherman's logic was impeccable. No modern army could stay in the field without massive support from the civilian population. If that population's will could be directly targeted and broken, then the armies that population was supporting would be forced to capitulate. Still, it had taken four grueling years of hard fighting before federal armies were in a position to take the war directly to the enemy population. By the First World War technology had provided the necessary means to directly attack the population without first having to destroy the enemy's armies. This resulted in a profound change in how war was to be waged. According to Gwynne Dyer,

> Bombing civilians in cities—not by accident while trying to hit military targets, but with the deliberate purpose of killing civilians and breaking their morale—was the final step in the brutal logic of war. If the civilian producing the weapons of war were now the real foundation of a nation's armed strength, then they were actually the most important target of all. [Certainly] . . . by 1915, everybody was a legitimate target.[27]

Although the weapons were still too primitive to do any significant damage, much less cause the population to demand an end to the war, the intent was still there. For instance, heavy-bomber crews were instructed by General Ludendorff in 1917 that their primary objective was the morale of the British population and that the disruption of the war industry, communications between London and the coast, and transportation across the Channel were secondary objectives.[28] Moreover, the British reaction clearly indicates that they perceived such force to be abnormal. As one minister of Parliament—Lord Montagu— quickly learned, the British populace was in no mood to hear that centers for the production of war materials such as London were perfectly legitimate military targets. Indeed, according to Neville Jones, reaction to Lord Montagu's comments by British civilians bordered on hysterical.[29] Despite the fact these air raids clearly affected British civilian morale, they certainly never came close to the stated objective of causing the British government to topple or sue for peace.[30]

When World War II began in September 1939, the British and Germans initially refrained from bombing each other's cities. But by the second summer of the war, both sides had again removed the kid gloves, and civilians once again became prime military targets. This, despite the fact that both the British and the Germans openly claimed that "indiscriminate" bombing of civilian targets was an abnormal use of lethal force. The Germans resurrected the term *Schrecklichkeit* or "frightfulness" (which had been originally used in conjunction with German submarine operations during World War I)[31] to describe their new aerial strategy. The British initially disguised their purpose with euphemisms, but eventually they, too, began to admit openly that their primary target was German civilian morale. By 1941 the chief of British Bomber Command, Sir Arthur "Bomber" Harris, was openly and vigorously calling for a policy of directly attacking German workers in their homes.[32]

By the end of the Second World War, technology had provided the ultimate terror weapon, the atomic bomb. That the American government considered this to be abnormal force, there can be little doubt. Moreover, its means of employment belied its terroristic nature. Indeed, according to Thomas Schelling, the purpose of employing atomic weaponry upon Hiroshima and Nagasaki was to make "noncapitulation terrible beyond endurance."[33] He continues by stating,

These were weapons of terror and [psychological] shock. They hurt and promised more hurt, and that was their purpose. . . . The bomb that hit Hiroshima was a [symbolic] threat aimed at all of Japan. The political target of the bomb was not the dead of Hiroshima or the factories they worked in, but the survivors of Tokyo.[34]

Bernard Brodie further reinforces this contention when he concludes that the final surrender of Japan resulted not from the atom bombs dropped on Hiroshima and Nagasaki, but from the implicit threat of more such attacks if the Japanese did not surrender right then.[35] Clearly, this represented the employment of terroristic force.

As early as 1943 there was already considerable and growing doubt as to whether terror bombing was having any effect on civilian morale at all. In retrospect, it is clear that neither the German Luftwaffe commanders nor those of the Royal Air Force truly understood what it would take to cause a civilian uprising against its government or to shatter the cohesion of that population.

Those who sought to cause the populace to rise up against its own government simply did not understand what such an enterprise required. As Skocpol has clearly pointed out, it is not enough for the population to want to overthrow the regime. So long as that regime is able to maintain control of coherent and effective coercive organizations, the regime can remain stable despite chronic, widespread discontent among the populace.[36] This was clearly a forlorn hope, particularly in the case of Nazi Germany, whose forces of coercion remained intact until the very last days of the Third Reich.

As for those who hoped to totally shatter the target population's morale, destroying its cohesion and making it entirely unmanageable by strategic aerial bombardment, they, too, did not fully understand the magnitude of what they sought to achieve. To begin with, it is a far more complex undertaking than those who advocated terror bombing were aware. It is a fallacy that bombing produces long-term, chronic terror among the populace. While it is true that air raid studies determined "that it was often not the countries responsible for the bombing that were blamed by the victims ... rather the victims blamed their own government for failing to protect them,"[37] these studies also established that "people found a succession of raids less disturbing than those which occurred at irregular intervals, [indicating that] sustained, intense, relentless terrorism is more likely to numb the target...."[38] Consequently, the more intense the bombing, the less overall effect it had. Moreover, those who sought to destroy enemy morale by terror bombing generally had an overly simplistic concept of what they were targeting. As Fred Ilke noted in his study, *The Social Impact of Bomb Destruction,*

> Before the end of World War II it was thought that bombing destruction would lower civilian morale and that low morale would lead to lessened war production or even to a revolt against the government, forcing it to surrender. The fallacy of this premise lies in the fact that *two different types of "morale" are involved*. . . . The German language has a different word for each kind of "morale." Consequently the German intelligence reports in World War II concerning the civilian home front always dis-

tinguished between the two. These reports correctly showed that bombing lowered *Stimmung*, the "passive morale" or the way people felt. But the low Stimmung did not destroy *Haltung*, the "active morale" or the way people actually behaved under stress. Habits, discipline, the fear of punishment, and the lack of alternative courses of action left the behavior (Haltung) of the civilian population unaffected by the low feelings and depressed mood (Stimmung).[39]

Not even the Japanese, who suffered far worse than the British or German populations from strategic bombing, lost their national cohesion or attempted to overthrow the government and sue for peace even after suffering the atomic attacks. The ultimate, tragic lesson is, then, that terror bombing simply does not work. Bombing alone could not crush an enemy's will to resist. It could, however, render him *unable* to resist.

Those, like Russell Weigley, who label American conventional bombing of Japan as terror bombing are simply using different criteria than we do in this book. Certainly the fire raids on Japan's cities were terrifying and devastating to Japan's civil population, but the decision by the American bomber commander Curtis LeMay to begin these raids was a technical one in which considerations of Japanese civilian morale were secondary at best. To be sure, the aim of the U.S. Army Air Force and Naval Air commanders was to defeat Japan without having to resort to a costly amphibious campaign against the Japanese home islands. But the means sought to bring this about were not something ephemeral, such as the loss of civilian morale, but the destruction of Japan's *ability* to wage war. This required the destruction of Japan's industrial capacity—particularly its manufacturing facilities. Unfortunately, unlike most European industrial targets, the ones in Japan were spread throughout highly populated centers. Moreover, within these populated areas were hundreds of "shadow" factories that fed finished products to the main industrial plants. Consequently, as Edward Jablonski correctly points out, "Defining the boundary between purely industrial and residential Japanese target was all but impossible."[40] It was found that, with the technical means then available, the most effective way to ensure the destruction of Japan's industrial capacity was to employ firebombing to destroy whole districts of Japanese cities. That this method caused tens of thousands of civilian casualties was seen as an unfortunate byproduct of the attacks, but these casualties certainly did not constitute the main objective.

When Japan finally did surrender, it was not because the morale of its civilian population had collapsed, nor even that of its still intact three-million-strong armed forces, but because Japan could no longer fight a war on modern terms. With its imports virtually cut off by submarine and surface naval forces and its production facilities demolished, Japan simply could not sustain the war effort any longer. As General MacArthur was to remark after the war, "At least 3,000,000 of as fine ground troops as I have ever known . . . laid down their arms because they didn't have the materials to fight with . . . and the potential to gather them . . . where we would attack. . . ."[41]

That Japanese civilian and military will to fight remained intact, even after suffering atomic attacks, is clearly indicated by the unprecedented intercession of the Japanese emperor in political decision making. Had the emperor not personally called for peace there is little doubt but that the war would have continued for many more weeks or even months. That virtually all, including most of the most ardent members of the faction calling for the continuation of the war, obeyed the emperor's command to cease hostilities is further indication that Japanese national cohesion remained intact until the final moment. It was Emperor Hirohito that removed the will of Japan's civilian population to continue fighting, not the American bombers. Japan was defeated, then, by technological and economic collapse, not psychological.

The ultimate question is, of course, is military terrorism war? Based upon the definition of war used by this book, the answer has to be yes. To begin with, military terrorism is simply a weapon or means of war. And, to the extent that all war is waged for political purposes, military terrorism qualifies as the employment of lethal force for a political end.

Military terrorism is also clearly tailored to destroy the enemy's will to resist. Indeed, one might say that this is the ultimate expression of this element of war. The fact that this form of war has proven to be unsuccessful (thus far) in either destroying the enemy's will to resist or shattering the social cohesion of the enemy populace is an interesting and instructional point, but it does not change the fact that it is still force employed for the purpose of undermining and destroying the enemy's will.

Finally, military terrorism is force applied against force, meeting the principle of engagement central to Clausewitzian principles of war. While noncombatants in World War II were clearly targeted in the employment of military terrorism, they were not defenseless—as anyone who flew missions in the night skies over Germany will clearly attest. Indeed, the most costly, single air bombardment mission of the entire war was the night terror-bombing raid on Nuremburg in March 1944.[42] While the individual, noncombatant civilian may not personally have anything with which to fight back, he or she is still protected by the armed forces of the government he or she supports. How well those forces protect the civilian noncombatant is another issue.

One final comment needs to be made before leaving this subject. The military terrorist can be either a soldier or a pure terrorist as defined above. That is to say, the soldier performing acts of military terrorism is still subject to certain rules of war and, whenever possible, respects the noncombatant status of a given individual. Even men who flew terror-bombing missions respected the territory of neutral countries and did not bomb open cities once they were abandoned by the enemy's armed forces and declared to be open. There are, however, pure terrorists, even in uniform, who do not respect noncombatant status, even when it is within their power to do so. The exploits of the 2d SS Panzer Division in France, previously mentioned, is a case in point, as are the infamous actions of American Lieutenant Calley during the Vietnam War. Thus, there is a distinction, and it bears remembering. Either way, however, military terrorism is still a form of war.

## State-Sponsored Terrorism

State-sponsored terrorism involves the employment of lethal force across international borders for the purpose of destroying or weakening the political cohesion of a targeted political entity. In this way, it is much like military terrorism. The primary difference, however, is that the state employing state-sponsored terrorism does *not* use its own military instrument to deliver the lethal force, but harnesses social elements within the targeted entity to do so. In short, it is a subcategory of social warfare and functions in the same way and for the same end as this form of war.

In the last chapter we concluded that revolutionary terrorism is a form of war. Certainly this condition would not change simply because the revolutionaries are being supported by an external sovereign power. As will be seen, however, state-sponsored terrorism can involve a wide array of revolutionary terrorist groups, including national revolutionary, international revolutionary and minute, political groups adhering to a revolutionary agenda. Although the goals and methods of each of these forms of revolutionary terrorism will be briefly discussed, the question this section seeks to answer is not whether these revolutionaries are conducting warfare, but whether the states sponsoring those revolutionaries are doing so.

## Types of State-Sponsored Terrorism

There are three basic types of terrorism employed by social forces that lend themselves to outside sponsorship. These are (1) national revolutionary terrorism, (2) international revolutionary terrorism, and (3) minute, political terrorist gangs. The first type was discussed in chapter 7, and a further description need not detain us here. It is sufficient to note that national revolutionary terrorism can be supported by sovereign states wishing to weaken or topple the incumbent regime of a targeted state. This type of terrorism involves what Ariel Merari calls "homofighters," that is, terrorists operating against their fellow countrymen. These terrorists include such organizations as the Italian Red Brigades, the German Red Army Faction, the Tupamaros, and the Contras, to name just a few. Merari points out that these are

> terrorists [who] usually refrain from activities that may alienate a major portion of the population. Indiscriminate murder of civilians, which is customary of groups that fight foreigners, is therefore unlikely to be adopted as an item in the domestic terrorists' arsenal, although selective killings or kidnappings of government officials, military and police personnel, or members of rival organizations are frequent.[43]

International revolutionary terrorists are those who employ terrorism against targets controlled and operated by persons other than the terrorists' fellow countrymen. These Merari calls "xenofighters" and include colonial terrorist organizations fighting against their colonial "masters," as well as irredenta contingents, such as the Palestine Liberation Organization (PLO), fighting those who currently control their homelands and those who are allied with them.[44] Other examples of xenofighters would include ideologically motivated terrorists having widespread popular support, such as the Islamic Jihad or other radical Islamic terrorist groups. Interestingly enough, the Irish Republican

Army (IRA) can fit in both groups. It is a homofighting group when it directs its lethal force against fellow Irishmen and a xenofighting group when directing such a force against the British.

States supporting international revolutionary terrorists are usually those having the same ideology as the terrorists or those wishing to destabilize and weaken the targeted entity politically. For instance, as Martin Arostegui notes,

> Radical Islamic groups operating under different names, Jihad, Martyrs of Baalbek, Islamic Liberation Front, soldiers of Allah and others are nothing less than Tehran's fifth column in its current war effort against Saddham Hussein's regime in Iraq, its conservative Arab supporters, and Western powers with strong interests in the area.[45]

Another very important difference between homofighters and xenofighters is that the latter tend to adopt more indiscriminate tactics. Again, according to Merari, "since xenofighters do not rely on the target population for support, as the homofighting type must do, they are relieved of the need to avoid harming the innocent."[46] This goes far in explaining the indiscriminate nature of the force used by international terrorists as opposed to national revolutionary terrorists. Just as in military terrorism, the international terrorist often seeks the complete destruction of the target entity's social cohesion, reducing the target population to a level of despair so as to make it unresponsive to its own government. Additionally, international terrorists are much more likely to need and to receive support from an outside source that, in turn, gives them greater technical ability to operate on a higher level of violence than their domestic counterparts. As Brian Jenkins notes, "State sponsorship puts more resources at the disposal of the terrorists: intelligence, money, sophisticated munitions, and technical expertise . . . reduc[ing] the constraints on the terrorists."[47]

The third type of terrorism likely to receive state sponsorship is what we call the micropolitical terrorist gangs. These groups include such organizations as the Baader-Meinhof gang and the Japanese Red Army. They seldom have membership over a dozen or so and, despite grandiose claims, have no popular support. As Paul Wilkinson points out,

> Ideological sects of this kind originate exclusively within the industrialized liberal democracies they profess to hate so heartily. . . . [Moreover],

their tiny memberships are drawn exclusively from the children of affluent and privileged homes. . . . Far from speaking the language of the working classes, they live in a kind of fantasy world concocted from vulgar neo-Marxist slogans and [other] half-baked and dangerous ideas. . . .[48]

While no sponsoring state is likely to expect such groups will successfully gain power, supporting these tiny organizations can disrupt the targeted entity, causing it to divert critical, finite resources and focus its attention within its own borders. This can be useful from a tactical perspective but is unlikely to cause a dramatic reduction in the targeted entity's will to resist. Still, a spectacular terrorist event, even by a minuscule terrorist organization, could discredit a specific leader of a Western power and may even result in a call for new elections and the ouster of a given regime. Although these micropolitical terrorists generally operate as homofighters, they can operate as xenofighters when targeting foreign elements within their own nation. Thus, operations by the German Red Army Faction are likely to be indiscriminate when employed against U.S. military bases and personnel in Germany.

These, then, are the three basic types of terrorist organizations likely to receive state sponsorship from some sovereign nation. As was noted earlier, the Brodie Paradox presents definite military benefits for using limited warfare having limited aims and employing limited means. Surrogate warfare, including the use of surrogate terrorists, clearly capitalizes upon the environmental factors highlighted by the Brodie Paradox. As will be seen, however, there are other, equally important factors for why states would want to sponsor terrorism, the most important of which is the utility of terrorism as a weapon within the current international infrastructure.

## International Terrorism

States sponsor terrorism for three basic reasons: (1) it is safe, (2) it is cheap, and (3) the current interstate infrastructure enhances and supports the employment of terrorism for political goals. These three elements combine to make it extremely easy to increase the expenditure of effort on the part of any targeted entity at little cost or risk to the sponsoring state. The first two points, of course, are germane to any surrogate warfare and are points that Queen Elizabeth I would readily recognize and with which she would undoubtedly concur. Consequently, they need little elaboration here. It is to the third point that we must turn our attention.

There are essentially two main factors making terrorism an effective tool in the international arena. The first is modern technology, and the second is the current structure of the international system and the problem it has in dealing with substate actors performing actions normally reserved for sovereign nation-states. Modern technology will be addressed first.

According to Donald H. Bell, there are two technological improvements that have made international terrorism more lucrative than before: (1) modern weaponry and (2) modern communications.[49] Clearly, modern explosives and light automatic weapons have greatly enhanced the lethality of the individual terrorist, such as hand-held, infrared-guided antiaircraft missiles (SA-7) and antitank rockets (RPG-7). Indeed, the continuous increase in the complexity of the technical means to employ terrorism has contributed to what Bell has called the transition from personal to impersonal terrorism wherein the target has changed from a specific tyrant to a randomly selected, symbolic individual remotely related to the target of terror.[50] To underscore this shift in the nature of terror he compares the nineteenth-century terrorist Nechayev's *Catechism of a Revolutionist* with Marighella's *Minimanual of the Urban Guerrilla:*

> Unlike Necha[y]ev . . . Marighella is absorbed with technical and pragmatic questions of armaments and their use. Instead of Nechaev's histrionic and even romantic statement, "The revolutionary is a doomed man," Marighella begins his tract by stating flatly, "the urban guerrilla . . . must be a good tactician and a good shot," . . . [which represents] quite a shift from typical nineteenth-century concerns with the connections of the means with the ends and with the need to justify one's action.[51]

As important as modern weaponry is, however, modern communications have had an even greater impact in the expansion in the use of international terrorism. Walter Laquer goes so far as to credit television with being "one of the main reasons for the shift from rural guerrilla to urban terror in the late 1960s; for in the cities the terrorists could always count on the presence of journalists and TV cameras and consequently a large audience."[52] Laquer goes on to point out that media coverage also determines the choice of target, ultimately driving even minuscule terrorist organizations into the international arena. As he puts it,

> Terrorist operations in Paraguay, the Philippines or Bangladesh will hardly ever be newsworthy, but an attack by Paraguayan or Philippine terrorists directed against their embassies in Washington, London, or Paris will receive extensive coverage, and if they . . . choose the president of some West European [government] as their victim they will receive even more publicity.[53]

Most terrorists, then, seek media coverage,* which is best obtained by operating internationally. Indeed, if an event is particularly spectacular, the media often seek out the terrorists. For instance, Bell notes that

> one is presented . . . with the unseemly competition of the three American networks during the [1985] hijacking of [TWA] Flight 847. Each network sought exclusive interviews with the hijackers themselves, and greatest media exposure was eventually achieved by that network— ABC—which was most forthcoming in presenting the views of the terrorists.[54]

Clearly, then, media exposure is a major factor in why certain terrorist groups conduct international terrorist operations. But this new technology is not the only reason for such operations. Much can be explained by the current international infrastructure as well.

The most salient factor, and one which drives all of the others, is the very complexity of the system itself. This provides the terrorists with a wide array of potential targets to attack, and these targets can be relatively "soft" since they often lie in areas of overlapping jurisdiction and responsibility. This, in turn, often results in cumbersome and inconsistent responses to the terrorist attacks, which affords the terrorists a greater likelihood of success than had they conducted such an attack in a purely intranational arena. As Merari has observed,

---

*A notable exception to this, of course, are the right-wing death squads, which have tried to avoid attention.

It should be recognized that the essential ingredient in the terrorists' tendency to operate outside the borders of their target country is simply weakness. For both practical and ideological reasons, [terrorists] . . . would prefer to stage their struggle "in the heart of the beast. . . ." Yet, this is often the most difficult place to operate. Target countries seem rather sensitive about terrorism. Even those countries that had shown amazing laxity toward captured terrorists whose spears were aimed at other nations regained their backbone . . . when they became the prime target.[55]

Overlapping jurisdiction also can quickly mitigate or even neutral-ize even the most successful countermeasures against terrorism. A prime example is the U.S. Navy intercept of an Egyptian airliner car-rying terrorists who had hijacked the passenger cruise ship the *Achille Lauro*. Because the airliner was forced down at an American base lo-cated in Sicily, Rome had jurisdiction over the captured terrorists. Al-though the Italians kept, and eventually prosecuted, the actual perpe-trators of the hijacking, Rome released the man who allegedly planned the operation, Abul Abbas, despite American requests for extradition. The key stumbling block here, of course, is the concept of national sovereignty. Political analyst Fehmy Saddy puts it this way:

International means of travel and communications, in particular, have made man international in a physical sense. Yet, perceptually and le-gally, he has remained captive of the geographical determinism of the nation-state. . . . For all practical purposes, and thanks to technology, the world has become one society as the interdependence of nation-states and transnational interactions have transcended all boundaries and barriers. Still, sovereignty has remained a sacrosanct concept and cornerstone of the international system.[56]

In short, technology has provided man with a de facto international system made up of juridically sovereign states having increasingly po-rous frontiers and borders. The result is that subnational actors are able to commit acts of lethal force against specific national targets that, in turn, unilaterally restrain the use of effective countermeasures by ad-herence to the very international norms that the terrorists have vio-lated. So long as such self-imposed weaknesses exist, international ter-rorists would be foolish not to capitalize upon them. Admittedly the problem is quite complex and one that no individual sovereign state can unilaterally solve. Some suggested solutions will, however, be addressed in the next chapter.

In effect, terrorists conduct international operations based upon sound military principles. From an offensive perspective, operating internationally gives the terrorists ample targets that are relatively easy to mass against and overwhelm, if for only a very short time. Since it would be virtually impossible for every state to adequately protect every potential target, the terrorists—providing they employ proper *security* and *surprise*—can usually depend upon their ability to attack and initially overwhelm any security forces that might be present. International operations also are sound from a defensive perspective as well. By operating in an international environment, effective countermeasures by the targeted entity usually require coordination between two or more sovereign states. This often results in slow, cumbersome, and ultimately ineffective responses on the part of the counterterrorists, greatly enhancing the terrorists' chances of emerging victorious. In short, from a purely military perspective, international terrorism has greater utility than national terrorism. But while this explains why terrorists employ this technique, it does not explain why states sponsor this form of terrorism.

## Analyzing State-Sponsored Terrorism as a Form of War

There can be little doubt that state-sponsored terrorism represents the employment of lethal force for political objectives. Consequently this type of terrorism meets the first basic test to determine whether it is a form of war. What is important to keep in mind, however, is that the political objectives of the sponsoring state are usually totally independent of those of the actual surrogate terrorists. For example, Imperial Russia provided clandestine support to Slavic movements in the Balkans with a view toward pan-Slavism. That is, the creation of a pan-Slavic state having Constantinople as its capital and led by Russia.[57] However, the Serbian, Montenegrin, and Bulgarian patriots receiving Russian support often had their own agendas. According to one French observer, although these movements were "very dissatisfied with the Ottoman [and later Austrian] regimes[. They were] determined not to substitute Russian domination for it."[58] Still, these movements could, and did, form a fifth column within the camp of the Ottoman and Austrian empires, diverting resources to defensive ends that might otherwise have been used offensively against Russia.

The states sponsoring terrorism are employing lethal force on both a moral as well as a physical plane. Specifically, they are targeting the cohesion of the targeted entity, whether it be an alliance system, an empire, or a nation-state. The purpose of such action is to disrupt the psychological ties that bind the constituent members together by placing asymmetrical stress on the targeted political structure. In this way, one member or element of the targeted entity perceives it is paying an inordinate price for its continued association with the larger whole and decides to cut its losses by withdrawing. Classical examples are the terrorism employed in colonial wars; terrorism during the Soviet-sponsored wars of national liberation—including those in Angola, Mozambique, and Vietnam—the Syrian-sponsored truck-bombing of the U.S. Marine barracks in Lebanon that caused the United States to drastically reduce its support to the Gemayel regime; and the North Vietnamese-sponsored Viet Cong attacks upon village-level authorities of the Saigon regime that undermined the authorities' willingness to support and serve the Diem regime.

It should be pointed out that the sufficient end sought by the sponsoring state is not necessarily the total destruction of the targeted entity through such means, but rather simply to destabilize or weaken the target. For example, as Claire Sterling has observed, the Soviets are not necessarily trying to cause "real revolutions" by employing and sponsoring terrorists but simply using them as a destabilizing factor within the capitalist camp.[59] Still, this clearly represents the use of lethal force on the moral plane to dissolve the cohesion of a targeted political entity. Consequently, it is safe to conclude that state-sponsored terrorism meets this, the second major criterion necessary for an activity to be considered a form of war.

The final test, of course, is to determine whether such force employment constitutes an engagement—i.e., does it represent the employment of force against force on the physical plane? As was concluded in the last chapter, revolutionary terrorism qualifies under this requirement due to the necessity for it to comply with the principles of combat that govern the employment of physical force against physical force. Regardless of whether the terrorists are national revolutionary, international revolutionary, or micropolitical, they must abide by these principles to be successful. Therefore, the immediate inclination is to conclude that state-sponsored terrorism meets this third and final test. But again, the question is not whether the terrorists themselves are waging war, but rather, are the states sponsoring them doing so?

In traditional warfare a nation is considered to be at war when combatants under that nation's direct authority and control commit lethal acts against a designated enemy political entity. Despite large amounts of circumstantial evidence and numerous claims to the contrary, there is no substantial proof that any nation is actually directing or controlling a given surrogate terrorist group or operation, much less a worldwide terrorist network. Moreover, the concept of sponsorship is *not* equivalent with control. For example, Syria is widely believed to sponsor many of the various terrorist factions currently operating in Beirut, Lebanon. In February 1987, however, Damascus had to step in to stop fighting between two factions it allegedly supports.[60] Moreover, Syrian armed forces actually became involved in fire fights with Syrian-backed Druse militia units.[61] The question becomes, then, whether sponsoring terrorist organizations constitutes the employment of lethal force by the sponsoring state against an enemy target.

To begin with, sponsorship entails many types of activities. It may include financial aid, weapons, training, intelligence, sanctuary, and bases for training and maintaining and staging terrorist forces. The sponsor may not directly control and employ these forces against specific targets, but the symbiotic relationship between the terrorists and their sponsors would clearly influence the terrorists' target selection. For instance, should the Soviet Union provide a terrorist organization with an SA-7 surface-to-air missile, Moscow could rest assured that the missile would not be used against an Aeroflot airliner, nor against an airliner of any Warsaw Pact nation. On the other hand, Moscow may have little control over whether the missile is used against an Israeli, U.S., or Japanese airliner. The choice of target, timing of the attack, and even the stated objective for the attack is generally up to the individual actor. In short, the sponsor acknowledges a certain degree of sovereignty on the part of the terrorist organization. But when these "sovereign" entities employ lethal force, does this constitute the use of force by the sponsoring state?

The answer to this question depends entirely upon the structural perspective you wish to take. If you perceive that war may only occur when a nation-state employs its military instrument for national, political goals, then the answer to the above question is no. But such a position cannot account for the use of force by subnational and revolutionary movements. Indeed, if war involves only an exchange of force between sovereign nation-states, then the American Revolutionary War is a misnomer. Moreover, even in traditional forms of war, nations have supported the employment of lethal force by nonnational actors, e.g., the partisan movements of World War II. Thus, there is a precedent for nation-states to ally themselves to subnational entities, even in a classical war setting. In this manner, a new type of political structure is created—one that constitutes an entity higher than the traditional nation-state.

To the degree that this higher entity has common or at least compatible political goals, it constitutes a political structure. The fact that only one or the other elements of this common structure employs force therefore becomes a moot point from the perspective of this book, since it has defined war as the employment of lethal force between any political entities—not merely states and their military instruments. Moreover, when one superimposes the concept of social warfare over this structure, it becomes obvious that the terrorists being sponsored are clearly agents of the sponsoring entity as well as being the military instrument for a supranational political structure within the international community. As with alliances of nations during World War II, absolute control over the armed forces of an ally is simply not a factor necessary for victory—although under the principle of unity of command it would certainly help. All that mattered in World War II was that each nation contributed to the effort of defeating a common enemy. For the Allies, the enemy during this war was defined as the ideology of national socialism, embodied in the nation-state of Germany and other Axis powers. In the postwar period, the enemy has been defined as capitalism or communism and is embodied not only in political entities defined as states but subnational revolutionary terrorist movements as well. The employment of lethal force by any element within one camp against any element of the other represents, then, an act of force between political entities. Given this, states that sponsor terrorism are performing an act of war.

## Summation

All three types of state terrorism employ force for a political objective. Repression terrorism seeks to compel the population to comply with the political will of the incumbent regime. Military terrorism attempts to compel an enemy state government to comply with the political will of the terrorizing state by robbing the targeted regime of the ability to control and use its own population. This is achieved by either undermining the population's *willingness* to support, or shattering its cohesion to make it *unable* to support, its own regime. State-sponsored terrorism represents an attempt to foster and support disaffected elements existing within the camp of the targeted political entity, whether that entity is a nation-state, empire, or alliance between ideologically compatible elements.

Despite the fact that all three types of state terrorism employ force for a political end, repression terrorism is not a form of war for two reasons. First, the state employing repression terrorism must avoid pressing the issue to its ultimate conclusion and causing the targeted population's cohesion to shatter. This introduces an element of moderation that von Clausewitz clearly rejects in any definition of war. Moreover, the force employed can be viewed as an end in itself so long as it keeps the regime in power. That is to say, unlike in war, "victory" does not result in a cessation of "hostilities," but simply the continuation of them. Secondly, there is no clash of arms between two contending political parties, which violates von Clausewitz's preeminent principle of war. The population is generally unarmed, supports no alternate political entity, and controls no territory. Consequently, force employed by the state is unilateral and unidirectional. The targeted population simply cannot reply in kind.

Military terrorism, on the other hand, very clearly is a form of war. Although it, too, is an attack on a civil population, that population is clearly a component of an *enemy* state's power structure. Destroying the cohesion of that population, or even simply undermining its willingness to support its own government, weakens the enemy state and makes it more susceptible to being compelled. Furthermore, although individuals within it may be unarmed, the targeted population is far from defenseless, since they have the regime's armed forces as a means of protection and/or replying in kind. Finally, force used in such a manner is a means to an end, and the force ceases when one of the belligerents realizes its political goals.

State-sponsored terrorism is also a form of war. Although the sponsoring state does not necessarily enjoy absolute control over the sponsored terrorist faction, that faction represents an active agent allied with the sponsoring entity. This alliance constitutes a supranational political structure having its own political agenda. The sponsorship of terrorist elements represents not only a form of social warfare but, under the restrictions of the Brodie Paradox, represents one of the few practical, efficient, and safe means of achieving political ends involving conflict between two nuclear-equipped political entities. The ultimate purpose of the sponsor's use of such means is to weaken the cohesion of the targeted entity, making it more vulnerable to being compelled. Finally, given that the terrorists constitute one element of the military instrument of this supranational political entity, any use of these forces against any other political entity—state, empire, or alliance system—represents an exchange of force between political entities. It is, therefore, a form of war.

## Notes

1. Andrew B. Schmookler, *The Parable of the Tribes: The Problem of Power in Social Evolution* (Berkeley: University of California Press, 1984; Houghton Mifflin Co., paperback edition, 1986), p. 92.

2. This definition of repression terrorism is a modification of one presented by Paul Wilkinson in his book, *Political Terrorism* (London: Macmillan Publishing Co., 1974), p. 40.

3. Alex P. Schmid, *Political Terrorism: A Research Guide to Concepts, Theories, Data Bases and Literature* (Amsterdam: North Holland Publishing Co., 1983; Transaction Books, 1985), p. 171.

4. Ted Robert Gurr, *Why Men Rebel,* 4th ed. (Princeton: Princeton University Press, 1974), p. 238.

5. Theda Skocpol, *States and Social Revolutions: A Comparative Analysis of France, Russia and China* (New York: Cambridge University Press, 1983), p. 32.

6. Schmookler, op. cit., p. 55.

7. Alexander Dallin and George Breslauer, *Political Terror in Communist Systems* (Stanford: Stanford University Press, 1970), p. 2. As quoted in Schmid, op. cit., pp. 172–73.

8. Owen Connelly, *French Revolution/Napoleonic Era* (New York: Holt, Rinehart and Winston, 1979), p. 142.

9. U.S. Congress, Senate, Subcommittee on Security and Terrorism, *The Historical Antecedents of Soviet Terrorism, Hearings Before a Subcommittee of the Senate Committee on the Judiciary,* J-97-40. 97th Cong., 1st sess., June 11 and 12, 1981 (statement of Stefan T. Possony), p. 57.

10. William Henry Chamberlin, *The Russian Revolution 1917–1921* (New York: Grosset & Dunlap, 1965) vol. 2, p. 81. As quoted in Skocpol, op. cit., pp. 215–16.

11. Eugene V. Walter, *Terror and Resistance: A Study of Political Violence with Case Studies of Some Primitive African Communities* (New York: Oxford University Press, 1969), pp. 341–42. As quoted in Grant Wardlaw, op. cit., p. 12.

12. Martha Crenshaw, ed., *Terrorism, Legitimacy and Power: the Consequences of Political Violence* (Middletown: Wesleyan University Press, 1984), p. 28.

13. Lyford P. Edwards, *The Natural History of Revolution* (Chicago: University of Chicago Press, 1927; Heritage of Sociology edition, 1973), pp. 175–76. (Emphasis added.)

14. Skocpol, op. cit., p. 231.

15. Adam Ulam, *Expansion and Coexistence: Soviet Foreign Policy 1917–1973* (New York: Praeger Publishers, 1974), p. 183.

16. Karl von Clausewitz, *On War,* edited and translated by Michael Howard and Peter Paret (Princeton: Princeton University Press, 1976), p. 76.

17. Richard Rubenstein, *The Cunning of History: The Holocaust and the American Future* (New York: Harper & Row, Publishers, Inc., 1978), pp. 72 and 75.

18. Schmid, op. cit., p. 81.

19. Ibid.

20. Samuel W. Mitcham, Jr., *Hitler's Legions: The German Order of Battle, World War II* (New York: Stein & Day Publishers, 1985), p. 442. The 2d SS Panzer Division hanged 95 Frenchmen at Tulle and gunned down over 400 men, women, and children at Oradour in retaliation for the murder of a German officer.

21. William V. O'Brien, "Counterterrorism: Lessons from Israel," *Strategic Review* (Fall 1985): 36.

22. Edwards, op. cit., pp. 177–78.

23. David Nevin, *Sherman's March: Atlanta to the Sea* (Alexandria, Va.: Time-Life Books, Inc., 1986), p. 15.

24. Ibid., p. 46.

25. R. Ernest Dupuy and Trevor N. Dupuy, *The Encyclopedia of Military History: From 3500 B.C. to the Present* (New York: Harper and Row Publishers, Inc., 1970), p. 900.

26. Russell F. Weigley, *The American Way of War: A History of the United States Military Strategy and Policy* (Bloomington: Indiana University Press, 1973; Indiana University paperback edition, 1977), p. 149.

27. Gwynne Dyer, *War* (New York: Crown Publishers, Inc., 1985), pp. 84–85.

28. Douglas Robinson, "Strategic Bombing," *Warplanes and Air Battles of World War I*, edited by Bernard Fitzsimmons (London: BPC Publishing, Ltd., 1973), p. 72.

29. Neville Jones, *The Origins of Strategic Bombing: A Study of the Development of British Air Strategic Thought up to 1918* (London: William Kimbest Co., Ltd., 1973), p. 133.

30. Robinson, op. cit., p. 72.

31. Jere C. King, *The First World War* (New York: Walker Publishing Co., 1972), p. 267.

32. Hanson Baldwin, *The Crucial Years, 1939–1941: The World At War—From the Beginning Through Pearl Harbor* (New York: Harper & Row Publishers, Inc., 1970), pp. 192–93.

33. Thomas Schelling, *Arms and Influence* (New Haven: Yale University Press, 1966), p. 15. As quoted in Schmid, op. cit., p. 68.

34. Ibid., pp. 15–17.

35. Bernard Brodie, "Changing Capabilities and War Objections," Lecture; Air War College; April 17, 1952; Maxwell AFB; p. 28. As quoted in Fred Kaplan, *The Wizards of Armageddon* (New York: Simon & Schuster, Inc., 1983; Touchstone Books, 1984), p. 47.

36. Skocpol, op. cit., p. 32.

37. Grant Wardlaw, *Political Terrorism: Theory, Tactics and Countermeasures* (Cambridge: Cambridge University Press, 1984), p. 36.

38. Ibid.

39. Fred Ilke, *The Social Impact of Bomb Destruction* (Norman, Oklahoma: 1958), p. 15. As quoted in Barrie Paskins and Michael Dockrill, *The Ethics of War* (Minneapolis: The University of Minnesota Press, 1979), p. 45.

40. Edward Jablonski, *Air War*, vol. 4, *Wings of Fire* (Garden City, N.Y.: Doubleday & Co., Inc., 1972), p. 169.

41. *Hearings on the Relief of General MacArthur* (Washington, D.C.: 1951), part 1, 57–58. As quoted in Theodore Ropp, *War in the Modern World,* revised edition (New York: Macmillan Publishing Co., 1962; Collier Books, 1985), p. 381.

42. James Campbell, *The Bombing of Nuremburg* (Garden City, N.Y.: Doubleday & Co., Inc., 1974), p. 147.

43. Ariel Merari, "A Classification of Terrorist Group," *Terrorism: An International Journal* 1, no. 3/4 (1978): 337.

44. Ibid., p. 333.

45. Martin C. Arostegui, "Special Reports of Risk International," *Terrorism: An International Journal* 7, no. 4 (1985): 417–18.

46. Merari, op. cit., p. 340.

47. Brian M. Jenkins, "Will Terrorists Go Nuclear?" *Orbis* 29, no. 3 (Fall 1985): 510.

48. Paul Wilkinson, "Terrorist Movements," *Terrorism: Theory and Practice,* edited by Yonah Alexander, David Carlton, and Paul Wilkinson (Boulder, Colo.: Westview Press, 1979), p. 107.

49. Donald H. Bell, "Comment: The Origins of Modern Terrorism," *Terrorism: An International Journal* 9, no. 3 (1987): 310.

50. Ibid., pp. 308–310.

51. Ibid., p. 311.

52. Walter Laquer, *Terrorism: A Study of National and International Political Violence* (Boston: Little, Brown & Co., Inc., 1977), p. 109.

53. Ibid., p. 110.

54. Bell, op. cit., pp. 310–311.

55. Merari, op. cit., p. 342.

56. Fehmy Saddy, "International Terrorism, Human Rights and World Order," *Terrorism: An International Journal* 5, no. 4 (1982):326–27.

57. L. S. Stavrianos, *The Balkans Since 1453* (New York: Holt, Rinehart and Winston, 1958), p. 398.

58. A. Leroy-Beaulieu, "Les reforms de la Turquie, la politque russe et la panslavisma," *Revue des Deux Mondes* XVII (December 1, 1876), p. 530. As quoted in Stavrianos, op. cit., p. 398.

59. U.S. Congress, Senate, Subcommittee on Security and Terrorism, *The*

*Origins, Direction and Support of Terrorism, Hearings before a Subcommittee of the Senate Committee on the Judiciary,* J-97-17. 97th Cong., 1st sess., April 24, 1981, p. 53. (Statement of Claire Sterling.)

60. Mohammed Salam, "Syrian Troops Skirmish With Druse Gunman," *The Herald* (Monterey), (February 24, 1987), p. 2.

61. Ibid.

# COUNTER-
# TERRORISM:
# CONCLUSIONS AND
# COUNTERMEASURES

■

## Introduction

We have identified war to be an activity that employs lethal force on
the moral and physical planes to achieve a political goal. Given this
basic paradigm, seven types of terrorism were tested to determine
whether they qualified as a form of war. Of these, three qualified: military terrorism, revolutionary terrorism, and state-sponsored terrorism.
To avoid more cumbersome means to collectively refer to these types
of terrorism qualifying as a form of war, these three will hereafter be
referred to as *war terrorism*.

This chapter seeks to identify the general methods necessary to
combat and neutralize war terrorism. It is important to understand
from the outset that what is suggested here is simply a starting point
and that, while the basic themes can be identified, each terrorist event
is in many ways unique and hence will require, as in any combat sit-

uation, considerable flexibility to neutralize the threat. Moreover, the countermeasures presented in this chapter are only applicable to those forms of terrorism qualifying as a form of war. Military solutions are clearly out of place and are even counterproductive in attempting to neutralize apolitical or repression terrorism. Neutralizing criminal, psychotic, or mystical terrorism falls mainly within the realm of law enforcement, jurisprudence, and public health, all of which are beyond the scope of this book.

Given the myriad possible scenarios involving a war terrorism event, tactical methodologies will also be avoided in this chapter. Police special weapon assault team (SWAT) units and counterterrorist forces are highly proficient at handling hostage situations, and little would be gained by a long discussion of tactical methods necessary to assault a building or hijacked aircraft. It is sufficient to note that when force is employed by these units, even at the microtactical level, they must adhere to the principles of combat.

Rather than tactical methodologies, then, this chapter will focus upon strategic methods and policies and the factors that govern them. In short, what will be presented are those factors a government should consider to (1) determine whether a military solution is called for; if so, (2) what the political objectives should be; (3) what the military objectives should be; and (4) how the military force should be applied to achieve these objectives.

It should also be pointed out that the primary focus of this chapter will be on the use of counterterrorism by democratic rather than authoritarian regimes. Because authoritarian regimes have fewer restrictions upon the means of force they may employ, they most often meet internal terrorist threats with internal repression, including large doses of repression terrorism, which has already been discussed in chapter 8. Democratic governments, however, face a much more complex dilemma in that they must not only protect the populace and defeat the terrorist threat, but must preserve their democratic institutions and way of life as well. Thus, the means of force employment open to democratic regimes are much more restricted than that available to authoritarian regimes. Indeed, as has been noted earlier, forcing democracies to employ increasingly heavy-handed tactics—thereby undermining the legitimacy of the incumbent regime—is a major element of classical revolutionary terrorist strategy. Still, the temptation to employ repressive countermeasures can be very great. It is therefore imperative that effective countermeasures be identified that will enable democracies to defeat the terrorist threat without destroying the fabric of their democratic societies.

It should also be noted here that very little will be said about military terrorism in this chapter. Military terrorism simply constitutes one of the many methods of force employment used in the context of a larger war. It is at best secondary to the main, more classical methods of force employment germane to traditional warfare and, therefore, represents an adjunct to the main effort. It is but one of many tactical methods a belligerent may select in employing his military instrument. Consequently, it is impossible to talk of defeating this form of terrorism except in the context of the war writ large. And, since the means to defeat an enemy in conventional, classical warfare have already been addressed in the earlier chapters, little more need be said of military terrorism here.

## What Is to Be Done?

The most important thing a government must do when confronted with revolutionary or state-sponsored terrorism is to realize that it is facing a military threat operating as a form of war. Consequently, although diplomacy, economic sanctions, social reforms, and political pressure may play very important roles in resolving the conflict, the ultimate arbiter of victory, as in traditional forms of war, remains the use of force. In war, it is force or the threat of force that will determine who is compelled and who achieves political goals. Once the regime realizes that it is facing a military threat, the next step is for the regime to ascertain the nature of the threat or, as Sun Tzu admonishes, "to know thy enemy." Here it is critical to gain an understanding of the terrorists' capabilities, weaknesses, methods, and above all, objectives. This knowledge will enable the regime to determine what its own *political* and *military objectives* should be as well as the best *military method* to adopt to neutralize the terrorist threat.

Objectives by themselves are useless, however, unless the will to achieve them exists. This is particularly problematical for a democratic regime, especially when it faces an internal revolutionary threat. Because democracies operate on the consent of the governed, the existence of an internal terrorist threat already connotes a serious problem within a democratic regime. Indeed, Martha Crenshaw suggests that revolutionary terrorists receive their claim to legitimacy from shortcomings in the "social contract" between the government and the governed. She has noted,

> For example, what legitimacy the Red Brigades possess (undoubtedly small, but a quality which is impossible to measure) is surely attributable to the Italian government's corruption, general inefficiency, and inability to solve persistent social and economic problems.[1]

A democratic regime facing a revolutionary terrorist threat is already suffering from at least some loss of legitimacy and will most likely experience considerable difficulty in convincing the population that some (or further) democratic rights must be given up to effectively fight a counterterrorist war. And, without mobilizing the population, the regime is unlikely to be able to generate sufficient popular will necessary to support the required military effort to neutralize the terrorist threat. This can have grave consequences for weak democracies. Either the regime will overreact, causing it to adopt a totally authoritarian form of government, as occurred in Uruguay, or if the regime is too weak, the terrorists will succeed, as occurred in the Weimar Republic. In certain cases the inability to mobilize popular support against a revolutionary terrorist threat has even resulted in virtual anarchy such as that which exists in present-day Lebanon.

The mobilization of the population is, then, clearly necessary for defeating the terrorist threat. It requires the democratic regime to convince the population that (1) the threat exists and (2) the ultimate aim of this threat runs counter to the will of the majority. The regime will therefore have to expend considerable effort to convince the populace that a military threat exists and that this threat may require the temporary loss of certain democratic rights and privileges until the threat is neutralized. By the same token the people must take great care not to permit the regime to go too far. Only the absolute minimum force necessary to neutralize the threat should be sanctioned, and it must be employed in accordance with the popular will. In short, the process by which the political decisions to employ lethal force are reached must be a dynamic one balancing the political requirements of protecting the regime and the democratic principles upon which it rests. What is abundantly clear, however, is that an effective counterterrorist strategy cannot ignore the necessity of popular support. Moreover, such a strategy must be based upon general principles agreed to in advance by the majority of the participants within the democratic process. Failure to do so will not only make it difficult—if not impossible—to arrive at a strategic policy that is supportable over the long term, it is also inherently dangerous to the same democratic institutions that are under attack by the terrorists.

This is clearly substantiated by the current state of affairs in the United States. At present, American foreign policy goals are largely being formulated and executed without the consent or even foreknowledge of the American people, particularly when achieving such goals requires the employment of military force. Indeed, as Richard J. Barnet contends,

> The American people, according to a barrage of polls, remains deeply divided about the wisdom and morality of interfering in the affairs of other nations. . . . [Moreover] not more than 40 percent of the electorate has ever subscribed to the official worldview undergirding the modernized intervention strategy or believed its major premises. Thus, the administration, as others before it, resorted to secrecy and deception to carry out policies that it could not defend in open political debate.[2]

Such secrecy is necessary, according to Barnet, because "there is a profound disagreement about when, where and how to use force in pursuit of the national interest."[3] Without a popular consensus, every president since Nixon has often felt compelled to employ military force *covertly*—not for military reasons, but under the presumption the American population would object if the truth were known.

This is clearly a self-defeating strategy. As this book has repeatedly pointed out, destroying an enemy's will to fight is central to the very concept of victory in any type of war. Failure to mobilize the will of the people to support the armed forces engaged in any conflict drastically restricts the administration's options and certainly risks defeat in any long-term struggle. Without popular support, the president must act unilaterally, hoping to secure a quick tactical success at low cost before negative public opinion can be aroused and brought to bear. Again, as Barnet notes, "The whole idea of [such] warfare is to avoid 'disturbing'—a euphemism for informing—public opinion in the United States."[4]

Under such conditions, long-term strategic offensive campaigns involving repeated employment of the military instrument are impossible to plan or conduct. Consequently, American counterterrorism objectives must remain strategically defensive with only occasional tactical offensive operations of short duration and limited effectiveness. Moreover, planning for such operations is done in an ad hoc fashion by a handful of trusted elites operating in accordance with a temporary political agenda and without accountability to any democratic institution within the American system of governance. As such, it poses a grave danger to the processes and institutions central to the American democratic system.

This is clearly substantiated by the Iran-Contra affair—a self-inflicted political crisis stemming from a failure to focus and mobilize American popular support for a well-articulated, counterterrorism policy. Indeed, this event fully emphasizes the danger of ad hoc policy formulation and execution without proper accountability to the popular will. As R. W. Apple notes in his introduction to the *The Tower Commission Report*, "It was an inept policy, poorly implemented . . . [wherein] a kind of parallel government came into being, operating in secret, paying scant heed to laws, deceiving congress and avoiding oversight of any kind."[5] And Morton Halperin sums it up this way:

> The Iran-contra affair . . . reveal[s] a system-wide breakdown in the democratic control of American foreign policy. In a country founded on the principle of shared powers in foreign affairs, the president has come to assert a unilateral authority over the use and support of military force by the United States. The officials behind the Iran-contra affair . . . completely by-passed every democratic check placed on the president. Their actions vividly demonstrate the deep incongruity and dangers that unauthorized covert action poses to democracy.[6]

The operative word in the above quote is *unauthorized* covert action. In and of itself, covert activity is not necessarily incompatible with Western democratic traditions and institutions. The problem arises when a government—assuming and fearing lack of popular support—adopts a covert strategy as a means to circumvent established democratic checks and balances. This is precisely what occurred in the Iran-Contra affair. The absurdity of such a strategy was clearly pointed out as far back as 1976 by the Church Committee, which noted that success in covert operations can only be assured "when covert operations have been consistent with . . . policies which have emerged from a national debate and established processes of government."[7] Certainly national debate is crucial to the entire process. Not only does it provide a means by which to test how the American public actually feels about given covert activities, but it is also the only safe means by which to ensure all sides of the given issue are aired and considered.

One of the most sinister elements of the Iran-Contra affair is presented by Robert Parry and Peter Kornbluh in an article entitled "Iran-Contra's Untold Story." Here they contend that the Reagan administration sought not to inform but to manipulate public opinion by creating "a sophisticated apparatus that mixed propaganda with intimidation, consciously misleading the American people and at times trampling on the right to dissent."[8] According to Parry and Kornbluh, the administration used this apparatus to carry out a huge psychological operation against the American public wherein congressmen were subjected to high-pressure lobbying, congressional elections were influenced, anti-Contra activists were targeted by FBI surveillance, and journalists were subjected to character assassination simply for questioning the administration's position on Nicaragua—all at the taxpayer's expense.[9] Even if these allegations are only partially true, they bespeak of a terrible erosion of democratic principles in U.S. governmental practices. As Parry and Kornbluh conclude in their article,

> Without accurate, honest information, citizens cannot participate meaningfully in democracy and cannot hold government officials accountable. . . . [A] pervasive system of deception and secrecy can only undermine the American people's trust and confidence in their government. . . . By intimidating innocent citizens who are exercising their constitutional right of dissent, this abuse deforms the public debate and guarantees misguided, and ultimately disastrous, decisions, as exemplified by the Iran-contra affair.[10]

Certainly this is *not* what this book is referring to when it recommends mobilizing popular support. Such support must be genuine if any counterterrorist strategy—covert or otherwise—is to be ultimately successful. But, is it possible to garner such support, and is it possible to debate covert operations openly, in a public forum? The answer to both of these questions is yes. In fact, we need look no further than the U.S. support of the Mujahadeen in Afghanistan.

The support for the Afghan rebels is still officially covert, affording the United States all of the benefits accruing to such operations. It has been, however, publicly authorized by Congress in an October 1984 resolution. Moreover, according to Halperin, such public acknowledgment and the subsequent congressional debate not only did not hinder U.S. aid to the rebels, it actually led to a larger and more effective operation.[11] At least in face of blatant Soviet aggression, the American people are quite willing to support covert military countermeasures. And certainly there is every reason to believe Americans would support similar methods against similarly aggressive enemies employing terroristic means.

Public debates of covert as well as counterterrorist operations need not—indeed, *should* not—go into operational details. But Congress should know of and approve the basic objectives of such operations, thereby affording the military or CIA the authority to perform those activities deemed tactically necessary and expedient. In this way, intelligence sources and methods are protected as are the agents in the field. More important, those agents have the psychological comfort afforded by the "absolute assurance that the operation is fully authorized."[12] Once this legitimate line of authority is clearly established, emanating from the genuine will of the populace through their duly elected and accountable officials, then, and only then, may a democratic government turn its attention to the selection of the proper political objective necessary for securing victory in any counterterrorist war.

Basically, a government can choose one of two political objectives: one seeking a total end or one seeking more limited ends. A total objective is one in which the target is to be completely destroyed as a political entity. A limited objective, however, is one in which the target is to be compelled to surrender or modify a given political objective but continues to exist within the political milieu as a functioning political entity after the war.

The political objective, of course, drives the military objective. It is here that von Clausewitz comes into play. As stated in chapter 4, to achieve a total objective the military must accomplish three things: (1) it must destroy the enemy's armed forces, (2) it must occupy the enemy's territory so that those forces cannot be reconstituted, and (3) it must destroy the enemy's will to resist. A limited objective, however, is achieved by making continuation of the struggle too costly for the enemy, forcing him to give up his political aims for which the war is being fought. This, according to von Clausewitz, is achieved through the simple expedient of increasing the enemy's expenditure of effort beyond which he is willing to bear. As will be seen, the means necessary to defeat revolutionary terrorism requires a total military objective, whereas state-sponsored terrorism can require either.

Once the regime has selected a political and military objective that is either total or limited, the next step in developing a counterterrorist strategy is to select the proper method of force employment to achieve them. Arriving at the proper military method in counterterrorist warfare is a dynamic process resting upon immutable principles of war on the one hand and on the vagaries of the political, social, and military environment in which the conflict is being waged on the other. Because these factors vary so widely between revolutionary and state-sponsored terrorism, each will be discussed separately.

## Countering Revolutionary Terrorism

Any nation-state can come under attack from a revolutionary terrorist threat, but mature democratic regimes are the least likely to be seriously threatened by this form of terrorism. Because states having democratic processes afford maximum access to nonviolent means of redressing grievances, the existence of disenfranchised elements within the populace is minimized, and revolutionary terrorism remains an attractive option only to the most extreme elements of the far right or left. In fledgling democratic regimes, however, in which there is no tradition of democracy and/or in which large segments of the population do not yet have access to these democratic processes, revolutionary terrorism can represent a very serious threat.

Regardless of whether it is a mature or a fledgling democracy, however, the regime must meet and destroy the terrorist threat, and it must do so by employing its armed forces in a way that neutralizes this threat without undermining its democratic institutions. This is not to say that there will not be any curtailment of individual democratic rights during this conflict. Even in traditional wars, democratic nations have had to place certain restrictions on both the population and democratic institutions. Some of these include setting limits on the freedom of the press, rationing, mandatory conscription, and even restriction of movement for large portions of the population. Still, these measures are temporary expedients implemented and retained only for the duration of the war, and great care must be taken to ensure a return of all democratic rights following the end of hostilities.

Given the nature of an internal, revolutionary threat, however, the regime will often have to resort to even more stringent curtailments. For instance, Israel often resorts to army and police "sweeps" through areas suspected of harboring terrorists. During these sweeps, all men over a certain age are rounded up, identified, and questioned, and homes are searched for weapons and other contraband. Suspected terrorists are detained, but the vast majority of those questioned are quickly returned to their homes.[13] In this way, Jerusalem is able to neutralize potential revolutionary terrorist threats with minimal disturbance to the daily life of the populace and usually without having to resort to the use of lethal force. As in every war, however, lethal force will ultimately be necessary to achieve political goals; to ensure victory, this force must be employed in accordance with the principles of war and combat.

A nation-state facing revolutionary terrorism must acknowledge that it is facing an internal enemy waging total war upon the regime. Consequently, the only proper political objective the regime can adopt is one that seeks the total destruction of the revolutionary terrorists and their political infrastructure. To achieve this end, the regime's military instrument seeks to achieve the three elements of the von Clausewitz trilogy just mentioned: to destroy the revolutionary terrorists' armed forces, to occupy their territory, and to destroy their will to resist. What this section seeks to show is *how* the military can achieve these objectives.

In traditional warfare, a belligerent enjoying absolute superiority in combat power may elect to wage an offensive war of annihilation in which the normal sequence of events is (1) the enemy's armed forces are defeated in battle, (2) the enemy's territory is occupied, and (3) the enemy's will to resist is neutralized. Given the nature of revolutionary terrorism, however, the regime—which almost always enjoys massive superiority in combat power—cannot quickly crush the revolutionaries in an offensive war of annihilation. The reason for this apparent contradiction is twofold. First, the regime's superior combat strength is greatly mitigated through its dispersal in garrison, police, and administrative duties. Second, and more important, the small size and intense security of revolutionary terrorist organizations make them extremely difficult to locate and neutralize, further reducing the actual utility of the regime's armed forces. Moreover, the utility of the regime's combat power can be further mitigated by operating within the regime's own cities and towns rather than in the less-populated rural areas. As Che Guevara learned in Bolivia, even a highly inefficient army is militarily superior to a fledgling revolutionary movement. By operating in sparsely populated rural areas not only are the revolution-

aries more easily located and isolated than in urban areas, but the regime can also employ heavy tactical weaponry, including artillery,
fighter-bombers and tanks, without risking large numbers of collateral
casualties among innocent civilians.[14] The utility of such weaponry in
densely populated cities, however, is virtually nil. Thus, as Carlos Marighella notes, the potential for revolutionary mobilization is much
higher in the rapidly growing and volatile atmosphere of the urban environment, and the revolutionaries are much safer operating there.[15]

This urban strategy of the revolutionary terrorists drastically erodes
much of the military superiority the regime would normally enjoy
from technological and administrative skills. And, while the regime
generally retains absolute superiority at the tactical level, from a strategic perspective neither the regime nor the terrorists enjoy sufficient
*usable* combat power to attack and annihilate their opponent's armed
forces in a single, short campaign—the terrorists because they are too
small and weak and the regime because it must restrain its use of force
to prevent the killing/alienation of innocent civilians. As was mentioned in chapter 7, the terrorists meet this situation by waging a war
of attrition against the regime wherein it secures victory by eroding
the populace's willingness to support the regime's war effort. The regime, on the other hand, continues to wage a total war of position and
annihilation in which it seeks to destroy the terrorists' armed forces
in combat, to occupy their "territory" to prevent these forces from
being reconstituted, and finally, to neutralize the will of the population
to support the revolutionaries' war effort. Due to urban terrorists' tactical ability to elude the regime's armed forces, the regime is often
forced to wage a war lasting many months or even years. And, given
that any modern war of long duration requires the mobilization and
support of the populace, the paramount skill required is not technical
or administrative, but social.

The key to victory in a classical social war is to undermine and
destroy the sociopolitical cohesion between the enemy populace and
its government, while protecting and sustaining this cohesion within
your own political structure. Revolutionary wars are unique in that
both sides seek to gain and/or maintain control over the same population. Consequently, it is the side that is able to forge and maintain
the strongest cohesion with the population that emerges victorious.
The role of force in such a conflict is to create a secure environment
wherein it is possible to establish and sustain an effective infrastructure of administration and control over the population, while destroy-

ing that of the enemy. As will be seen, the regime has two, interdependent means of defeating the revolutionary terrorists' endeavors to gain influence and control over the populace: physical isolation and moral isolation. Once this is achieved, the regime will be in a much better position to locate the revolutionary terrorists, occupy their "territory," and destroy their armed forces.

The first step in isolating the terrorists from the population is what John McCuen has called counterorganization.[16] Counterorganization affords the regime better command, control, and protection on the physical plane and provides a means to establish stronger psychological bonds and increased cooperation between the regime and populace on the moral plane. According to McCuen,

> The governing authorities must keep in mind that most countries struck by revolutionary warfare have had adequate military forces based upon conventional requirements for internal security. . . . Nevertheless, these forces, however superior, have never in themselves proved to be an adequate defense against the revolutionaries. . . . [Rather] massive counter-organization is the most effective strategy to defeat revolutionary organization. . . . This strategy [includes] such techniques as effective administration, civic training, counter-organization of the population, establishment of popular self-defense, implantation of an intelligence system, organization of a territorial defense, and improvement of mobile forces.[17]

These counterorganizing efforts, of course, do not occur in a vacuum. To be successful, they require the regime not only know and understand the revolutionary terrorists' goals, but what effect these are having upon the local populace. Clearly the regime will have different operational strategies when dealing with a population that is in general opposed to the terrorists' goals and/or methods, as opposed to dealing with a populace in which the revolutionaries enjoy widespread support. For instance, as the British learned in Malaya, when the populace was neutral or hostile toward the regime it was often necessary to concentrate on physically isolating that population from the terrorists before civic action projects could move in to begin the moral isolation of the insurgents.[18] In areas where regime support remained strong, however, civic projects could begin immediately, and as the legitimacy of the regime was thereby further reinforced, the increasing moral isolation of the revolutionaries was translated into an increasingly hostile physical environment. The result is that the revolutionary terrorists are pushed more and more into a defensive posture where they become increasingly concerned with problems of survival and are less able to concentrate on offensive operations of their own.[19]

The objectives necessary to effect the moral and physical isolation of the terrorists are clearly interdependent. For the sake of clarity, however, we will examine each separately, beginning with physical isolation.

The elements of the strategy suggested by McCuen germane to physically isolating the terrorists are civic training, popular self-defense, territorial defense, and the creation of mobile forces. While McCuen proferred these as a means to counter revolutionary warfare that had already reached the guerrilla phase of the revolutionary mobilization process, they are equally applicable and perhaps even more effective in the earlier terrorist phase. The basic purpose of each of these four elements is to establish the regime's physical presence among the populace presenting the revolutionaries an obstacle they must contend with and neutralize before they can establish their own means of controlling the populace. For instance, the civic training program suggested by McCuen is necessary to provide "the large number of local officials required to [maintain] . . . the necessary 'human contact' with the population."[20] This human contact reinforces in the minds of the populace the fact that the regime is not some abstract entity existing far away and having no responsibilities to the people, but is an active, positive influence in each person's daily life. Although this may appear to be appropriate only to rural areas far from the central government, it is also critical within large cities. The regime's counterorganization must physically reach down to each city block, ensuring to the maximum extent possible that human contact is established and sustained with all those living there. For maximum legitimacy, these block organizations should be made up of people elected from and by the residents of the block and not simply appointed by the regime.

The same can be said for establishing local, popular defense units. Whether these units are rural militia or auxiliary police patrolling the streets and alleys of a large city, their purpose again is to establish a viable presence by the regime that the revolutionaries must overcome before they can successfully mobilize the revolution.

There is, of course, the danger that the presence of armed militia and/or auxiliary police could cause widespread resentment among a populace used to living in an open democratic society. And, since the support of the populace is critical to winning any social war, any loss of regime legitimacy in the eyes of the populace can clearly spell disaster for the government. This will be addressed in greater detail when moral isolation of the terrorists is discussed. McCuen goes so far as to suggest that local defense is perhaps the most important element (at least on the physical plane) in the government's counterorganization strategy:

> Unless the people themselves have the means and commitment to resist, their desire for personal security is likely to overpower their loyalty to the government or neutrality. Even in this early phase of the [revolutionary mobilization process] . . . organization of the local auxiliary police and militia units should be a first priority task of the governing authorities.[21]

The purpose of these local security forces is to create a physical environment in which any offensive operation by the revolutionary terrorists will cause them heavy casualties, particularly should they attempt any shock operations such as assassinations, bank robberies, or political kidnapping. Moreover, by increasing the security of the most critical nodes of command, control, service, and other high-risk facilities through the installation of concrete barriers, fences, alarms, and other passive measures, these facilities can be made virtually impervious to any but the most determined terrorist attacks. Such measures have been undertaken at most airports, nuclear energy facilities, and military installations even in the most democratic states.

In such a physical environment the terrorists are exposed to potentially prohibitive losses unless (1) they attack less well-protected targets—i.e., the general populace—(2) they eschew shock actions altogether and employ only less discriminate fire attacks using bombs and other fire weapons, or (3) they employ only shock actions in which they prevent themselves from being overwhelmed by the regime's massive tactical superiority by seizing hostages. Should the terrorists employ option 1 or 2 they clearly risk their claim to having any moral superiority over the regime, which Marighella, Mao, and others have insisted is critical to mobilizing the revolution. Consequently, operations involving the seizure of hostages obviously remain one of the few options open to revolutionary terrorists when operating in a high-threat environment.

Hostage-taking is attractive to the terrorists because it neutralizes the superior physical combat power of the regime at the tactical level and places the regime in the moral predicament of having to choose between giving in to the terrorists' demands and risking the lives of the hostages in an assault. If improperly executed, an assault on a hijacked aircraft, building, or other structure can result in scores of casualties among the hostages who would have lived had the government given in to the terrorists' demands. Such heavy casualties, particularly if they are children, can seriously erode the population's moral support for the regime. It is here that the highly mobile, specially trained and equipped units of the special weapons assault team (SWAT) variety employed by many metropolitan police forces come into play. If properly trained and equipped, these forces have a truly impressive advantage over ad hoc assault forces facing a terrorist-hostage situation.

Regular police or poorly trained SWAT units can spell disaster, however. For instance, in comparing the Philadelphia police assault on the revolutionary group MOVE in May 1985 with the SAS (the British special forces team) assault on the Iranian embassy in London, Gayle Rivers notes that after firing 10,000 rounds of ammunition, killing six adults and five children, and burning down sixty-one houses, the Philadelphia police finally terminated all resistance. A SWAT unit trained to the degree of the SAS or the American Delta force, notes Rivers,

> could have covered the Philadelphia house in forty-five seconds to one minute. The armed people would have been shot or disabled. The women, if not armed, and the children would have been moved out. The assault team would withdraw, leaving the law enforcement people to move people back into the neighborhood. . . . No deaths of innocents. No burning down of sixty-one houses, leaving 250 people homeless. No city-wide shame. No flare-up of racial antagonisms. Just an efficient— and by SAS or Delta standards—relatively easy operation.[22]

It is obvious that forces capable of this degree of discriminate force, applied rapidly and efficiently, can clearly neutralize almost any terrorist-hostage situation. In creating such forces, the regime removes the final shock option available to terrorists operating in a high-threat physical environment. And, as mentioned above, if the terrorists are forced to employ the much less discriminate fire attacks, they lose much of their moral superiority over the regime and severely jeopardize any hopes they have of mobilizing the revolution.

The regime should, of course, endeavor to foster this lowering of the revolutionary's moral superiority and, in particular, do everything possible to avert atrocities committed by its own security forces—especially where it concerns the employment of wanton and indiscriminate force. The regime has two means to achieve this, which should be employed simultaneously. The first is to recruit and employ security forces from within the local populace. When a militiaman or auxiliary police officer is operating in his own neighborhood, he is much less likely to employ indiscriminate force than when he is patrolling in a strange environment among people he does not know. Secondly, the regime should insist on maximum discipline and proper training for its regular armed forces when they are employed to counter internal threats. Even then, these regular armed forces should be used only sparingly and as a last resort. During the terrorist phase of the revolutionary mobilization process this military presence is probably best provided by what Grant Wardlaw has called the Third Force,[23] which is essentially the SWAT-type of special ground combat units described above, since they are most likely to employ lethal force in a disciplined and highly discriminate manner. Without such precautions, the democratic institutions of the regime are placed in jeopardy, and the government runs the risk of poorly trained and undisciplined troops committing atrocity after atrocity, ultimately resulting in the moral bankruptcy of the incumbent leadership. Indeed, as Wardlaw has observed,

> The containment of terrorism should as far as possible be a police matter dealt with by existing police force. Each police force should have a unit which is able to deal with public order situations involving firearms, explosives, and/or hostage-taking. . . . In extreme situations with which the police are unable to cope it should be acceptable to call upon the armed forces. If large numbers of armed personnel are called out they should have received adequate training in both civilian security operations and their powers and duties.[24]

We see, then, that by properly employing the regime's police and armed forces it is possible to go a long way toward physically protecting both the regime's mechanisms of command and control as well as the general populace from terrorist attack. This is not to suggest that every, or even most, terrorist attacks can be prevented, but rather that the physical environment can be made so costly for the terrorists that such attacks are few and of limited effectiveness. Moreover, if the terrorists can be compelled to use only indiscriminate forms of force, their claims to moral superiority over the regime is drastically eroded, particularly if the latter avoids employing equally indiscriminate methods. Up to this point, however, we have only addressed counter-organization from a physical perspective. This is clearly not enough. The population must also be counterorganized on the moral plane as well.

From a moral perspective, counterorganizing the rural and urban populations reinforces their psychological and emotional identification with the regime in areas where the revolutionaries are not yet operating and provides an alternative in those areas already subjected to revolutionary terrorism. The key to this counterorganization on the moral plane is to establish small, local groups wherein strong bonds of friendship and loyalty to one another can be translated into loyalty to the incumbent regime and its ideology, traditions, and institutions. Additionally, these counterorganizations can be instrumental in alleviating much of the discontent experienced by the population by providing education, health care, construction projects, child care, organized sports, etc. These organizations can also provide a means by which grievances can be aired and action initiated to correct them.[25] Indeed, one of the most effective means to morally isolate the revolutionary terrorists, according to Conor Cruise O'Brien, is to remove the necessity of violence to achieve political change. It is here democracies have a decided advantage over totalitarian regimes. Writing of the American Civil Rights movement of the 1960s O'Brien notes that

> Southern blacks were the most politically—and otherwise—disadvantaged and deprived minority that has existed in any democracy in modern times. If their political disadvantages could be largely removed by democratic process, it is hard to see any good case for political violence on behalf of minorities less disadvantaged.[26]

Although systemic and social inequities undoubtedly served as the primary reasons for the formation of the Black Panthers and other black groups seeking to use lethal force to cause social and political change, the existence of nonviolent, democratic means provided an alternative means obviously supported by the majority of disenfranchised American blacks of the early 1960s. Clearly, by providing more effective administration coupled with functioning democratic processes available to all citizens, a regime can undermine the legitimacy of the terrorists' use of lethal force and morally isolate the revolutionaries from the mass of the populace.

Moral isolation also serves to increase the expenditure of effort on the part of the revolutionary terrorists, particularly as many people—even many belonging to the terrorists' reference group—become willing to provide intelligence information to the regime and its armed forces. For instance, when the Catholic clergy interceded to stop the 1981 hunger strikes by Irish Republican Army (IRA) inmates of a British prison (in which ten IRA members, including Bobby Sands, had starved themselves to death), the clergy found itself under attack by the IRA leadership, which wanted more deaths to show the barbarity of the British system.[27] What actually occurred was to cause a backlash among Irish Catholics against the IRA. As O'Brien notes,

> This ... seems to have caused widespread reaction against the IRA among those who had rallied to its "humanitarian" cause in the early days of the hunger strikes. Certainly the Catholic clergy now became more explicit and businesslike in its opposition to the IRA. The Bishop of Derry ... told his congregation, after an IRA murder outside his cathedral, that it was their duty to cooperate with the police in the apprehension of murderers. He thus broke the old taboo against "informing"; an important step.[28]

This increasing moral isolation of the IRA has recently had dire consequences for that revolutionary terrorist organization. According to certain accounts it was through an informer that Belfast police were alerted to an IRA attack on a police station on the night of May 8, 1987. The attack was repulsed by the alerted police in what was described as "the bloodiest single blow against the ... [IRA] in 18 years...."[29] In the attack, eight senior IRA members were killed. As seen here, the loss of moral support of the populace can clearly cause the terrorists to operate at a much higher expenditure of effort level.

Such counterorganization can also positively affect offensive operations conducted by the regime against the revolutionary terrorists, particularly in situations in which the terrorists have lost much of their claim to moral superiority over the regime. Here, the population can be quite helpful in providing information concerning the location of the terrorists' "territory"—such as safehouses, training and storage facilities, and staging areas—as well as the location of the actual terrorists themselves. Just as with classical guerrilla operations, once the terrorists lose their ability to move among a friendly or at least indifferent populace, their security is jeopardized. Once identified, they are easily overwhelmed by the security forces, and escape and evasion become increasingly difficult as safehouses are occupied by the regime, and arms caches, printing presses, and other revolutionary paraphernalia are discovered and destroyed. Finally, most damaging of all, is the arrest or killing of senior cadre members. These represent the center of gravity for revolutionary movements still operating in the terrorist phase of the revolutionary mobilization process. Two excellent examples of this occurred in the United States with the ambush of the Black Panther leaders in Chicago in December 1969 and the attack on the Symbionese Liberation Army headquarters in Los Angeles in May 1974.[30] In both cases the "revolution" was terminated by a single lethal act.

Clearly, then, countermobilizing the population is the key to defeating revolutionary terrorism. This is done through positive action that endeavors to establish and maintain human contact between the regime and the populace, by taking the necessary steps to protect both the regime command and control infrastructure as well as the population from terrorist attacks and by creating a physical environment that compels the terrorists to use less discriminate forms of lethal force. So long as the regime uses only the most discriminate force, the moral superiority of the terrorists comes into question, and the sociopolitical cohesion the revolutionaries seek to create between themselves and the populace becomes increasingly difficult. In such a situation, the isolated and weak revolutionary terrorist forces are more easily located and dispatched by the overwhelming superiority enjoyed by the regime's armed forces.

## Countering State-Sponsored Terrorism

Unlike revolutionary terrorism, which always seeks a total end and is therefore a form of total war, state-sponsored terrorism can be employed for either a total or a limited end. For instance, the Palestine Liberation Organization is sponsored by many Arab states and employs force for both limited and total ends. Clearly, the PLO seeks a total end against Israel but by the same token seeks only a limited end against Israel's allies, most notably the United States. Thus, how a state responds to state-sponsored terrorism will depend upon whether that state perceives its very existence to be at stake or whether only a given foreign policy objective is at risk. This section seeks to identify the range of military options a state may use to neutralize state-sponsored terrorism.

In the last section, solutions for dealing with an *internal* terrorist threat were presented. These remain applicable here insofar as defeating sponsored terrorists operating within the state's own territory is concerned. Therefore, the means by which states defeat sponsored terrorists operating internally will not be addressed in this section. Rather, the current subject will center on how to defeat state-sponsored terrorism at its roots. That is where it finds support, training, and sanctuary by operating out of another sovereign nation.

To begin with, the nation defending itself against state-sponsored terrorism has in reality two enemies: the actual terrorists and the state that sponsors them. Yet there is still only one center of gravity: the will of the sponsoring state to support the terrorists. If the targeted regime can successfully destroy the will of the sponsoring state to support the terrorists, then the cohesion between the two is shattered, and the terrorists must find a new sponsor and sanctuary or perish. In this way, the terrorists are denied territory essential for training, staging, and supporting operations. There are, of course, many examples of this technique, but probably best known is the break between Jordan and the PLO in September 1970. Following two years of increasingly heavy Israeli attacks on Jordanian bases and towns suspected of providing support to the PLO, Jordan had the organization expelled. According to William V. O'Brien, the rift occurred after "King Hussein apparently considered excessive the price his country and regime were paying for giving sanctuary and support to the PLO's war against Israel."[31]

What is being proposed, then, is that a nation that is the target of state-sponsored terrorism initiate and conduct a limited war against the sponsoring state. The purpose of the war is to increase the sponsor's expenditure of effort until he is no longer willing to sponsor the terrorists and withdraws his support. The force employed against the sponsoring state should, of course, be commensurate with the threat. In this regard, Israel—surrounded as it is by states seeking its total destruction and under attack by terrorist organizations waging total war on the Israeli regime—will have to use greater force than say, the United States or France, which are secondary targets against which the Middle Eastern terrorists are waging a limited war. Even so, this force must also be employed within the context of social warfare, where technological and administrative skills remain critical yet secondary to social skills. Here the emphasis should rest upon taking advantage of any social or political cleavages that might exist within the sponsoring state so as to employ force in a manner that exacerbates and widens any existing polarizing factors. In this manner, the regime of the sponsoring state becomes embroiled in efforts to put its own house back in order and may become less sanguine about continuing its support of terrorist offenses launched by forces trained in its own territory.

A case in point is the April 15, 1986, attack on terrorist bases in Libya by the United States. Although certainly a step in the right direction, the United States, by relying exclusively upon technical means, lost an excellent opportunity to rock the foundations of and possibly even topple the Kaddhafi regime. For example, in addition to the actual bombing attacks, the American aircraft could have dropped thousands of leaflets over Tripoli and Benghazi explaining to the Libyan people exactly why the attacks had occurred. The leaflets could have shown a picture of the body of 11-year-old Natasha Simpson (or better, non-American and non-Jewish victims), killed in Rome by the Abu Nidal terrorist group operating out of Libya. Accompanying this photo should have been the statement that the United States was not seeking to kill Libyan civilians or soldiers, but merely the terrorists the Libyan government was supporting, and that to prevent any future attacks the Libyan people should appeal to their government to expel the terrorists immediately. As it was, the attack proved very successful from a technical perspective. The camps were hit and apparently suffered heavy damage for the loss of only one of the attacking F-111 fighter-bombers. Additionally, the psychological effect on Kaddhafi of directly attacking his living quarters was, from the American perspective, quite positive. In the two years following the attack, no known Libyan-sponsored terrorist groups made an attack against U.S. citizens or property. Consequently, it appears the U.S. raid on Libya may have caused the terrorist sword to drop from Kaddhafi's "paralyzed hand." But damage to the sociopolitical cohesion of the Libyan regime was not as heavy as it could have been due to the fact that Kaddhafi was allowed to interpret the attack for his own people and could therefore more easily convince them that Libya was a victim of American barbarity rather than the other way around.

Other countries, such as Syria, with its Sunni-Shiite religious cleavage, or Iran, with its Arab-Persian ethnic cleavage, have even greater vulnerabilities to their social cohesion. Moreover, the Soviet Union, which some consider to be the ultimate sponsor of international terrorism, has twenty-two major national ethnic groups having a population of more than one million, many of whom have openly protested or rioted against the Soviet government within the last two decades. By targeting or even threatening to target these cleavages, it may be possible to reduce Soviet support for international terrorism. This is not to suggest that it is necessary to attack the Soviet Union with armed forces in the hopes of causing it to lose its sociopolitical cohesion. Indeed, such an attack could possibly have the opposite effect. Instead, there are other, more subtle and hence (given the Brodie Paradox) much less dangerous weapons available in the arsenal of social warfare. One of the most effective is suggested by Gayle Rivers:

> When the Western democracies feel really threatened they are quite capable of setting up terrific covert intelligence operations. . . . [Such operations] should now be applied [in a manner] . . . that is not passively collecting information but actively supplying disinformation to Libya, Syria, Iran and the Soviet Union, specifically designed to make them distrustful of their internal security and of each other. . . . Any network composed of such disparate ethnic groupings can become a playing field for mischievous "black" intelligence. . . . Nothing is more disorienting as distrust within one's own ranks.[32]

What is abundantly clear, however, is that the state sponsoring the terrorism will continue to do so until forced to make an expenditure of effort that it is unwilling to sustain. But the force employed against the states sponsoring terrorism must be highly discriminate, ideally hitting only the terrorists and their supporting infrastructure. Little is gained from directly attacking the civilian population of the sponsoring state, especially within the context of social warfare. Consequently, conventional armed forces, particularly long-range naval or land artillery, have very limited utility against terrorists located within a city of a sponsoring state. Air power enjoys a somewhat higher utility in that it has the range and accuracy—under current conditions—to hit and destroy specific targets. But even air power will undoubtedly cause large numbers of casualties among the local population when attacking terrorists who often have deliberately collocated with "refugee camps."[33] At present the Israelis, who are fighting a total war for survival, are willing to accept the necessity of having to cause collateral damage and casualties among those living near the targets they strike, considering this to be an unavoidable byproduct of a counterterrorist campaign and a means by which to inflict an unacceptable expenditure of effort on the sponsoring state.[34] Still, despite its inaccuracies, air power provides one of the few means of hitting point targets in a high-threat environment with any measure of success. There are, however, even better and even more promising means.

The most discriminate use of force possible is the use of specialized ground forces capable not just of hitting general target areas but of killing or capturing the terrorists themselves. These forces, such as the Israeli Mossad, German GSG-9, British SAS, and American Delta Force, are generally thought of as quick-reaction teams capable of neutralizing an ongoing terrorist attack. Examples include the Entebbe raid and the October 1977 GSG-9 assault on a hijacked airliner in Mogadishu, Somalia. But these are essentially defensive operations, employing lethal force against the terrorists only after they have perpetrated an attack. In this way the terrorists are permitted the luxury of having the initiative, engaging in combat only when and where they choose. As has been mentioned before, by fighting purely on the defensive an entity loses any chance it may have for ultimate victory and at best can only manage to preserve itself. Consequently, elite, specialized forces such as SAS and Delta should also be employed offensively to neutralize not only given terrorist bases located within a sponsoring state, but specific terrorists as well. There are already precedents of this type of action having quite promising results. Gayle Rivers alludes to many of these in his book *The War Against The Terrorists*,[35] and Albert Parry describes several others. One such offensive operation by these specialized ground troops Parry describes in this manner,

> On April 10, 1973, in a predawn raid upon Beirut and Saida on the Lebanese coast, well-armed Israeli commandos, landing from boats, their intelligence scouts preceding them, penetrated the main guerrilla offices not only in the refugee camps but in a Beirut residential sector as well. They hit and wrecked the headquarters of Fatah and of Hawatmah's Popular Democratic Front. In the heart of Beirut, smashing apartment doors, they shot dead three prominent Fatah leaders. . . . As the Israelis reboarded their boats, they carried not only their wounded with them, but also bags of captured documents. With the help of these, [Israeli] intelligence men made many arrests of secret guerrilla agents throughout the country.[36]

Another example, of course, is the more recent April 1988 Israeli commando raid in Tunisia that resulted in the assassination of PLO military commander Al-Wazir. In a well-orchestrated operation involving naval units, an electronic countermeasures aircraft, and a single, twenty-man commando unit, the Israelis successfully eliminated a very high-ranking terrorist leader who, in all likelihood, had planned numerous terrorist operations against Israel.[37] These possibly include the March 7, 1988, hijacking of an Israeli bus—in which three Israelis were killed—and an earlier amphibious commando-style raid on Israel, similar to the one in which Al-Wazir himself was killed.[38]

Not all of the offensive operations need be this large and risky. Rivers notes the success of the German GSG-9 in tracking down and capturing individual terrorists who move throughout Europe. In one case, the GSG-9 tracked three known terrorists to Bulgaria and in June 1978 sent a small team into that Warsaw Pact nation, captured the terrorists, and successfully returned them to West Germany where they are now in prison.[39]

The benefits of such small teams conducting offensive operations is clear. They cause maximum damage to the terrorists and their infrastructure with minimum force that functions under extremely tight command and control. This heightens, to the greatest possible degree, the probability that lethal force will be applied only against the designated enemy and that collateral damage to innocent civilians is minimized. Additionally, these forces are not only more effective, but they are also, on the whole, cheaper than conventional forces. As Rivers has observed,

> A raid on terrorist camps in Libya or Lebanon by professionals would be less destructive of civilian life than retaliatory bombing raids and less expensive than using the [U.S.] Sixth Fleet in the Mediterranean. The preoccupation of the Sixth Fleet with terrorism must be viewed by the Soviets with some amusement.[40]

To be totally effective these forces must be self-contained combat units having command and control over all of the assets necessary to execute a specific mission. According to Charlie Beckwith, the commander of the Iranian hostage rescue mission, one of the most serious limitations—and the one that ultimately resulted in the failure of the mission—was that Delta Force was dependent upon ad hoc airlift assets composed of aircraft and aircrew designated and trained for conventional combat missions. As Beckwith notes, "The normal Navy crews who trained on the [RH-53 Sikorsky helicopters] had no experience in the type of mission we envisioned [*sic*]. In fact, there were no pilots in any of the services who had been trained to fly in the conditions this mission required."[41] In response to a question from the Senate Armed Services Committee as to why the Iranian hostage rescue mission was a failure, Colonel Beckwith's answer sums up the situation perfectly:

> In Iran we had an ad hoc affair. We went out, found bits and pieces, people and equipment, brought them together occasionally and then asked them to perform a highly complex mission. The parts all performed, but they didn't necessarily perform as a team. . . . My recommendation is to put together an organization which contains everything it will ever need, an organization which would include Delta, the Rangers, Navy SEALS, Air Force pilots, its own staff, its own support people, its own aircraft and helicopters. Make this organization a permanent military unit. . . . Allocate sufficient funds to run it. And give it sufficient time to recruit, assess, and train its people. Otherwise, we are not serious about combating terrorism.[42]

The answer to the need for effective counterterrorist combat units is thus one with which Napoleon would be familiar. That is, to create a self-contained, mission-oriented strategic unit, with its own commander and staff, and made up of all the necessary combat and combat-support personnel and equipment it requires to operate independently.[43] The United States made a tentative move in that direction when, in April 1987, it formed the U.S. Special Operations Command (USSOCOM). According to Robert S. Dudney, the basic mission of this command "is to build military tools capable of intervening in local wars, beefing up friendly forces, carrying out antiterrorist actions or striking behind Warsaw Pact lines in a major war."[44] But while this is a step in the right direction, it is only a half-step. Currently, USSOCOM is not an independent combat command but rather a training and providing organization. When its units go into combat they will be under the control of whatever Unified Command is responsible for that geographic region of the world. Moreover, the forces making up USSOCOM come from the four services—each of which has its own priorities, agendas, and mission. This greatly erodes the independence of the Special Operations Command and relegates it to developing common doctrine and tactics, conducting training, and competing against the much larger, better established branches of service for the funding necessary to properly equip special operations forces (SOF). This is certainly a far cry from the self-contained, mission-oriented strategic unit referred to above.

There is, however, one additional factor to consider: state-sponsored terrorism is a multinational problem and therefore requires a multinational response to be truly effective. At present each state is on its own to build, train, equip, and employ counterterrorist forces. Indeed, sovereignty is becoming an increasingly troublesome barrier to the effective response to international terrorism. As Rivers emphasizes, state sovereignty presents one of the major hindrances to the creation of a centralized chain of command and control necessary to create a truly effective counterterrorist force capable of operating internationally.[45] As noted in chapter 8, international terrorism owes much, if not most, of its success to being able to take advantage of a cumbersome international milieu made up of political entities that have their own means and methods of meeting the problem. Simply by crossing an artificial line known as an international border, terrorists who have committed lethal acts in one area of jurisdiction can avoid prosecution or extradition from another. Indeed, during the 1970s, many countries sought to solve their terrorist problems by deporting terrorists rather than by putting them in prison. Clearly, what is needed is a common policy consistently executed by all those subjected to international, state-sponsored terrorism. In short, it is necessary to create a supranational political entity having sovereign control over its own counterterrorist forces, yet remaining responsible to its constituent members.

It is ironic, therefore, that perhaps the ultimate legacy of international, state-sponsored terrorism will be to have served as the catalyst for the first truly international government project enjoying both the responsibility and the power to protect its collective citizenry. There is already considerable evidence that humankind is moving toward this form of global superstate. People are already operating as international citizens in many ways, and national allegiances are increasingly being usurped by psychological bonds to other structures, including international entities. For instance, many European nations are, after centuries of warring against each other, now beginning to realize they have common goals, needs, and relatively similar cultures. This represents a major step toward the realization of a United European political entity. Indeed, according to Barry Buzan's argument presented in chapter 4, at the most basic level of analysis a state is in reality "more a metaphysical entity, an idea held in common by a group of people, than it is a physical organism."[46] Moreover, this metaphysical entity has, over the past several millennia, consistently grown until it in some cases encompasses entire continents. As Gwynne Dyer has observed,

> There is a slow but quite perceptible revolution in human consciousness taking place: the last of the great redefinitions of humanity. At all times in our history we have run our affairs on the assumption that there is a special category of people . . . whom we regard as full human beings, having rights and duties approximately equal to our own, and whom we ought not to kill even when we quarrel. Over the past fifteen or twenty thousand years we have successfully widened this category from the original hunting-and-gathering band of a couple of hundred people to encompass larger and larger groups. First it was the tribe of some thousand of people bound together by kinship and ritual ties; then the state, where we recognized our shared interests with millions of people whom we don't know and will never meet; and now, finally, the entire human race.[47]

These redefinitions, as Dyer notes, occur not out of sentiment, but out of a necessity of collective security and because it proved to be a useful means of advancing humankind's material well-being.[48] Clearly, the greatest threat facing mankind is nuclear holocaust. But, so far, this has remained *potential* force rather than *kinetic*. It is state-sponsored terrorism that currently kills and maims people for a political objective, and it is this form of war that must be met and neutralized.

This, of course, represents an ideal; that is, a goal toward which the democratic nations of the world should work. Although the present situation is one in which each state jealously guards its sovereignty, there are already promising signs that a multinational entity having certain powers approaching those of a traditional nation-state is coming into being. The first step is to establish a collective extradition treaty wherein all member states agree to extradite captured terrorists to any other member state for the purposes of trial and punishment. The next step should be a common agreement between all members of this "superstate" of proper punitive sanctions to be taken against a state known to be sponsoring terrorism.

The last step, of course, is the creation of a jointly trained and controlled special counterterrorist force that can be employed offensively against the international terrorist bases located within the sponsoring states. This force can be made up of units from each of the signatory members of the superstate. The employment of this force on a given mission would require the consent of all members, with perhaps a means to override a veto by one of the signatory powers with a two-thirds' majority vote. Additionally, this joint counterterrorist force (JCF) would be on call to assist in neutralizing a terrorist incident within each member nation. It should be understood, however, that this force cannot substitute for local defense forces or other counter-organizing measures. Its sole purpose in internal actions would be to lend expertise in dealing with a specific hijacking or other hostage situation or perhaps to assault a position held by a terrorist combat unit—particularly where absolute discriminate force is called for. The ultimate purpose of the JCF would be offensive: to subject the international terrorists to total war in which their forces are destroyed, their will to resist is attacked and undermined, and their territory denied them. This latter is provided by conducting limited war upon the sponsoring states with an aim toward increasing their expenditure of effort beyond which they are willing to sustain.

By creating such a superstate having both the means and will to protect their collective interests, it becomes possible to establish a consistent, coherent counterterrorist strategy. It denies the terrorists and their sponsors the strategic advantage they currently enjoy through self-imposed restrictions by the targeted states and the overly cumbersome, ad hoc agreements that are quickly made during a specific terrorist attack or event. Failing to achieve this superstate throws each nation back upon its own resources, which are greatly mitigated by the existence of man-made boundaries delineating sovereign states. In such a situation, tactical victories against terrorism may be possible, but each state remains essentially on the strategic defensive in which—at best—all that can be hoped for is to preserve the current, unsatisfactory, and dangerous situation.

## Summation

This chapter has offered some general prescriptive methods for dealing with and neutralizing the threat from those types of terrorism that are a form of war. Military terrorism is essentially a tactic of employment used by forces engaged in a conventional, classical war. Consequently, no specific means of defeating this form of terrorism can be addressed except within the context of the larger war itself. Since the means to defeat an enemy in conventional or classical warfare formed the basis for the first four chapters of this book, it was deemed not necessary to reiterate these in this chapter.

Revolutionary terrorism represents a form of total war in that the revolutionaries are seeking the total destruction of the targeted regime. Given this, coupled with the fact that this threat is operating internally, the regime's only proper response is to wage total war on the terrorists—destroying their armed forces, occupying their "territory," and undermining their will to resist. Because this war is being fought among the populace and infrastructure of the regime, the regime must employ limited means involving highly discretionary force. Above all, the populace must be counterorganized to avoid the physical and moral efforts of the revolutionaries to gain the allegiance of the population. By counterorganizing the populace the regime creates a physical environment that is extremely dangerous to terrorist operations. This, in turn, forces the terrorists to use increasingly indiscriminate forms of force to avoid the heavier casualties germane to the more discriminate shock operations. This indiscriminate force can result in the moral isolation of the revolutionaries from the populace, particularly if the regime's armed forces avoid committing atrocities or other excesses. Once the terrorists are morally and physically isolated from the population, the regime will have much less difficulty locating them, destroying their armed forces, and occupying their "territory."

State-sponsored terrorism offers a much more complex problem, however. Here there are two enemies with which the targeted regime must contend. Despite this, there is but one center of gravity, and this is the cohesion between the terrorists and their sponsor. By destroying this cohesion the terrorists are denied territory essential for creating, training, and employing their combat forces. Interdicting this cohesion is accomplished by increasing the sponsoring state's expenditure of effort until it is beyond that which it will continue to bear. At the same time, the regime must also take the war to the terrorists themselves by launching direct attacks upon the terrorists' bases and infrastructure—even if it is located in a sponsoring state. Because the regime conducting such operations does not want to alienate the population of the sponsoring state, the force employed in such counterterrorist operations should be highly discriminate—ideally eliminating (physically, or in terms of their will to fight) only the terrorists and their immediate supporters. Indeed, within the context of social warfare, every effort should be made to cause the population of the sponsoring state to rebel against its government and demand the removal of the terrorists. Given the lethality of modern conventional weapons and their relative inaccuracy, the ideal counterterrorist weapon to employ in a sponsoring state is not conventional armed forces, but light, highly specialized forces capable of closing with a specific target, employing lethal force only against the various elements of that target and returning, when possible, with prisoners and intelligence material. Ideally, this would be a multinational force having the authority to operate within any of the nations belonging to some form of supranational government. In lieu of this, states suffering international terrorist attacks should cooperate as much as possible, sharing intelligence and permitting extradition of captured terrorists.

Failure to have a common approach against international, state-sponsored terrorism means having weaknesses the terrorists can capitalize on. Only by treating state-sponsored terrorism as a form of war can consistently correct responses be achieved. Certainly a strong alliance of democratic nations, having the necessary resources and resolve to neutralize the threat from these minute proxy forces, can do so without endangering the democratic institutions these nations cherish. The necessity for collective security is there. The question is, will the Western democratic nations be able to set aside petty differences long enough to meet this threat? This is the ultimate challenge of the modern democracies. Failure to meet this challenge means victory for terrorism and those who employ it.

## Notes

1. Martha Crenshaw, ed., *Terrorism, Legitimacy and Power: The Consequences of Political Violence* (Middletown: Wesleyan University Press, 1984), pp. 32–33.

2. Richard J. Barnet, "The Costs and Perils of Intervention," *Low Intensity Warfare: Counterinsurgency, Proinsurgency, and Antiterrorism in the Eighties,* edited by Michael T. Klare and Peter Kornbluh (New York: Pantheon Books, 1988), pp. 217–18.

3. Ibid., p. 218.

4. Ibid.

5. *The Tower Commission Report: The Full Text of the President's Special Review Board*, introduction by R. W. Apple, Jr. (New York: Joint Publication of Bantam Books, Inc., and Time-Life Books, Inc., 1987), p. xv.

6. Morton H. Halperin, "Lawful Wars," *Foreign Policy* no. 72 (Fall 1988): 173.

7. Ibid., p. 178 (quoting the 1976 Select Committee to Study Governmental Operations with Respect to Intelligence Activities, known as the Church Committee).

8. Robert Parry and Peter Kornbluh, "Iran-Contra's Untold Story," *Foreign Policy* no. 72 (Fall 1988): 3.

9. Ibid., pp. 20–25.

10. Ibid., pp. 29–30.

11. Halperin, op. cit., p. 183.

12. Ibid., p. 185.

13. For a description of a typical Israeli sweep, see the newspaper article entitled "More Than 60 Arabs Arrested In Israeli Raid on Refugee Camp" (Associated Press) *The Herald* (Monterey), (June 1, 1987), p. 2.

14. John W. Sloan, "Political Terrorism in Latin America: A Critical Analysis," *The Politics of Terrorism*, edited by Michael Stohl (New York: Marcel Dekker, Inc., 1979), p. 305.

15. Ibid.

16. John J. McCuen, *The Art of Counter-Revolutionary War: A Psycho-Politico-Military Strategy of Counter-Insurgency* (Harrisburg: Stackpole Books, 1966), p. 124.

17. Ibid.

18. Ibid., pp. 152–53.

19. Ibid., p. 150.

20. Ibid., pp. 94–95.

21. Ibid., p. 107.

22. Gayle Rivers, *The War Against the Terrorists: How to Win It* (New York: Stein & Day Publishers, 1986), pp. 46–47.

23. Grant Wardlaw, *Political Terrorism: Theory, Tactics and Countermeasures* (Cambridge: Cambridge University Press, 1984), pp. 97–100.

24. Ibid., p. 100.

25. McCuen, op. cit., p. 98.

26. Conor Cruise O'Brien, "Terrorism Under Democratic Conditions," *Terrorism, Legitimacy and Power,* Martha Crenshaw, ed., op. cit., p. 95.

27. Ibid., p. 103.

28. Ibid.

29. "Senior IRA Men Lost In Ambush," (Associated Press) *The Sunday Herald* (Monterey), (May 10, 1987), p. 6A.

30. P. N. Grabosky, "The Urban Context of Political Terrorism," *The Politics of Terrorism,* edited by Michael Stohl, op. cit., p. 71.

31. William V. O'Brien, "Counterterrorism: Lessons From Israel," *Strategic Review* (Fall 1985): 38.

32. Rivers, op. cit., pp. 243–44.

33. William V. O'Brien, op. cit., p. 36.

34. Ibid.

35. Rivers, op. cit., pp. 210–17.

36. Albert Parry, *Terrorism: From Robespierre to Arafat* (New York: Vanguard Press, Inc., 1976), p. 466.

37. Jill Smolowe, "Assignment Murder: How Israel Planned the Killing of Arafat's Right-hand Man," *Time* (May 2, 1988): 36.

38. Ibid., p. 37.

39. Rivers, op. cit., pp. 213–14.

40. Ibid., p. 217.

41. Charlie A. Beckwith and Donald Knox, *Delta Force* (New York: Harcourt, Brace, Jovanovich, Inc., 1983; Dell Publishing Co., Inc., 1985), p. 203.

42. Ibid., p. 268.

43. Martin van Creveld, *Command In War* (Cambridge, Mass.: Harvard University Press, 1985), p. 97.

44. Robert S. Dudney, "Toward a Fifth Service?" *Air Force Magazine* (May 1988): 24.

45. Rivers, op. cit., p. 230.

46. Barry Buzan, *People States and Fear: The National Security Problem in International Relations* (Chapel Hill: University of North Carolina Press, 1983), p. 83.

47. Gwynne Dyer, *War* (New York: Crown Publishers, Inc., 1985), p. 263.

48. Ibid.

# THE NEWEST FACE
# OF WARFARE

■

T his book has sought to establish that certain forms of terrorism are a form of war. To determine this, it was necessary to
establish a clear understanding of what constituted the phenomenon called war and from this understanding examine the phenomenon
called terrorism. To avoid a shallow tautology, however, more than just
a simple definition of war was necessary. It had to be isolated in not
only its *purpose* but also in how it *functions*. Once these special activities were isolated and clearly understood, it was possible to construct
a paradigm to test the various forms of terrorism. Consequently, this
book is divided into two basic parts, the first dealing with war and the
second aimed at defining and testing terrorism in its various manifestations to determine if it or any of its subtypes qualifies as a form of
war.

Coming to grips with the phenomenon called war was, in many
respects, the most difficult aspect of this book. As was seen in chapter
1, there are four major approaches to the study of war, each of which

provides insight into how man views the phenomenon, but each having weaknesses in terms of providing a total understanding of all aspects of warfare. The primary approach chosen in this book is the technological approach. This approach was chosen over the others because it is the least subjective and provides insight not only to *why* warfare exists, but *how* it functions.

According to the technological approach, the purpose of warfare is to compel other actors to do one's will through the application of physical force. Physical force is chosen and used because it has utility in compelling others and because there is no higher authority than a decision made by force. Consequently, the first test we use to determine whether a type of terrorism qualifies as a form of war is if it involves lethal force employed by one organized political entity against another political entity for the purpose of compelling it to meet certain political ends.

In the second chapter we were introduced to a much closer examination of the phenomenon of force. In this chapter we saw that force and power were not equivalent concepts but that power is in reality a product of force, which functions on the physical as well as the psychological, or moral, plane. Of these two manifestations of force, we saw that it is the operation of force on the moral plane that results in the greatest realization of power. Indeed, nearly every classical military thinker analyzed in this book contends that moral force is by far the most important determinant of victory, both on the battlefield and in the war in general. As a consequence, military organizations the world over have spent considerable time and energy to maximize the ability of their own forces to withstand the threat of force on the psychological plane. This is measured in terms of unit cohesion, the loss of which invariably means defeat for that unit. Due to the decisive nature of force operating on this plane, military organizations have also sought means to maximize the moral influence of their own forces, seeking not to *physically* compel every enemy combatant, but rather to do so *psychologically*. Thus, the second test of our paradigm is to determine whether the entities employing lethal force have taken special steps to maintain their own cohesion and at the same time have made a special effort to target the cohesion of the enemy's forces.

In chapter 3 we saw how force functioned on the physical plane. It is here that the immutable principles of war come into play. Clearly, the most critical element involves the employment of force against force in physical combat. Von Clausewitz refers to this as the principle of engagement, which essentially expresses the idea that warfare entails the reciprocal use of force by both political entities involved. Thus, if a form of terrorism involves the employment of force only by the terrorists, then it is not a form of war. This is not to suggest that the reciprocal use of force must be simultaneous, only that both political entities involved are employing lethal force against each other for political ends. Moreover, when this force is employed, it must meet the principles of combat. These define how physical force can overcome physical force in an engagement. Again, if it can be shown that a form of terrorism need not comply with these principles and can still consistently emerge victorious, then this form of terrorism does not involve the principle of engagement and is not a form of war.

The first three chapters thus provide the basic paradigm by which different types of terrorism are tested to ascertain whether each qualifies as a form of war. This paradigm consists of three basic questions: (1) does this activity involve lethal force by a political entity for a political end, (2) does this activity involve the employment of lethal force against the cohesion of the targeted political entity, and (3) does this activity involve the reciprocal use of lethal force by both sides employed in accordance with the principles of combat? These three questions provide answers regarding *why* this force is being employed and *how* is it used. It thereby affords a method of testing that is complex enough to validate the presence of war on more than one simple and possibly arbitrary measurement.

Clearly, however, even if it is based upon the same immutable principles and laws, warfare has *many* differences as well. In chapter 4 it was determined that there are many types of warfare that devolve from differences in (1) the objectives sought in the war and (2) the methods used to attain these objectives. Here we saw that war could be waged for basic political objectives: *total* or *limited*. Moreover, war could be waged in accordance with one of two general military objectives, *annihilation* or *attrition*, and in accordance with one of two general military methods, *positional* or *evasive*. Using these three general groupings it is possible to come up with eight combinations of types of war ranging from a total, positional war of annihilation to a limited, evasive war of attrition. Moreover, the type of war that a belligerent employs rests upon not only what he wishes to accomplish, but also upon the size and capability of his forces in relation to those of his enemy. Understanding the dynamic interaction of these six elements makes it possible to understand how different types of terrorism can employ force based upon the same immutable principles as classical forms of war in a unique manner. In this way, we can analyze critical differences between repression terrorism, revolutionary terrorism, and state-sponsored terrorism.

In addition to these different types of war, chapter 4 also introduced the idea that the way war functions cannot be separated from its environment. Over time, new technologies and organizational structures have changed the factors influencing the shape and nature of war, and it is here that the analysis of the evolution of warfare comes into play.

According to chapter 4, warfare evolves as part of a dialectical process wherein what exists at any given moment in time represents a synthesis of a previous thesis and a later antithesis. In analyzing this evolution we saw that the modern epoch contains five major evolutionary phases, each of which is governed by a specific paramount war skill. The side capable of fielding the largest force that can fight at a given era's paramount skill level would invariably emerge victorious—providing they were able to sustain that advantage. What is critical to this book is that the current, or nuclear era, is governed by social warfare, wherein the decisive factor is the ability to employ social skills—the ability to employ force in a manner so as to destroy the sociopolitical cohesion between the enemy's population and its government while protecting your own. Given the dangers of direct confrontation between the armed forces of nuclear-equipped powers—the Brodie Paradox—the most stable and efficient means of waging war in the nuclear era is by sponsoring social forces within the enemy's camp to undermine and weaken the enemy's government and power base. Perhaps the most efficient and effective means to bring this about is to sponsor the employment of terroristic methods to mobilize a revolution against the enemy's regime.

Chapter 5 introduced us to terrorism per se. Here, terrorism was defined as a deliberate attempt to create terror through a symbolic act involving the use or threat of abnormal lethal force for the purpose of influencing a target group or individual. Armed with this definition we then examined how terrorism functions. As was quickly seen, terrorism is not limited to any specific ideology or method of government but simply represents a specific method of force employment. This can occur in two ways: triadic or quadratic. In triadic terrorism abnormal lethal force is employed against a symbolic victim to terrorize and influence the behavior of all who identify with the victim. In quadratic terrorism, the influenced group is separate from the terrorized group.

Either way, however, terrorism represents an extremely efficient use of force. This is what makes it the favorite method of force employment of the very weak. Given the definition and understanding of the role of force in the terrorist process, it becomes possible to identify the types of terrorism that might qualify as a form of war. Here, three major groupings were found: apolitical terrorism, revolutionary terrorism, and state terrorism. Within two of these groups, several subtypes of terrorism exist, and each of these was tested against the paradigm constructed in the first part of this book.

The three subtypes of terrorism found in apolitical terrorism are psychotic, criminal, and mystical terrorism. As was noted in chapter 5, the lack of a political purpose alone would seem sufficient to disqualify these forms of terrorism as a form of war, but there are many who suggest that psychotic or criminal terrorists are in fact unwitting political terrorists subconsciously reacting to their sociopolitical environment, and that mystical terrorists seek to maintain a political environment in which they can continue to practice their deadly rites. Thus, they can be construed to have a political purpose.

Upon examining each of these forms of terrorism, however, it was found that none qualifies as a form of war. Psychotic terrorism fails to qualify due to the fact that the terrorists employ this form of lethal force primarily to satiate their own psychological needs and that those who identify with the symbolic victim are unable to determine how they should modify their behavior to avoid future violence. In a similar vein, criminal terrorism fails to qualify as a form of war because the terrorists again employ force simply to satiate personal needs, and any impact upon the political system is essentially incidental and unintended. Although mystical terrorism seeks to maintain a given political environment wherein the terrorists may continue to perform their lethal religious activities, this form of terrorism, too, fails to qualify as a form of war. It fails for two reasons. First, the lethal force being employed is clearly an end in itself. There is absolutely no way in which the target of terror can modify behavior to avoid future terrorism. Secondly, this form of terrorism clearly violates the principle of engagement in that the employment of force is unilateral. Thus, there is no clash of arms and therefore no need for the principles of combat. Consequently, mystical terrorism, like criminal and psychotic terrorism, is not a form of war.

Revolutionary terrorism is the one major form of terrorism having no subtypes. Moreover, it very clearly is a form of war. It involves lethal force for the political purpose of toppling the incumbent regime. It also represents the employment of lethal force to both the physical and moral planes. Its utilization of force on the moral plane can be easily seen in the role of revolutionary terrorism within the revolutionary mobilization process. Here we see that the force employed has utility in both mobilizing the populace and undermining the ability and the will of the regime to resist. On the physical plane, revolutionary terrorism employs force in accordance with both the principle of engagement and the seven principles of combat. For instance, by adhering to these principles, the Lebanese terrorists were able to launch the spectacularly effective attack on the Marine barracks in Beirut in 1983. By the same token, as the Tupamaro and Argentinian ERP examples described in chapter 7 underscore, failure to adhere to these principles has proven time and again to be disastrous for revolutionary terrorist organizations. Clearly, then, revolutionary terrorism qualifies as a form of war.

State terrorism consists of three subtypes: repression terrorism, military terrorism, and state-sponsored terrorism. Of these only repression terrorism fails to qualify as a form of war. Although repression terrorism clearly represents the use of lethal force by a political entity for a political purpose, it fails to meet the principle of engagement. The populace being subjected to the lethal force perpetrated by the regime has no means to resist, has no political structure, and has no territory. Moreover, they cannot truly be considered the enemy by the regime since the population actually functions as an element of the regime's own power structure. Therefore, to take the "war" to its ultimate conclusion and destroy the populace represents a logical absurdity and cannot be done. Repression terrorism therefore does not qualify as a form of war.

Military terrorism, on the other hand, very clearly qualifies as a form of war. It represents the employment of terroristic force against the population of an enemy regime for the purpose of shattering their will to support their government and its war effort. Thus, it clearly represents the employment of force on the moral plane. It also quite clearly involves the use of force on the physical plane in accordance with the principles of war and combat, since military terrorism is employed by a nation's military instrument against a political entity that can both defend itself and reply in kind. Finally, of course, it represents the use of force for a political objective. What should be emphasized, however, is that military terrorism, particularly when applied through air bombardment, has never yet proven effective. Even the Japanese, who suffered tremendous civilian casualties from air bombardment, never lost their will to continue to war, and it was only the unprecedented intercession of the Japanese emperor that terminated the war.

State-sponsored terrorism also qualifies as a form of war. In this form of terrorism, the government of a sovereign nation-state provides overt or covert support to terrorist organizations that operate within the enemy's camp for the purpose of undermining a specific targeted entity, usually the regime of another nation-state. This form of terrorism is actually no more than a subtype of social warfare, wherein one state targets the sociopolitical cohesion of a second state to weaken it so that it will divert its resources into defensive measures and/or to make it more vulnerable to an offensive attack. This clearly represents the use of force for a political objective. Moreover, given that the sociopolitical cohesion of the targeted entity is being attacked, this means of force employment also represents the use of force on the moral plane. It is in the concept of the principle of engagement that state-sponsored terrorism may not appear to qualify as a form of war. This question arises because terrorists are not subject to the sponsoring state's absolute authority. Consequently, we have to ask if sponsoring a terrorist organization—which has the authority to choose its own targets and means of attack—represents the employment of lethal force by the sponsoring entity against the target. Here again, if viewed from the perspective of social warfare, the answer has to be that, indeed, a clash of arms between two political entities does occur. Thus, state-sponsored terrorism is a form of war.

Of the seven forms of terrorism tested, three qualify as a form of war. These are revolutionary terrorism, military terrorism, and state-sponsored terrorism. The significance of these findings is obvious. To neutralize these forms of terrorism they must be treated as a form of war, and only by waging war upon them in accordance with the principles of war and combat is it possible to defeat this threat. Of course, given that military terrorism represents a military tactic within the context of a larger war, it is not possible to talk about waging war against this form of terrorism per se. Rather, it is defeated in conjunction with defeating the enemy's conventional armed forces. Revolutionary and state-sponsored terrorism, however, represent individual categories of types of war and can exist independently from other, larger forms of war. Consequently, engaging and defeating these can be achieved and require a specific mode of force employment to do so.

Defeating revolutionary terrorism poses particularly difficult problems in that the regime is waging war against an enemy that is operating in and among its own population. Consequently the chances of causing casualties among innocent civilians is very high unless only the absolute minimum of force is employed in a highly discriminate fashion. Defeating the revolutionary terrorists involves employing force in essentially the same basic manner as in conventional, classical warfare. Since the revolutionary terrorists are waging a total war against the regime and are an internal threat, the regime must wage total war against the revolutionaries. It is essential that the revolutionary terrorists' armed forces are destroyed, their "territory" is occupied, and their will to resist is neutralized. As was shown in chapter 9, this is achieved by creating a physical and moral environment that forces the terrorists to operate at an expenditure of effort level well above that which they can sustain. By creating a physical environment wherein the most critical nodes of the regime's command and control infrastructure are "fortified" along with the establishment of local means of resistance that can be rapidly reinforced by highly mobile, extremely disciplined, and well-trained special forces, the terrorists will be forced to risk prohibitive casualties in shock operations or else employ less discriminate fire attacks that would put innocents at risk. This, in turn, can lead to the revolutionaries losing any moral support they may have had among the populace. This loss of moral support can be reinforced by the state's counterorganizing the population to ensure that psychological bonds form between the people and the regime. This can pay dividends in the form of intelligence information concerning where the terrorists' "territory" is located or even who the terrorists are. In that way the regime is able to identify and neutralize the enemy by direct action.

In combating state-sponsored terrorism, the targeted regime has two enemies: the terrorists and their sponsors. Although the targeted regime will usually have to wage total war against the terrorists, it will normally wage only limited war against the sponsor. The targeted regime attacks the sponsoring state to increase the sponsor's expenditure of effort beyond what it is willing to bear, thereby having it withdraw support for the terrorists. Indeed, it is this cohesion between the sponsoring state and the terrorists that represents the center of gravity. Once this cohesion fails, the targeted regime can dispatch the internal terrorist threat in a manner suggested in the previous paragraph. What is abundantly clear is that any attack by the targeted regime upon the terrorist sponsor should be in the context of social war seeking to capitalize upon the internal cleavages existing within the sponsoring state. This is particularly necessary when the sponsor has nuclear-equipped armed forces. In this way, the targeted entity can cause the maximum expenditure of effort for the sponsoring state with the minimum force. Moreover, just as with an internal threat, every effort should be made *not* to kill innocent civilians but, to the greatest degree possible, kill or capture only terrorists.

This requires highly specialized forces capable of long-range ingress and egress with sufficient force to neutralize any threat encountered. Air power represents one such weapon, although its inherent inaccuracies make it less appropriate to such warfare. Ideally, such a force would be a highly reliable ground force equipped, trained, and authorized to perform hit-and-run attacks directly upon terrorist bases located in the sponsoring nation. Examples of these operations were described in chapter 9. Only by employing force in such a manner is it possible to neutralize the state-sponsored terrorist threat.

In conclusion, then, certain types of terrorism are a form of war, meeting the same criteria and functioning in the same manner as traditional or classical forms of war. These forms of war exist as the latest evolutionary step in the evolution of warfare, one in which social skills are paramount. Technical, administrative, organizational, and physical skills all remain extremely important to securing victory, but without the social skills to back them up, at best all the targeted entity can do is delay the inevitable. Given that these terrorist threats qualifying as a form of war must function and operate in accordance with the immutable laws and principles, however, the formulas for defeating these threats are neither remarkable nor complex. Military personnel throughout the world should be able to accept the validity of both the principles and the formulas that have been offered here to defeat those forms of terrorism that are a form of war. What remains to be seen is whether the democratic nations of the West have the political resolve to implement these solutions in a consistent, coherent fashion.

# Bibliography

■

## Books

Adomeit, Hannes. *Soviet Risk-Taking and Crisis Behavior: A Theoretical and Empirical Analysis.* Boston: Allen & Unwin, 1982.

Alexander, Yonah; Carlton, David; and Wilkinson, Paul, eds. *Terrorism: Theory and Practice.* Boulder, Colo.: Westview Press, 1979.

Arendt, Hannah. *On Violence.* New York: Harcourt Brace Jovanovich, 1970. Quoted in Alex P. Schmid, *Political Terrorism,* p. 13. Amsterdam: North Holland Publishing Co., 1983; Transaction Books, 1985.

Asprey, Robert. *War in the Shadows: The Guerrilla in History.* 2 vols. Garden City, N.Y.: Doubleday Co., Inc., 1975.

Bainton, Roland H. *Christian Attitudes Toward War and Peace: A Historical Survey and Critical Re-evaluation.* New York: Abingdon Press, 1960.

Baldwin, Hanson. *The Crucial Years, 1939–1941: The World At War—From the Beginning Through Pearl Harbor.* New York: Harper & Row, Publishers, Inc., 1970.

Beckwith, Charlie A. and Knox, Donald. *Delta Force.* New York: Harcourt Brace Jovanovich, Inc., 1983; Dell Publishing Co., Inc., 1985.

Bell, J. Bowyer. *A Time of Terror: How Democratic Societies Respond to Revolutionary Violence.* New York: Basic Books, 1978. Quoted in Alex P. Schmid, *Political Terrorism,* p. 6. Amsterdam: North Holland Publishing Co., 1983; Transaction Books, 1985.

———. *Transnational Terror.* Washington, D.C.: American Enterprise Institute for Public Research, 1975.

Belloc, Hilaire. *Poitiers.* London: 1913. Quoted in Harry H. Turney-High, *Primitive War,* p. 29. Columbia, S.C.: University of South Carolina Press, 1949; 2d ed., 1971.

Bloch, Ivan. *The Future of War in its Technical, Economic and Political Relations.* Translated by R. C. Long, Boston: 1903. Quoted in Theodore Ropp, *War in the Modern World,* pp. 218–22. New York: Macmillan Publishing Co., 1959; Collier Books, 1962.

Blumenson, Martin and Stokesbury, James L. *Masters of the Art of Command.* Boston: Houghton Mifflin Co., 1975.

Burke, James. *Connections.* Boston: Little, Brown & Co., Inc., 1978.

Buzan, Barry. *People, States and Fear: The National Security Problem in International Relations.* Chapel Hill: University of North Carolina Press, 1983.

Campbell, James. *The Bombing of Nuremburg.* Garden City, N.Y.: Doubleday & Company, Inc., 1974.

Chaliand, Gerard, ed. *Guerrilla Strategies: An Historical Anthology from the Long March to Afghanistan.* Berkeley: University of California Press, 1982.

Chamberlin, William Henry. *The Russian Revolution, 1917–1921.* New York: Grosset and Dunlap, 1965. Quoted in Theda Skocpol, *States and Social Revolutions,* pp. 215–16. New York: Cambridge University Press, 1983.

Coleman, James C. and Brown, William E., Jr. *Abnormal Psychology and Modern Life.* Glenville, Ill.: Scott, Foresman and Co., Inc., 1972.

Connelly, Owen. *French Revolution/Napoleonic Era.* New York: Holt, Rinehart and Winston, 1979.

Costello, John. *The Pacific War.* New York: Rawson, Wade Publishers, Inc., 1981.

Crenshaw, Martha., ed. *Terrorism, Legitimacy and Power: The Consequences of Political Violence.* Middletown: Wesleyan University Press, 1984.

Dallin, Alexander and Breslauer, George. *Political Terror in Communist Systems.* Stanford: Stanford University Press, 1970. Quoted in Alex P. Schmid, *Political Terrorism,* pp. 172–73. Amsterdam: North Holland Publishing Co., 1983; Transaction Books, 1985.

Dallin, Alexander. *Black Box: KAL 007 and the Superpowers.* Berkeley: University of California Press, 1985.

Deighton, Len. *Blitzkrieg: From the Rise of Hitler to the Fall of Dunkirk.* New York: Alfred A. Knopf, Inc., 1980.

Dobson, Christopher and Payne Ronald. *The Terrorists: Their Weapons, Leaders and Tactics.* New York: Facts on File, Inc., 1982.

Du Picq, Ardant. *Etudes sur le Combat.* Paris: 1914. Quoted in J. F. C. Fuller, *The Conduct of War, 1789–1961*, pp. 121–22. New York: Funk and Wagnalls, Inc., 1961; Minerva Press, 1968.

Dupuy, R. Ernest and Dupuy, Trevor N. *The Encyclopedia of Military History: From 3500 B.C. to the Present.* New York: Harper and Row, 1963.

Durant, Will. *The Story of Civilization.* vol. 1. *Our Oriental Heritage.* New York: Simon & Schuster, Inc., 1954.

Durant, Will and Durant, Ariel. *The Story of Civilization.* vol. 7. *The Age of Reason Begins.* New York: Simon and Schuster, 1961.

———. *The Story of Civilization.* vol. 8. *The Age of Louis XIV.* New York: Simon & Schuster, Inc., 1963.

———. *The Story of Civilization.* vol. 11. *The Age of Napoleon.* New York: Simon & Schuster, Inc., 1975.

Dyer, Gwynne. *War.* New York: Crown Publishers, Inc., 1985.

Earle, Edward M., ed. *The Makers of Modern Strategy: Military Thought From Machiavelli to Hitler.* Princeton: Princeton University Press, 1943; Princeton Paperback Edition, 1973.

Edwards, Lyford P. *The Natural History of Revolution.* Chicago: University of Chicago Press, 1927; Heritage of Sociology Edition, 1973.

Engels, Donald W. *Alexander the Great and the Logistics of the Macedonian Army.* Berkeley: University of California Press, 1978.

Fanon, Frantz. *The Wretched of the Earth.* London: Hamandsworth, 1967. Quoted in Paul Wilkinson, "Terrorist Movements," *Terrorism: Theory and Practice,* Edited by Yonah Alexander, David Carlton, and Paul Wilkinson, p. 113. Boulder, Colo.: Westview Press, 1979.

Fitzsimons, Bernard, ed. *Warplanes and Air Battles of World War I.* London: BPC Publishing, Ltd., 1973.

Franklin, Noble and Dowling, Christopher, eds. *Decisive Battles of the 20th Century: Land, Sea and Air.* New York: David McKay Co., Inc., 1976.

Friedland, William. *Revolutionary Theory.* Totowa, N.J.: Rowman & Allanheld Publishers, 1982.

Fuller, J. F. C. *The Conduct of War, 1789–1961.* New York: Funk & Wagnalls Inc., 1961; Minerva Press, 1968.

Gabriel, Richard and Savage, Paul L. *Crisis in Command: Mismanagement in the Army.* New York: Hill and Wang, 1978; reprinted, 1979.

Gardner, Michael. *A History of the Soviet Army.* New York: Praeger Publishers, 1966.

Gaucher, R. *Les Terroristes.* Paris: 1965. Quoted in Alex P. Schmid, *Political Terrorism,* p. 206. Amsterdam: North Holland Publishing Co., 1983; Transaction Books, 1985.

Goldstone, Jack, ed. *Revolutions: Theoretical, Comparative, and Historical Studies.* New York: Harcourt Brace Jovanovich, Inc., 1986.

Greene, Thomas H. *Comparative Revolutionary Movements: Search for Theory and Justice.* Englewood Cliffs, N.J.: Prentice-Hall, Inc., 1984.

Grundy, Kenneth W. *Guerrilla Struggle in Africa: An Analysis and Preview.* New York: Grossman Publishers, 1971.

Guevara, Che. *Guerrilla Warfare.* New York: Monthly Review Press, 1961.

Gurr, Ted Robert. *Why Men Rebel.* 4th ed. Princeton: Princeton University Press, 1974.

Hacker, Frederick J. *Crusaders, Criminals, Crazies: Terror and Terrorism in Our Time.* New York: Bantam Books, 1978. Quoted in Austin T. Turk, *Political Criminality,* p. 74. London: Sage Publications, Ltd., 1982.

Harrison, James Pinckney. *The Endless War: Vietnam's Struggle for Independence.* New York: McGraw-Hill Book Co., Inc., 1982.

Hart, Basil Liddell. *Strategy.* New York: Praeger Publishers, 1968.

Heinl, Robert D., Jr. *Dictionary of Military and Naval Quotations.* Annapolis, Md.: The United States Naval Institute Press, 1985.

Henderson, William D. *Why the Vietcong Fought: A Study of Motivation and Control in a Modern Army in Combat.* Westport, Conn.: Greenwood Press, Inc., 1979.

Herzstein, Robert E., ed. *Adolf Hitler and the Third Reich, 1933–1945.* Boston: Houghton Mifflin Co., 1971.

Hobsbawm, E. J. *Primitive Rebels.* New York: Norton and Co., 1965. Quoted in Martin Oppenheimer, *The Urban Guerrilla,* pp. 33–34. Chicago: Quadrangle Books, 1969.

Holsti, K. J. *International Politics: A Framework for Analysis:* Englewood Cliffs, N.J.: Prentice-Hall, Inc., 1983.

Howard, Michael. *The Causes of Wars: And Other Essays.* 2d ed., enlarged. Cambridge, Mass.: Harvard University Press, 1984.

———. *The Franco-Prussian War: The German Invasion of France, 1870–1871.* New York: Macmillan Publishing Co., 1961; Collier Books, 1969.

Ilke, Fred. *The Social Impact of Bomb Destruction.* Norman, Oklahoma: 1958. Quoted in Barrie Paskins and Michael Dockrill, *The Ethics of War,* p. 45. Minneapolis: University of Minnesota Press, 1979.

Jablonski, Edward. *Air War.* vol. 4. *Wings of Fire.* Garden City, N.Y.: Doubleday & Co., Inc., 1972.

Janowitz, Morris. *Military Conflict: Essays in the Institutional Analysis of War and Peace.* London: Sage Publications, Ltd., 1975.

Jenkins, Brian. *International Terrorism: A New Mode of Conflict.* Los Angeles: Crescent Publications, 1975.

Jomini, Antoine H. *Precis d'art de la Guerra.* Paris: 1838. Quoted in Craine Brinton, Gordon Craig, and Felix Gilbert, "Jomini," *Makers of Modern*

*Strategy*, edited by Edward M. Earle, p. 254. Princeton: University of Princeton Press, 1943; Princeton Paperback Printing, 1973.

Jones, Neville. *The Origins of Strategic Bombing: A Study of the Development of British Strategic Air Thought and Practice up to 1918*. London: William Kimber and Co., Ltd., 1973.

Josephus. *The Jewish War*. Translated by G. A. Williamson. New York: Dorset Press, 1985.

Kaplan, Fred. *The Wizards of Armageddon*. New York: Simon & Schuster, Inc., 1983; Touchstone Books, 1984.

Karnow, Stanley. *Vietnam: A History*. New York: Viking Press, 1983.

Keegan, John. *The Face of Battle: A Study of Agincourt, Waterloo and the Somme*. New York: The Viking Press, 1976; Penguin Books, 1985.

King, Jere C. *The First World War*. New York: Walker Publishing Co., 1972.

Komer, R. W. *Bureaucracy Does Its Thing: Institutional Constraints on US-GVN Performance in Vietnam*. Santa Monica, Calif.: Rand Corporation, 1972. Quoted in Harry G. Summers, *On Strategy*, p. 147. Novato, Calif.: Presidio Press, 1984.

Koch, H. W. *The Rise of Modern Warfare: 1618–1815*. London: Hamlyn Publishing Group, Ltd., 1981.

Laquer, Walter. *Terrorism: A Study of National and International Political Violence*. Boston: Little, Brown & Co., Inc., 1977.

———. *The Terrorism Reader: A Historical Anthology*. New York: New American Library, 1978; Meridian Books, 1978.

Lawrence, T. E. *Seven Pillars of Wisdom*. New York: Doubleday & Co., Inc., 1935; Penguin Books, 1985.

Lenski, Gehard. *Power and Privilege: A Theory of Social Stratification*. New York: McGraw-Hill Book Co., 1966.

Lincoln, W. Bruce. *Passage Through Armageddon: The Russians in War and Revolution*. New York: Simon & Schuster, Inc., 1986.

Livingston, Marius H., ed. *International Terrorism in the Contemporary World*. London: Greenwood Press, 1978.

Lumpkin, Henry. *From Savannah to Yorktown: The American Revolution in the South*. Columbia, S.C.: University of South Carolina Press, 1981.

Luttwak, Edward N. *The Grand Strategy of the Roman Empire: From the First Century A.D. to the Third*. Baltimore: The Johns Hopkins University Press, 1976; Johns Hopkins Paperback Edition, 1981.

Mao Tse-Tung. *On Guerrilla Warfare*. Translated and edited by Samuel B. Griffith. New York: Praeger Publishers, 1961.

Marighella, Carlos. *Minimanual of the Urban Guerrilla*. Havana: Tricontinental Congress, No Date. Quoted in Robert Moss, *Urban Guerrillas*, p. 198. London: Temple Smith, 1972.

Marshall, S. L. A. *Men Against Fire*. New York: William Morrow Co., Inc.,

1947. Quoted in John Keegan, *The Face of Battle,* pp. 71–72. New York: Viking Press, 1976; Penguin Books, 1985.

Marx, Karl. *Das Kapital.* Translated by Eden and Cedar Paul. London: J. M. Dent and Sons, 1933. Quoted in Robert C. Tucker, *The Marxian Revolutionary Idea,* pp. 23–24. New York: W. W. Norton & Co., Inc., 1969.

McCuen, John J. *The Art of Counter-Revolutionary War: A Psycho-Politico-Military Strategy of Counter-Insurgency.* Harrisburg, Pa.: Stackpole Books, 1966.

McKee, Alexander. *Dresden 1945: The Devil's Tinderbox.* London: Souvenir Press, Ltd., 1982.

Mitcham, Samuel W., Jr. *Hitler's Legions: The German Order of Battle, World War II.* New York: Stein & Day Publishers, 1985.

Moss, Robert. *Urban Guerrillas.* London: Temple Smith, 1972.

Nevin, David. *Sherman's March: Atlanta to the Sea.* Alexandria, Va.: Time-Life Books, Inc., 1986.

Oman, C. W. C. *The Art of War in the Middle Ages.* Revised and edited by John H. Beeler. London: 1885; Cornell Paperback Edition, 1973.

O'Neill, Bard E.; Heaton, William R.; and Alberts, Donald J. *Insurgency in the Modern World.* Boulder, Colo.: Westview Press, 1980. Quoted L. C. Green, "Terorrism and Its Responses," *Terrorism: An International Journal* 8, no. 1 (1985).

Oppenheimer, Martin. *The Urban Guerrilla.* Chicago: Quadrangle Books, 1969.

Palmer, David R. *Summons of the Trumpet: US-Vietnam in Perspective.* San Rafael, Calif.: Presidio Press, 1978. Quoted in Harry G. Summers, *On Strategy,* p. 68. Novato, Calif.: Presidio Press, 1984.

Parry, Albert. *Terrorism: From Robespierre to Arafat.* New York: Vanguard Press, Inc., 1976.

Paskins, Barrie and Dockrill, Michael. *The Ethics of War.* Minneapolis: The University of Minnesota Press, 1979.

Pfaltzgraff, Robert L. and Doherty, James. *Contending Theories of International Relations: A Comprehensive Survey.* New York: Harper & Row, Publishers, Inc., 1981.

Porter, Horace. *Campaigning With Grant.* New York: 1897; Da Capo Press, Inc., 1986.

Quick, John. *Dictionary of Weapons and Military Terms.* New York: McGraw-Hill Book Co., 1973.

Rausching, Herman. *Gesprache mit Hitler.* Vienna: 1940. Quoted in Alex P. Schmid, *Political Terrorism,* p. 90. Amsterdam: North Holland Publishing Co., 1983; Transaction Books, 1985.

Rivers, Gayle. *The War Against the Terrorists: How To Win It.* New York: Stein & Day Publishers, 1986.

Ropp, Theodore. *War in the Modern World.* Revised edition. New York: Macmillan Publishing Co., 1962; Collier Books, 1985.

Rubenstein, Richard. *The Cunning of History: The Holocaust and the American Future.* New York: Harper & Row Publishers, Inc., 1978.

Saxe, Maurice de. *Mes Reveries.* Paris: 1732. Quoted in Robert D. Heinl, Jr., *Dictionary of Military and Naval Quotations,* p. 196. Annapolis, Md.: U.S. Naval Institute Press, 1985.

Schelling, Thomas. *Arms and Influence.* New Haven: Yale University Press, 1966. Quoted in Alex P. Schmid, *Political Terrorism,* p. 68. Amsterdam: North Holland Publishing Co., 1983; Transaction Books, 1985.

Schmid, Alex P. *Political Terrorism: A Research Guide to Concepts, Theories, Data Bases and Literature.* Amsterdam: North Holland Publishing Co., 1983; Transaction Books, 1985.

Schmookler, Andrew B. *The Parable of the Tribes: The Problem of Power in Social Evolution.* Boston: Houghton Mifflin Co., 1986.

Skocpol, Theda. *States and Social Revolutions: A Comparative Analysis of France, Russia, and China.* New York: Cambridge University Press, 1983.

Smith, V. A. *Oxford History of India.* Oxford: Oxford University Press, 1923. Quoted in Will Durant, *The Story of Civilization,* vol. 1. *Our Oriental Heritage,* pp. 499–500. New York: Simon & Schuster, 1954.

Starr, Richard F. *USSR Foreign Policies After Detente.* Stanford, Calif.: Hoover Institution Press, 1985.

Stavrianos, L. S. *The Balkans Since 1453.* New York: Holt, Rinehart and Winston, 1958.

Sterling, Claire. *The Terror Network: The Secret War of International Terrorism.* New York: Holt, Rinehart and Winston, 1981; Berkeley Books, 1984.

Stoessinger, John G. *Why Nations Go to War.* 4th ed. New York: St. Martin's Press, Inc., 1985.

Stohl, Michael, ed. *The Politics of Terrorism.* New York: Marcel Dekker Inc., 1979.

Strachan, Hew. *European Armies and the Conduct of War.* 2d ed. London: Allen & Unwin, Inc., 1983.

Summers, Harry G. *On Strategy: A Critical Analysis of the Vietnam War.* 4th ed. Novato, Calif.: Presidio Press, 1984.

Sun Tzu. *The Art of War.* Edited and translated by Samuel B. Griffith. London: Oxford University Press, 1963.

Thucydides. *The Peloponnesian Wars.* Translated by Benjamin Jowett, revised and abridged by P. A. Brunt. New York: Washington Square Press, 1963.

*The Tower Commission Report: The Full Text of the President's Special Review Board,* Introduction by R. W. Apple, Jr. New York: Joint Publication of Bantam Books, Inc., and Time-Life Books, Inc., 1987.

Tucker, Robert C. *The Marxian Revolutionary Idea.* New York: W. W. Norton & Co., Inc., 1969.

Turk, Austin T. *Political Criminality: The Defiance and Defense of Authority.* London: Sage Publications, Ltd., 1982.

Turney-High, Harry H. *Primitive War: Its Practice and Concepts.* Columbia, S.C.: The University of South Carolina Press, 1949; Reprint Edition, 1971.

Ulam, Adam. *Expansion and Coexistence: Soviet Foreign Policy 1917–1973.* New York: Praeger Publishers, 1974.

Van Creveld, Martin. *Command in War.* Cambridge, Mass.: Harvard University Press, 1985.

———. *Fighting Power: German and U.S. Army Performance, 1939–1945.* Westport, Conn.: Greenwood Press, 1982.

von Clausewitz, Carl. *On War.* Edited by Michael Howard and Peter Paret. Princeton: Princeton University Press, 1976.

von der Goltz. *The Conduct of War: A Brief Survey of its Most Important Principles and Forms.* Translated by Joseph T. Dickman. Kansas City, Mo.: Franklin Hudson Publishing Co., 1896. Quoted in Harry G. Summers, *On Strategy*, p. 110. Novato, Calif.: Presidio Press, 1984.

Walter, Eugene V. *Terror and Resistance: A Study of Political Violence With Case Studies of Some Primitive African Communities.* New York: Oxford University Press, 1969. Quoted in Grant Wardlaw, *Political Terrorism*, p. 12. Cambridge: Cambridge University Press, 1984.

Wardlaw, Grant. *Political Terrorism: Theory, Tactics and Countermeasures.* Cambridge: Cambridge University Press, 1984.

Watson, Peter. *War on the Mind: The Military Uses and Abuses of Psychology.* New York: Basic Books, Inc., Publishers, 1978.

Weigley, Russell F. *The American Way of War: A History of the United States Military Strategy and Policy.* Bloomington, Ind.: Indiana University Press, 1973; Indiana University Paperback Edition, 1977.

Wilkinson, Paul. *Political Terrorism.* London: Macmillan and Co., 1974. Quoted in Alex P. Schmid, *Political Terrorism*, p. 93. Amsterdam: North Holland Publishing Co., 1983; Transaction Books, 1985.

Wise, Terence. *Medieval Warfare.* New York: Hastings House, Publishers, 1976.

Wright, Quincy. *A Study of War.* 2 vols. Chicago: The University of Chicago Press, 1941.

## Articles and Chapters

Ahmad, Eqbal. "Revolutionary Warfare and Counterinsurgency." In *Guerrilla Strategies: An Anthology from the Long March to Afghanistan*, Edited by Gerard Chaliand. Berkeley: University of California Press, 1982.

Allen, William S. "The German People and National Socialism: The Experience of One Town." In *Adolf Hitler and the Third Reich, 1933–1945.* Edited by Robert E. Herzstein. Boston: Houghton Mifflin Co., 1971.

Arostegui, Martin C. "Special Reports of Risks International," *Terrorism: An International Journal* 7, no. 4 (1985).

Aspaturian, Vernon. "Soviet Global Power and the Correlation of Forces" *Problems of Communism,* May–June, 1980.

Barnet, Richard J. "The Costs and Perils of Intervention." *Low Intensity Warfare: Counterinsurgency, Proinsurgency, and Antiterrorism in the Eighties.* Edited by Michael T. Klare and Peter Kornbluh. New York: Pantheon Books, 1988.

Bell, Donald H. "Comment: The Origins of Modern Terrorism." *Terrorism: An International Journal* 9, no. 3 (1987).

Berg, Richard. "1066: Year of Decision." In *Strategy and Tactics Magazine* no. 110 (November–December 1986) pp. 17–21.

Bonaparte, Napoleon. "Correspondance Inedite de Napoleon Ier, Conserve Aux Archives de la Guerre." Edited by Ernest Picard and Louis Tuety. Paris: 1912. Quoted in J. F. C. Fuller, *The Conduct of War, 1789–1961,* p. 50. New York: Funk & Wagnalls Inc., 1961; Minerva, 1968.

Bond, Brian. "Battle of France." In *Decisive Battles of the 20th Century: Land, Sea and Air.* Edited by Noble Franklin and Christopher Dowling. New York: David McKay Co., Inc., 1976.

Brinton, Craine; Craig, Gordon; and Gilbert, Felix. "Jomini." In *Makers of Modern Strategy: Military Thought From Machiavelli to Hitler.* Edited by Edward M. Earle. Princeton: Princeton University Press, 1943; Paperback Printing, 1973.

Burke, Arleigh. "Power and Peace." In *Peace and War in the Modern Age: Premises Myths and Realities.* Edited by Barnett, Frank R.; Mott, William C.; and Neff, John C. Garden City, N.Y.: Doubleday & Co., Inc., 1965; Anchor Books, 1965.

Carlton, David. "The Future of Political Substate Violence." In *Terrorism: Theory and Practice.* Edited by Yonah Alexander, David Carlton, and Paul Wilkinson. Boulder, Colo.: Westview Press, 1979.

Chessman, Caryl. "A Letter to the Governor." In *Criminal Life: Views from the Inside.* Edited by David M. Petersen and Marcello Truzzi. Englewood Cliffs, N.J.: Prentice-Hall, Inc., 1972.

Craig, Gordon. "Delbruck: The Military Historian." In *Makers of Modern Strategy: Military Thought From Machiavelli to Hitler,* Edited by Edward M. Earle. Princeton: Princeton University Press, 1943; Paperback Printing, 1973.

Crenshaw, Martha. "The Causes of Terrorism." In *Comparative Politics* (July, 1981). Quoted in Alex Schmid, *Political Terrorism,* p. 386. Amsterdam: North Holland Publishing Co., 1983; Transaction Books, 1985.

Dudney, Robert S. "Toward a Fifth Armed Service?" *Air Force Magazine* (May, 1988).

Emerson, Ralph Waldo. "Nature" and "The American Scholar," *The Heart of Emerson's Essays*. Edited by Perry Bliss. Boston: Houghton Mifflin Co., 1933. Quoted in Andrew B. Schmookler, *The Parable of the Tribes*, pp. 91–92. Boston: Houghton Mifflin Co., 1986.

Freedman, Lawrence A. "Why Does Terrorism Terrorize?" In *Terrorism: An International Journal* 6 (1983).

Galanter, M. "Engaged Members of the Unification Church: Impact of a Charismatic Large Group of Adaptation and Behavior." In *Archives of General Psychiatry*. (In Press). Quoted in Jerrold M. Post, "Notes on Psychodynamic Theory of Terrorist Behavior." In *Terrorism: An International Journal* 7, no. 3 (1984).

Gilbert, Felix. "Machiavelli: The Renaissance of the Art of War." In *Makers of Modern Strategy: Military Thought from Machiavelli to Hitler*. Edited by Edward M. Earle. Princeton: Princeton University Press, 1943; Paperback Printing, 1973.

Grabosky, P. N. "The Urban Context of Political Terrorism." In *The Politics of Terrorism*, Edited by Michael Stohl. New York: Marcel Dekker, Inc., 1979.

Green, L. C. "Terrorism and Its Responses." In *Terrorism: An International Journal* 8, no. 1 (1985).

Griffith, Samuel B., ed. "Sun Tzu and Mao Tse-Tung." In *The Art of War*. Oxford: Oxford University Press, 1963; Oxford Paperback, 1971.

Guillen, Abraham. "Urban Guerrilla Strategy." In *Guerrilla Strategies: An Historical Anthology from the Long March to Afghanistan*. Edited by Gerard Chaliand. Berkeley: University of California Press, 1982.

Halperin, Morton H. "Lawful Wars," *Foreign Policy* No. 72 (Fall 1988).

Holborn, Hajo. "Moltke and Schlieffen: The Prussian School." In *Makers of Modern Strategy: Military Thought From Machiavelli to Hitler*. Edited by Edward M. Earle. Princeton: Princeton University Press, 1943; Paperback Printing, 1973.

Holton, Gerald, "Reflections on Modern Terrorism." *Terrorism: An International Journal* 1, nos. 3/4 (1978).

Iyad, Abu. "Al Fatah's Autocriticism." In *Guerrilla Strategies: An Historical Anthology from the Long March to Afghanistan*. Edited by Gerard Chaliand. Berkeley: University of California Press, 1982.

Jenkins, Brian. "Will Terrorists Go Nuclear?" *Orbis* 29, no. 3 (Fall 1985).

Johnpoll, Bernard K. "Perspectives on Political Terrorism in the United States." In *International Terrorism: National, Regional, and Global Perspectives*. New York: Praeger Publishers, 1976.

Kupperman, Robert M. "Terrorism and National Security." *Terrorism: An International Journal* 8, no. 3 (1985).

Lasswell, Harold D. "Terrorism and the Political Process." In *Terrorism: An International Journal* 1, nos. 3/4 (1978).

Leroy-Beaulieu, A. "Les reformes de la Turquie, la politique russe et le pan-slavisme," *Revue des Deux Mondes.* XVIII, (December 1, 1876). Quoted in L. S. Stavrianos, *The Balkans Since 1453,* p. 530. New York: Holt, Rinehart and Winston, 1958.

Loh, Jules. "Big-Time Crime Hits Kentucky Hill Country," (Associated Press) *San Jose Mercury News* (July 20, 1986), p. 11A.

Merari, Ariel. "A Classification of Terrorist Groups." *Terrorism: An International Journal* 1, nos. 3/4 (1978).

"More Than 60 Arabs Arrested In Israeli Raid on Refugee Camp," *The Herald* (Monterey) (June 1, 1987).

Nechayev, Sergei. "Catechism of a Revolutionist." In *The Terrorism Reader: A Historical Anthology.* Edited by Walter Laquer. New York: New American Library, 1978.

O'Brien, Conor Cruise. "Terrorism Under Democratic Conditions." In *Terrorism, Legitimacy and Power: The Consequence of Political Violence.* Edited by Martha Crenshaw, Middletown, Conn.: Wesleyan University Press, 1984.

O'Brien, William V. "Counterterrorism: Lessons From Israel." *Strategic Review* (Fall 1985).

Odom, William. "Soviet Force Posture: Dilemmas and Directions." In *Problems of Communism,* July–August 1985.

Parry, Robert and Kornbluh, Peter. "Iran-Contra's Untold Story." *Foreign Policy,* no. 72 (Fall 1988).

Possony, Stefan T. and Mantoux, Etienne. "Du Picq and Foch: The Military School." In *Makers of Modern Strategy: Military Thought from Machiavelli to Hitler.* Edited by Edward M. Earle. Princeton: Princeton University Press, 1943; Princeton Paperback Printing, 1973.

Post, Jerrold M. "Notes on Psychodynamic Theory of Terrorist Behavior." *Terrorism: An International Journal* 7, no. 3 (1984).

Powell, Roland. "Weinburger Discusses Anti-Terrorist Attacks." *Monterey Peninsula Herald* (January 7, 1986), p. 2.

Rhyme, Russell. "Patterns of Subverson by Violence." *Annals* 341 (May, 1962). Quoted in Martin Oppenheimer, *The Urban Guerrilla,* p. 75. Chicago: Quadrangle Books, 1969.

Robinson, Douglas. "Strategic Bombing." In *Warplanes and Air Battles of World War I.* Edited by Bernard Fitzsimons. London: William Kimber and Co., Ltd., 1973.

Rothfels, H. "Clausewitz." In *Makers of Modern Strategy: Military Thought From Machiavelli to Hitler.* Edited by Edward M. Earle. Princeton: Princeton University Press, 1943; Princeton Paperback Printing, 1973.

Saddy, Fehmy. "International Terrorism, Human Rights and World Order." *Terrorism: An International Journal* 5, no. 4 (1982).

Salam, Mohammed. "Syrian Troops Skirmish With Druse Gunmen." *The Herald* (Monterey) (February 24, 1987), p. 2.

"Senior IRA Men Lost in Ambush." (Associated Press) *The Sunday Herald* (Monterey) (May 10, 1987), p. 6A.

Sergiyev, A. "Leninism on the Correlation of Forces as a Factor of International Relations." In *International Affairs* (May 1975). Quoted in Vernon Aspaturian, "Soviet Global Power and the Correlation of Forces." *Problems of Communism* (May–June 1980), p. 10.

Sewell, Alan F. "Political Crime: A Psychologist's Perspective." In *International Terrorism and Political Crime.* Edited by M. Bassiouni. Springfield, Ill.: Charles C. Thomas, 1975. Quoted in Alex P. Schmid, *Political Terrorism*, p. 29. Amsterdam: North Holland Publishing Co., 1983: Transaction Books, 1985.

Sloan, John W. "Political Terrorism in Latin America: A Critical Analysis." In *The Politics of Terrorism.* Edited by Michael Stohl. New York: Marcel Dekker, Inc., 1979.

Smolowe, Jill. "Assignment Murder: How Israel Planned the Killing of Arafat's Right-Hand Man." *Time* (May 2, 1988).

Stepniak-Kravchinsky, Serge. "Underground Russia." London: n.p., 1883. In *The Terrorism Reader: A Historical Anthology.* Edited by Walter Laquer. New York: New American Library, 1978.

Stohl, Michael, ed. "Myths and Realities of Political Terrorism." In *The Politics of Terrorism.* New York: Marcel Dekker, Inc., 1979.

Taylor, Robert W., and Kim, Byong-Suh. "Violence and Change in Postindustrial Societies: Student Protest in America and Japan in the 1960s." *International Terrorism in the Contemporary World.* Edited by Marius H. Livingston. London: Greenwood Press, 1978.

Thornton, Thomas P. "Terror as a Weapon of Political Agitation." In *Internal War: Problems and Approaches.* Edited by Harry Eckstein. New York: The Free Press of Glencoe, 1964.

Tromp, Hylke. "Politek Terrorisme: De Derde Wereldoorlog in een Volstrekt Onverwachte Vorm?" [Political Terrorism: The Third World War in a Totally Unexpected Form?] In *Universitskrant*, Groningen, The Netherlands: 1978. Quoted in Alex P. Schmid, *Political Terrorism*, p. 208. Amsterdam: North Holland Publishing Co., 1983; Transaction Books, 1985.

Vernon, P. E. "Psychological Effect of Air Raids." In *Journal of Abnormal and Social Psychology* (1941), pp. 36 and 457–76. Quoted in Grant Wardlaw, *Political Terrorism*, pp. 35–36. Cambridge: Cambridge University Press, 1984.

Wilkinson, Paul. "Terrorist Movements." In *Terrorism: Theory and Practice.*

Edited by Yonah Alexander, David Carlton, and Paul Wilkinson. Boulder, Colo.: Westview Press, 1979.

Williams, Carol J. "Separate Cultures, Societies Pose Problems for Kremlin." (Associated Press) *The Sunday Herald* (Monterey) (May 10, 1987), p. 5B.

Withey, Stephen and Katz, Daniel. "The Social Psychology of Human Conflict," In *The Nature of Human Conflict.* Edited by Elton B. McNeil. Englewood Cliffs, N.J.: Prentice-Hall, Inc., 1965.

Wolf, John B. "Organization and Management Practices of Urban Terrorist Groups." In *Terrorism: An International Journal* 1, no. 2 (1978).

Wood, Gordon. "The American Revolution." In *Revolutions: A Comparative Study.* Edited by Lawrence Kaplan. New York: Vintage Books, 1973. Quoted in Theda Skocpol, *States and Social Revolutions,* p. 18. New York: Cambridge University Press, 1983.

Wright, Jeffery W. "Terrorism: A Mode of Warfare." *Military Review.* Ft. Leavenworth, Kansas: U.S. Army Command and General Staff College (October, 1984).

Yadin, Y. "A Strategic Analysis of Last Year's Battles." *The Israeli Forces Journal* (September 1949).

# Manuals, Reports, Lectures

Brodie, Bernard. "Changing Capabilities and War Objectives." Lecture; Air War College; April 17, 1952; Maxwell AFB. In Fred Kaplan, *The Wizards of Armageddon,* p. 47. New York: Simon and Schuster, 1983; Touchstone Books, 1984.

Field Manual 100-1, *Field Service Regulations–The Army.* Washington, D.C.: Government Printing Office, 1982.

Field Manual 100-5, *Field Service Regulations–Operations.* Washington, D.C.: Government Printing Office, 1983. Quoted in Harry G. Summers, *On Strategy,* pp. 199–204. Novato, Calif.: Presidio Press, 1984.

U.S. Congress. Senate. Subcommittee on Security and Terrorism. *The Historical Antecedents of Soviet Terrorism. Hearings before a Subcommittee of the Senate Committee on the Judiciary.* J-97-40. 97th Cong., 1st sess., June 11 and 12, 1981.

U.S. Congress. Senate. Subcommittee on Security and Terrorism. *The Origins, Direction and Support of Terrorism. Hearings before a Subcommittee of the Senate Committee on the Judiciary.* J-97-17. 97th Cong., 1st sess., April 24, 1981.

U.S. Congress. House (Select Committee to Investigate Covert Arms Trans-
actions with Iran) and Senate (Select Committee on Secret Military Assis-
tance to Iran and the Nicaraguan Opposition). Hamilton, Lee H. (Chairman,
House Select Committee), and Inouye, Daniel K. (Chairman, Senate Select
Committee). *Report of the Congressional Committees Investigating the
Iran-Contra Affair: Executive Summary with Supplemental, Minority, and
Additional Views. House Report no. 100-433/Senate Report no. 100-216.*
100th Cong., 1st sess., November 13, 1987.

# The Author

■

Donald J. Hanle is an active duty U.S. Air Force officer. His bachelor's degree is from the University of South Carolina, and he has an M.A. in national security affairs from the Naval Postgraduate School, Monterey, California. Major Hanle is presently assigned to the Air Force Intelligence Agency's Directorate for Research and Soviet Studies.